CW01510315

WALK ON

JAMES PEARCE

WALK ON

INSIDE ARNE SLOT'S LIVERPOOL

Harper
North

HarperNorth
Windmill Green
24 Mount Street
Manchester M2 3NX

A division of
HarperCollins*Publishers*
1 London Bridge Street
London SE1 9GF

www.harpercollins.co.uk

HarperCollins*Publishers*
Macken House, 39/40 Mayor Street Upper
Dublin 1, D01 C9W8, Ireland

First published by HarperCollins*Publishers* 2025

1 3 5 7 9 10 8 6 4 2

© James Pearce 2025

James Pearce asserts the moral right to
be identified as the author of this work

A catalogue record of this book is
available from the British Library

HB ISBN 978-0-00-877472-1
TPB ISBN 978-0-00-877473-8

Printed and bound in the UK using 100%
renewable electricity at CPI Group (UK) Ltd

All rights reserved. No part of this publication may be
reproduced, stored in a retrieval system, or transmitted,
in any form or by any means, electronic, mechanical,
photocopying, recording or otherwise, without the
prior written permission of the publishers.

Without limiting the exclusive rights of any author, contributor
or the publisher of this publication, any unauthorised use of
this publication to train generative artificial intelligence (AI)
technologies is expressly prohibited. HarperCollins also exercise
their rights under Article 4(3) of the Digital Single Market
Directive 2019/790 and expressly reserve this publication
from the text and data mining exception.

MIX
Paper | Supporting
responsible forestry
FSC™ C007454

This book contains FSC™ certified paper and other controlled
sources to ensure responsible forest management.

For more information visit: www.harpercollins.co.uk/green

To mum and dad for always encouraging
me to follow my dreams.

CONTENTS

INTRODUCTION

Captain Virgil van Dijk planted a kiss on the Premier League trophy, strolled in front of his team-mates and thrust it triumphantly towards the heavens.

Fireworks and red ticker tape filled the early evening air as a roar of delight swept around Anfield.

It was 25 May 2025 and Liverpool had been crowned champions of England for a record-equalling 20th time.

'It feels amazing,' Van Dijk told the jubilant crowd. 'You guys deserve it. We deserve it as well. We love you guys. I'm so proud of the boys. Let's enjoy the biggest party ever.'

On his first trip back to Merseyside since stepping down as manager a year earlier, a beaming Jurgen Klopp stood applauding in the directors' box as the man who succeeded him, Arne Slot, accepted the acclaim of Anfield. Slot's name was chanted repeatedly.

Replacing such an iconic figure as Klopp had been widely regarded as the most difficult transition facing a major Premier League club since summer 2013, when Sir Alex Ferguson's near 27-year trophy-laden tenure at Manchester United came to an end.

But Slot had made a mockery of that assessment by taking the fast-track to joining the pantheon of Liverpool greats. All expectations had been exceeded.

The Dutchman became just the fifth manager in Premier League history to win the league title in his first season in English football – following on from José Mourinho (Chelsea, 2004/05), Carlo Ancelotti (Chelsea, 2009/10), Manuel Pellegrini (Manchester City, 2013/14) and Antonio Conte (Chelsea, 2016/17).

Only Matt McQueen (1922/23), Joe Fagan (1983/84) and Kenny Dalglish (1985/86) had previously led Liverpool to title glory in their debut campaign at the helm. But that trio had already been well established figures at Anfield before being given the top job, rather than new to the club like Slot.

Having equalled Manchester United's record tally of 20 league titles, and their superior haul of six European Cups compared to United's three, Liverpool's claim to be England's most successful club was undeniable. They were back on their perch.

The sense of euphoria at Anfield was magnified by the fact that it had been 35 years since the club had last been able to celebrate winning the league in front of their supporters. Some had waited their entire lives for that moment.

When Klopp ended Liverpool's long title drought in 2019/20, they had been denied all the trappings that should have come with such an achievement as the season was completed behind closed doors due to restrictions imposed during the global pandemic. This time there was no holding back.

More than a million fans lined the streets of the city for the open-top bus parade which spanned 10 miles and lasted nearly four hours.

The party had actually started a month earlier. With four matches still to play, Liverpool thrashed Tottenham Hotspur 5–1 at home to move an unassailable 15 points clear of nearest rivals

Arsenal. The final whistle had triggered an explosion of joy. Mohamed Salah sank to the turf and pointed to the heavens, while Van Dijk raised both arms aloft. Overcome with emotion, goal-keeper Alisson Becker collapsed in a heap.

There were tears both on the field and in the stands. A red fog hung over Anfield from the flares which had been lit when the players charged towards the Kop. They danced to 'One Kiss' by Dua Lipa and 'Freed From Desire' by Gala. So calm and composed for most of the season, Slot donned a special 'champions 24/25' shirt and unleashed some Klopp-style fist pumps.

Van Dijk called players and staff together to lock arms for a spine-tingling rendition of the club's anthem 'You'll Never Walk Alone'. Liverpool's principal owner John W. Henry stood on the pitch filming the scenes on his mobile phone.

After blowing kisses to his family in the directors' box, Slot had embraced his backroom staff before taking the microphone to address the fans. 'It feels great,' he said. 'I don't think I want to say a lot. The only thing I can do now is send my appreciation to Jurgen.'

A smile crept across his face before he burst into song. '*Jurgen Klopp, na-na-na-na-na,*' he chanted to the tune of 1980s hit 'Live Is Life' by Austrian pop rock band Opus.

Slot was interrupted by the spray unleashed in his direction from shaken alcohol-free sparkling wine bottles by Van Dijk, Andy Robertson, Cody Gakpo and Harvey Elliott. As the head coach was drenched, the home supporters kept the rendition going.

Paying tribute to his predecessor during his own moment of glory was a classy act from Slot. It was impromptu, it was modest and it was also deeply symbolic.

The previous May, Klopp had stood close to the same spot in the Anfield centre circle and delivered a farewell speech. The curtain had just come down on the charismatic German's glittering eight-

and-a-half year Liverpool reign following a 2–0 victory over Wolverhampton Wanderers.

'It doesn't feel like an end, it just feels like the start,' Klopp told supporters. 'I saw a football team playing full of talent, full of youth, full of creativity, full of desire, full of greed. People told me I turned them from doubter to believer. That's not true. Believing is an active act, you have to do it yourself. I just said we have to and you did it. That's a big difference.

'Nobody tells you now to stop believing. This club is in its best moment for a long time. We have this wonderful stadium, wonderful training centre, and we have you, the superpower of world football. Since today I am one of you and I keep believing in you.

'I saw a lot of people crying and it will happen to me tonight as well because I will miss people, but change is good. You never know exactly what to expect, but if you go with the right attitude into that then everything will be fine because the basics are 100 per cent there with the team and the new coach.'

Since Klopp had delivered his bombshell announcement four months earlier that he would be leaving at the end of the 2023/24 season, it had become a running joke that supporters had increasingly ignored his request not to chant his name during matches. Klopp had previously urged them to focus their attention on inspiring the players instead.

'I know you don't give a shit what I want you to sing, but I have an idea,' Klopp grinned. 'Let's see how the response will be … *Arne Slot, na-na-na-na-na.*' Anfield joined in as Slot's name boomed around the stadium for the first time.

The baton had been publicly passed on, even if Klopp had jumped the gun slightly given that Liverpool didn't officially confirm the appointment of his successor until 24 hours later. Klopp's gesture meant a great deal to Slot, who was saying his own goodbyes in the Dutch city of Rotterdam the same day as his successful three-year spell in charge of Feyenoord ended with an emphatic 4–0 win over Excelsior.

The departure of Klopp had been eagerly anticipated by Liverpool's rivals, who expected the club's fortunes to nosedive in his absence.

On the morning of 26 January 2024, shortly after Klopp's decision to step down was made public, Liverpool legend Jamie Carragher was in the ski resort of Courchevel in the French Alps when his phone buzzed. It was a message from former Manchester United defender and fellow Sky Sports pundit Gary Neville.

It read: 'Your manager is fucking off and that's you lot fucked for another 30 years.' It was tongue in cheek, but the sentiment was clear. Even among Liverpool's fanbase there was a feeling of apprehension about what the future would hold.

Ferguson's successor at Manchester United, David Moyes, lasted less than 12 months at Old Trafford and they had remained in an almost constant state of flux since. By the end of the 2024/25 season United had plumbed new depths under manager Ruben Amorim: their 15th-placed league finish was the lowest since 1974/75. The 42-point gap to Liverpool was the biggest-ever between the clubs at the end of a top-flight campaign.

United's title drought had been extended to 12 years – despite spending more than £1.5 billion on transfers during that period.

Internally, senior Anfield figures never feared a similar implosion. For a start, the squad Klopp left behind was younger and more talented. The ownership of Boston-based Fenway Sports Group (FSG) provided stability off the field and they had plenty of time to plan for the new era given Klopp's long goodbye.

However, the fact that the initial target for Slot, who signed a three-year contract, was qualifying for the Champions League showed where the bar was set. His record in Holland was impressive having reached the UEFA Conference League final, won the Eredivisie title and lifted the Dutch Cup with Feyenoord.

But he hadn't coached outside of his homeland and the pressure and scrutiny of managing a global powerhouse like Liverpool represented a big step up. At the age of 45, he also arrived on Merseyside at a time when Manchester City were enjoying a spell of unprecedented dominance.

Pep Guardiola's City had become the first team in the history of English football to be crowned top-flight champions in four successive seasons. As Liverpool's title challenge wilted towards the end of Klopp's reign, Mikel Arteta's Arsenal had been City's nearest challengers.

When BBC Sport asked 30 of their pundits for their Premier League predictions on the eve of the 2024/25 season, not one of them tipped Liverpool to win it. Only two had them down to finish as runners-up and three had them missing out on the top four entirely.

At that stage, Liverpool were the only Premier League club who hadn't made a single signing. They had been poised to trigger the £51 million release clause in the contract of Real Sociedad's Martin Zubimendi, but the Spanish midfielder changed his mind over moving to Anfield and ended up staying put.

By the time the window closed at the end of August, they had bought Federico Chiesa from Juventus for an initial fee of £10 million as a back-up attacker and struck a £29 million agreement with Valencia for goalkeeper Giorgi Mamardashvili to join Liverpool in the summer of 2025.

However, with the sales of Fabio Carvalho, Sepp van den Berg and Bobby Clark generating £62 million, Liverpool had made a healthy profit on their summer dealings. There had been no statement of ambition in the transfer market and a section of the fanbase were restless, given the money invested by their rivals.

Throw into the mix that Slot was without most of his star names until late in pre-season due to their extended breaks following international commitments at the European Championships and the Copa América. There was also growing uncertainty over the futures of captain Virgil van Dijk, Mohamed Salah and Trent Alexander-Arnold as they entered the final year of their contracts.

But through his tactical acumen and expert man-management, Slot took the squad he inherited from Klopp to the next level. There was no title race, simply a procession as Liverpool embarked on an astonishing 26-game unbeaten league run between September and April. They set standards that no-one else came close to replicating as they led the way from early November onwards and never looked back. When the title was secured, they had been beaten just twice in 34 matches.

Slot was helped by one of the greatest individual seasons in the history of English football. Salah not only won the Premier League Golden Boot with 29 league goals (34 in all competitions) but also walked away with the Playmaker award after contributing 18 league assists (23 in all competitions).

The prolific Egyptian attacker broke the record for most goal involvements over a 38-game Premier League season which was previously held jointly by Arsenal's Thierry Henry (2002/03) and Manchester City's Erling Haaland (2022/23) with 44.

Salah was crowned the Football Writers' Association Footballer of the Year for a record-equalling third time after receiving almost 90 per cent of the votes, the biggest margin of victory this century. At the other end of the field, Slot benefited from the inspirational leadership of Van Dijk, who became the first Dutch player to captain a side to the English top-flight crown and also the first non-British player to skipper Liverpool to the league championship.

The feelgood factor during the run-in had been fuelled by the sight of both Salah and Van Dijk signing two-year extensions. Confirmation that Alexander-Arnold would be leaving for Real Madrid created a side-show, but ultimately it didn't detract from the enormity of Liverpool's achievement.

The summer of 2025 should have been one of celebration and unbridled optimism on Merseyside as the champions' squad evolved with the biggest transfer spending spree in the club's history.

However, just 39 days after the trophy lift, the mood at Anfield was one of shock and devastation. On the morning of 3 July 2025 the news broke that Liverpool forward Diogo Jota and his brother André Silva had died in a car accident in Spain. They had been en route to Santander to catch a ferry to England when the Lamborghini they were travelling in careered off the road.

Jota had married his childhood sweetheart Rute Cardoso in their home city of Porto less than a fortnight earlier and they had three young children. Professionally, the 28-year-old had followed up clinching the Premier League title with Liverpool by helping Portugal win the Nations League. It was all so unimaginably cruel.

Suddenly, a tale of glorious triumph was also one of heartbreaking tragedy. Grieving supporters descended on Anfield in their thousands to pay their respects and leave flowers, cards, shirts, scarves, banners, flags, hats and even PlayStation controllers, a nod to Jota's love of gaming. The shrine outside the Main Stand quickly spanned the entire length of the stadium.

Liverpool permanently retired his No. 20 shirt. It was an unprecedented gesture by the club in memory of a player who touched the hearts of millions around the world, not just with his talent with a ball at his feet, but also with his humble, kind and genuine personality.

Among the tributes, one written on a Liverpool shirt outside Anfield read: 'He signed in 2020, he wore the No. 20, and he won us No. 20. Forever a Red.'

Rest in peace Diogo.

1

THE TRANSFORMER

'It's not so important what people think when you come in, it's much more important what they think when you leave.'

Jurgen Klopp

The Titanic Hotel – close to Liverpool's iconic waterfront – was the setting for a lavish farewell party.

After all the emotion of Jurgen Klopp's Anfield send-off a few hours earlier, it was time for players and staff to unwind with family and friends. The champagne flowed on the evening of 19 May 2024 and an orchestral band played before the DJ, Twotone, took over.

As Liverpool legend John Barnes delighted the crowd with a rendition of 'Rapper's Delight' by the Sugarhill Gang, Klopp made his way up to the stage. They formed an unlikely double act as Barnes rapped and Klopp, wearing a black shirt, blue jeans and a black baseball cap on back to front, showed off his dance moves.

The array of silverware won during Klopp's tenure was on display and there was a photo booth for guests to get prints emblazoned with the caption 'Danke Jurgen'. The celebrations went on until 4 a.m.

At one point the big screen showed a collection of video messages from current and former players thanking Klopp for the impact he had made on their careers. There were also tributes paid to defender Joel Matip and midfielder Thiago, who were both leaving the club as free agents at the end of the 2023/24 season.

Klopp's diary had been packed during his final week at the helm. The players were given the following day off after a chaotic 3–3 draw at Aston Villa on the Monday night, but Klopp headed to Anfield.

After walking across the pitch and standing on the Kop with a Liverpool scarf around his neck filming a goodbye video with the in-house LFCTV crew, he attended a special event for around 700 club staff from across all departments in the Main Stand's biggest executive lounge.

There was an hour-long Q&A during which he talked about what it meant to be part of the 'LFC family'. There was both laughter and tears. Despite having spent nearly a decade living in England, he conceded that some things still baffled him: 'Cricket! I hear the scores announced and I still have no idea who has won.'

Klopp revealed that he would be back at Anfield sooner than anyone anticipated as his wife Ulla had got them tickets to attend Taylor Swift's concert in the stadium the following month and he started singing her hit song 'Shake It Off'.

His advice for building a great team? 'Build it around Bobby Firmino.' Klopp went on to explain that his favourite Scouse word was 'luv' and it had taken him years to understand why the ladies in the canteen at the training ground would say to him each morning: 'Do you wanna coffee, luv?'

It was Klopp's idea to have 'Thank you luv' emblazoned on the front of the hoodies that departing staff put on after his final game in charge against Wolverhampton Wanderers. On the back of them it read: 'I'll Never Walk Alone Again'.

At the end of the Q&A, Liverpool chief executive Billy Hogan presented Klopp with a book full of photos and heartfelt messages written by staff members. Flicking through it, he spotted a photo of himself looking fresh faced at his Anfield unveiling in October 2015.

'This is proof of why I have to leave,' he chuckled. 'It was only eight-and-a-half years ago, but it looks like 500!'

Klopp couldn't stay for the refreshments because he had accepted an invitation to have dinner with Sir Alex Ferguson. Despite Liverpool's intense rivalry with Manchester United, there had been a long-standing mutual respect between them. Klopp had described encountering the United managerial legend for the first time as 'like meeting the Pope'.

When Klopp was crowned the League Managers' Association Manager of the Year after ending Liverpool's 30-year title drought in 2019/20, Ferguson had been effusive in his praise. 'Incredible and thoroughly deserved,' Ferguson said. 'The performance level of your team was outstanding. Your personality went right through the whole club. I'll forgive you for waking me up at half past three in the morning to tell me you'd won the league!'

Liverpool weren't just losing Klopp in May 2024. Assistant managers Peter Krawietz and Pep Lijnders, elite development coach Vitor Matos, goalkeeping coaches John Achterberg and Jack Robinson, head of fitness Andreas Kornmayer, head of recovery and performance Andreas Schlumberger, and first-team operations manager Ray Haughan were all moving on.

Klopp spent his last Wednesday evening in charge in his local pub, The Freshfield, in the town of Formby, 12 miles north of Anfield, drinking beer and reminiscing with Krawietz and members of the club's media department.

The following day Van Dijk delivered a moving speech at a barbecue held at the club's AXA Training Centre in Kirkby. The squad presented Klopp and each of his coaches with a Rolex watch as a leaving gift.

After overseeing his final training session on the Saturday, Klopp cleared out his office. He broke down while reading letters from fans who detailed how he had changed their lives. The *Liverpool Echo* newspaper published his open letter to the fans in which he described Liverpool as 'the city of open arms'.

Much to the amusement of the players, given his repeated warnings to them over the years about the perils of using social media, Klopp launched his own Instagram account. Within 48 hours, @Kloppo had gathered more than two million followers.

With Liverpool already destined to finish third in the Premier League, there was little riding on the game against Wolves but a 2–0 win was secured by goals from Alexis Mac Allister and Jarell Quansah. After returning to the home dressing room, Klopp addressed the squad for one final time.

'I love you, that's all I can say,' he said. 'The football you are able to play is absolutely ridiculous. I can't wait, watching you developing, making the next steps. Thank you for the ride. I'm so proud of you, and I'm so proud that I have been allowed to be part of this. The sky is the limit for you boys.'

When Klopp finally conducted his post-match press conference some two hours after the final whistle, he got his mobile phone out and took a photo of the journalists sitting in front of him. 'In case I miss you,' he joked.

Nine days later, following a holiday in Majorca, there was one final date on his goodbye tour as 10,000 supporters packed into Liverpool's M&S Bank Arena for 'An Evening With Jurgen Klopp'. Hosted by comedian John Bishop and LFCTV presenter Peter McDowall, it raised funds for the charitable work of the LFC Foundation. Klopp had agreed to become an honorary ambassador and made a personal donation of €100,000 (around £86,000).

The event started with a video message from James Bond actor Daniel Craig: 'In the few precious moments I spent with you, I said, hand on heart, I would follow that man anywhere.

'Thank-you for what you've achieved at Liverpool Football Club. It's been quite a ride. Your ability to cut through the bullshit and get to the heart of what really matters has inspired me and millions of people around the world. Wherever you go and whatever you do, I wish you and your family only joy.'

There was music from singer Alfie Boe and Liverpool bands the Lightning Seeds and the Zutons, but Klopp took centre stage. He joked that he was the third 'Scouser' to sell out the arena after Paul McCartney and Jamie Webster.

'What you did here tonight no other club in the world would have done,' he said. 'If another club had done this nine days after the last fella had left then it would have been empty.

'I don't think the human race is made for getting as much attention as I've had over the past few weeks. I wasn't ready to receive this much love. I've known myself the longest, nearly 57 years, how can you imagine that something like this would happen? If my best friend was in the same situation I'd sit up there and think: "He's probably a decent fella." But unfortunately, you're talking about me and I can't get my head around that.'

Klopp described taking the Liverpool job in 2015 as the best decision of his life after marrying his wife Ulla. 'If it was easy to leave then what would that say about the time we had together? It's really difficult to leave and that's how it should be. Let's not be sad that it's ending, be happy that it happened.'

Asked about his reasons for standing down, Klopp added: 'A lot of people don't believe me when I say I'm running out of energy. It's not that I can't get up in the morning. Being manager of Liverpool, you can't do it at 90 per cent. You have to be on top of your game and I'm not anymore. I cannot be here as a passenger.

'Announcing it early was important. Imagine we played against Wolves, the families were walking around and then I said: "By the way, I fuck off!" That doesn't work. The club would have problems. When you are responsible for a club like this you have to make sensible decisions and that's what I did. Was it right? Absolutely and the timing we couldn't change. It was a good season, not a perfect season. It's a basis. We helped the new manager already by not winning everything so he can improve things.'

After a montage of highlights from his Liverpool reign was played on the big screen, the night ended with Klopp being sere-naded by supporters for nearly two minutes to the tune of the famous Beatles song 'I Feel Fine'.

Jurgen said to me you know
We'll win the Premier League you know
He said so
I'm in love with him and I feel fine
I'm so glad that Jurgen is a Red
I'm so glad he delivered what he said.

Puffing out his cheeks and wiping tears from his eyes, Klopp got to his feet before delivering his customary fist pumps one last time.

Liverpool Football Club were in a mess.

Two days after Fenway Sports Group (then known as New England Sports Ventures) won a London High Court battle to complete a £300 million takeover of the Premier League club in October 2010, principal owner John W. Henry and chairman Tom Werner took their seats for the Merseyside derby at Goodison Park.

It was an unpleasant experience in more ways than one. Roy Hodgson's Liverpool slumped to a dismal 2–0 defeat which left them 19th in the table – only goal difference kept them off the bottom.

'After Everton scored one of their goals, one of their supporters spat at John and me,' Werner recalled. 'It was a somewhat rude welcome to English football. Gradually, the enormity of the task we had taken on unfolded and revealed itself.'

The debt-ridden and divisive reign of former American owners Tom Hicks and George Gillett had taken its toll both on and off the pitch with Liverpool pulled back from the brink of administration.

Within three months Hodgson had been sacked and Kop legend Sir Kenny Dalglish returned for a second spell in charge to spearhead the resurgence. He galvanised the fanbase and won the League Cup, but was relieved of his duties in May 2012 after a disappointing eighth-placed finish.

The owners had expected Champions League qualification after sanctioning a £113 million outlay on transfers, including a club record £35 million on Newcastle United striker Andy Carroll. Director of football Damien Comolli was also dismissed.

FSG then put their faith in Brendan Rodgers, who came agonisingly close to winning the Premier League in 2013/14. It was breathtaking to watch as the lethal front two of Luis Suárez and Daniel Sturridge, who scored 52 league goals between them that season, spearheaded an unexpected title challenge. Rodgers' Liverpool needed just seven points from their remaining three league games to be crowned champions.

However, there was heartbreak as Steven Gerrard's cruel slip against José Mourinho's Chelsea at Anfield consigned them to a damaging defeat. A late capitulation at Crystal Palace then sealed their fate as Manchester City pipped them to the big prize.

After hitting such heights, the wheels came off under Rodgers. Suárez left for Barcelona and Liverpool made a hash of replacing him as they missed out on Alexis Sanchez, who joined Arsenal instead. They ended up signing the erratic Mario Balotelli, who scored just four times in 28 appearances before being cast aside.

The nadir was a humiliating 6–1 thrashing at Stoke City on the final day of the 2014/15 season – the final appearance of Gerrard's stellar Liverpool career. It was a sad way for the club's greatest player of the modern era to sign off. Despite a sixth-placed finish, Rodgers limped on into the following season but with little discernible improvement FSG took action. The Northern Irishman was relieved of his duties after a 1–1 draw at Everton on 4 October 2015. Liverpool were 10th in the Premier League with just 12 points from eight matches.

By then Klopp had already agreed to cut short his sabbatical after stepping down as Borussia Dortmund boss five months earlier. He had flown from Munich to New York with his agent Marc Kosicke to meet Liverpool's owners at the Lexington Avenue offices of law firm Shearman & Sterling, having already spoken extensively with FSG president Mike Gordon on the phone.

FSG also met with Italian coach Carlo Ancelotti, who was available after parting company with Real Madrid, but Klopp was always their top target. It wasn't just the success he had masterminded at Dortmund with back-to-back Bundesliga titles, lifting the German Cup and reaching the Champions League final, but the manner in which it had been achieved with such an exciting attacking brand of football and his sheer force of personality.

The data provided by Liverpool's director of research Ian Graham told the owners not to be concerned about the downturn in Dortmund's fortunes in Klopp's final season there: the underlying numbers were much better than the results. Whereas Ancelotti talked about the need for a rebuilding job at Anfield, Klopp saw plenty of untapped potential in the existing squad.

'After that first meeting, we turned to each other and said: "Forget his tactical strategy, he's absolutely the right person for this club,"' Werner told *The Athletic* in 2024. 'We had interviewed other coaches but he was just extraordinarily charismatic. He could be the CEO of any number of big companies outside of football. He has this remarkable ability to motivate people.'

It was just after 5.30 p.m. on Thursday 8 October 2015 when Klopp arrived at Liverpool's Hope Street Hotel in a Mercedes V-Class and headed for The Sixth boardroom to sign a three-year contract. At his Anfield unveiling in front of the world's media the following day, Klopp delivered a masterful display as he described himself as 'the normal one' and urged fans to 'change from doubters to believers'.

'If we want, this could be a very special day,' he said. 'If you are prepared to work for it, if you are patient enough. If I'm sat here in four years, I think we will have won one title in this time. If not, the next one [job] may be in Switzerland!'

'It's not so important what people think of you when you come in, it's much more important what they think when you leave.'

No managerial appointment in Liverpool's history had created such fervour or been so universally popular among supporters, but the scale of the task facing Klopp was immense.

This was a club which had won just a solitary League Cup in the previous nine years and had only qualified for the Champions League once in the previous six seasons. They were competing against opponents with much deeper pockets. Manchester City were bankrolled by the riches of Abu Dhabi, while Chelsea had the financial backing of Russian billionaire Roman Abramovich.

Klopp had turned down an approach from Manchester United the previous year after discussions in Germany with their executive vice-chairman Ed Woodward, who had described Old Trafford as 'like an adult version of Disneyland'. That didn't appeal to Klopp. But the self-confessed 'football romantic' was energised by the prospect of reviving Liverpool's fortunes.

He quickly established that the downward spiral of the previous 18 months and a torrent of negativity had left the Liverpool players feeling inhibited and devoid of confidence. He told them: 'The only criticism which is really important is mine.' Time off was reduced and training sessions became much more intense as he sought to instil his gruelling counter-pressing style.

In one of his first team meetings with the squad he wrote on the board:

T – TERRIBLE
E – ENTHUSIASTIC
A – AMBITIOUS
M – MENTALLY-STRONG MACHINES

'He said that terrible was how opponents were going to feel after going up against us for 90 minutes,' recalls goalkeeper Simon Mignolet. 'It was all about being part of a team – everyone working together and being a machine to break opponents down.'

Klopp asked all the staff based at the club's Melwood training complex to pass through the room one by one and told his players: 'Everyone has to know everyone's name. These people are here to help you perform. We're all one family. Everyone is responsible for everything.'

Kenny Grimes had worked on the gate as security at Melwood since 1994. 'The culture soon changed,' he said. 'Everyone just seemed happier and more relaxed. Jurgen made you feel part of Liverpool FC to a much greater extent.'

Klopp also had to change attitudes at Anfield. A month into the job, he was baffled by the sight of fans heading towards the exit gates with Liverpool 2–1 down at home to Crystal Palace with a few minutes remaining. 'I felt pretty alone,' Klopp admitted in his post-match press conference. 'We decide when it's over.'

When Divock Origi scored a stoppage-time equaliser against West Bromwich Albion a month later, Klopp made the players hold hands afterwards in front of the Kop. He was mocked by critics for 'celebrating' a draw against mid-table opposition but they missed the point. It was simply a show of togetherness and a thank-you to supporters who had stuck by the team during a difficult afternoon.

The players had expected their Christmas party at Formby Hall Golf Resort and Spa to be cancelled after a chastening 3–0 loss at Watford, but much to their surprise they all received a text message from Klopp which read: 'Whatever we do together, we do as well as we can, and tonight that means we party.' They were told they had to stay until at least 1 a.m.

Klopp reached two finals with the squad he inherited. Defeat to Manchester City on penalties in the League Cup final at Wembley was followed by an unexpected run to the final of the Europa League in Switzerland.

Liverpool trailed 4–2 on aggregate with just 25 minutes remaining of the quarter-final second leg against Klopp's former club Borussia Dortmund before staging a stunning fightback. Dejan Lovren's 91st minute header sent Anfield into raptures. 'The Kop created the best half an hour I've ever had in football,' Klopp said.

Sturridge fired them ahead against Sevilla in the final but they fell apart in the second half and were beaten 3–1. Klopp was determined to lift the despondent mood back at Basel's Novotel and gathered players and staff together on the dance floor. Taking the microphone, he said: 'Two hours ago you all felt shit. Now hopefully you all feel better. This is just the start for us. We will play in many more finals.' Klopp then launched into a rendition of 'We are Liverpool, tra-la-la-la!'

After finishing eighth in the Premier League, reinforcements arrived in the summer of 2016 in the form of Sadio Mané,

Georginio Wijnaldum, Joel Matip and Loris Karius. Both Mané and Wijnaldum had also been targeted by Tottenham, but Klopp's sales pitch ensured they were Anfield-bound.

In his attempt to raise standards, Klopp made it abundantly clear that indiscipline would not be tolerated. Defender Mamadou Sakho was sent home in disgrace from the pre-season tour of America after being late for the team flight to California, late for a team meal and then failing to turn up to a treatment session. 'We have rules. If somebody doesn't respect it or somebody gives me the feeling he is not respecting it, then I have to react,' Klopp said.

The French centre-back had missed the end of the previous season following a failed UEFA drugs test. He was subsequently cleared but Klopp was furious that he had taken weight-loss supplements without the club's knowledge. Sakho joined Crystal Palace, initially on loan the following January, and never played for Liverpool again.

Roberto Firmino, who had struggled under Brendan Rodgers after arriving from Hoffenheim, was transformed after being moved into a central attacking role. Klopp's side were also indebted to the goals of Philippe Coutinho and Mané as they secured a top-four finish and Champions League qualification by beating Middlesbrough 3–0 on the final day of the 2016/17 season.

Nurturing young talent proved to be a theme of the Klopp era with academy graduate Trent Alexander-Arnold soon establishing himself as the first-choice right-back after being handed his debut at the age of 18.

'Especially early on, as a young player coming through at such a big club, you go through a lot: the demands, the pressure, the expectation,' Alexander-Arnold told *The Athletic* in 2024. 'Jurgen helped me so much. He put an arm around me and took the pressure off. He talked to me about managing my emotions. He knew when a bollocking was needed or a little bit of love. He helped me go from being a young player breaking through to being a leader. I owe him so much.'

Prior to Klopp's appointment, Liverpool's recruitment process had been dysfunctional. Rodgers' refusal to work with a sporting director meant that a transfer committee was formed comprising of the manager, chief executive Ian Ayre, technical director Michael Edwards, head of recruitment Dave Fallows and chief scout Barry Hunter.

Director of research Ian Graham, who boasts a PhD in biological physics from the University of Cambridge, was an 'unofficial member' of the committee after being headhunted by Edwards from data company Decision Technology in 2012. The Welshman was tasked with building the first in-house analytics department in the Premier League. FSG's data-led approach was designed to find value in the market, but there was friction behind the scenes over which players should be pursued.

'The typical experience of a data person going into a club back in the early 2010s was you come in with some bright ideas straight out of university and some old football guys think, "This is all rubbish; we're not going to listen to this stuff",' Graham told *The Athletic* in 2024. 'There was resistance – and there was certainly resistance from Brendan.'

Rodgers had wanted Ashley Williams and Ryan Bertrand but ended up with Sakho and Alberto Moreno. The manager got his own way with the signing of Fabio Borini, who he had previously managed at Swansea City, when other members of the committee felt that Daniel Sturridge was a better option. Sturridge was belatedly bought from Chelsea six months later.

It became well known publicly which players were 'Rodgers' signings' such as Joe Allen, Rickie Lambert and Adam Lallana, and which players were 'committee signings' such as Iago Aspas, Emre Can and Lazar Markovic.

'In the first few years of the transfer committee, those failed signings, most of them were because the players we wanted to bring in Brendan vetoed,' Graham added. 'And the ones Brendan wanted to bring in we vetoed. So at times we ended up with fifth or sixth choice players. We just weren't getting our top targets.'

In the summer of 2015, Graham had opposed Rodgers' plan to buy Aston Villa striker Christian Benteke because the data suggested he would be a poor fit for Liverpool's style. However, the owners agreed to trigger his £32.5 million release clause with the compromise being that Rodgers would accept the signing of Firmino from Hoffenheim for £29 million. Firmino, who was greatly admired by Edwards, went on to score 111 goals in 362 games for Liverpool, while Benteke was off-loaded after just one season having netted 10 times in 42 appearances.

With Klopp at the helm, the following summer window was much less fraught. 'The difference was Jurgen's open-mindedness,' Graham said. 'The data gradually became more sophisticated and the models improved, but there wasn't a step-change in the quality of our analysis when Brendan left and Jurgen arrived. It was the same processes and the same people. Jurgen saw players in the same way as Michael Edwards, whereas Brendan didn't.

'Jurgen believed in experts and that they can make a difference. He knew that data informed our recruitment process and the feed-back he got after games from our video analysis department and he was receptive to that. In those first two seasons in particular, Jurgen was suggesting players I would have been suggesting to him. What he saw in a player was the same as what we saw in a player. We didn't have to fight.'

There was a clear strategy but good fortune also played a part. Klopp had initially targeted Bayern Munich's Mario Gotze before Mané was signed from Southampton for £30 million in June 2016. Gotze, who scored the winning goal for Germany in the 2014

World Cup final against Argentina, visited Klopp's house in Formby, but opted to stay in his homeland and joined Borussia Dortmund instead because they could offer Champions League football.

The following summer Klopp held talks with Bayer Leverkusen's Julian Brandt before being convinced that Mohamed Salah was actually the best wide forward available on the market. The Egyptian attacker had been branded a Premier League flop after an unsuccessful stint at Chelsea, but Liverpool's scouting reports and data analysis of his performances in Italy, first for Fiorentina and then Roma, were glowing. Edwards, who by then had been promoted to the role of sporting director, agreed a £43.9 million deal.

'We couldn't believe that we were able to sign Mo,' Graham said. 'We didn't understand why Man City or Arsenal weren't putting in bids. From a complicated data point of view, he ticked all the boxes. Mo came with the baggage of having failed in the Premier League, but our data analysis helped us to understand that we could ignore that. Michael Edwards, Dave Fallows and Barry Hunter convinced Jurgen to go for Mo and he was gracious enough to speak publicly about the part they played in that.

'Signing Mo because he had failed at Chelsea was doing something different, but we didn't care about looking stupid. That was the difference between us and a lot of clubs at that time. We just cared about making the right decision and we believed in the process. It was similar with Firmino and Mané, who came from mid-table clubs. They were the three stars. Everyone at the club was really excited we could get them. We didn't care that the rest of the world didn't feel that way.'

Shortly after Salah's arrival, data also played an important role in the £10 million signing of left-back Andy Robertson from relegated Hull City, who had the worst defensive record in the Premier League. 'It's pretty rare that a big club signs you off the back of something like that,' Graham said. 'The club had just got back into the Champions League and it felt like the first steps of the journey. You could see how much belief everyone had in Jurgen. The whole club was connected. Before, from the outside looking in, it didn't look that way. Part of that was signing good characters: people who could carry his messages within the changing room as his eyes can't be everywhere.'

Salah rewrote the Premier League record books in 2017/18, setting a new best of 32 league goals over a 38-game season as he scored 44 times in all competitions. As well as the Golden Boot, he landed the PFA Player of the Year and the FWA Footballer of the Year double. The three-pronged attack of Salah, Firmino and Mané contributed a staggering 91 goals between them.

Fears that the mid-season sale of Coutinho to Barcelona for £142 million would derail the club's resurgence proved misplaced as Klopp's side excelled. Liverpool reached their first Champions League final for 11 years and secured back-to-back top-four finishes in the Premier League for the first time since 2009.

Five days before Coutinho's exit, Liverpool shattered their transfer record to sign Southampton centre-back Virgil van Dijk for £75 million. It proved to be one of the most transformative signings of the Premier League era.

Buying a player for that kind of money was alien to Klopp. He had always developed elite talent rather than bought the finished article. 'I want to do it differently,' Klopp had told reporters 18 months earlier after Manchester United had made Paul Pogba the most expensive player in world football following a £89 million move from Juventus.

Accused of hypocrisy after Van Dijk became the most expensive defender on the planet, Klopp grinned and said: 'Did I change my opinion? Yes. That is true. But it is better to change your opinion than never have one.'

Van Dijk's arrival solved one area for weakness as Liverpool finally had the defensive leader they had lacked since Jamie Carragher's retirement in 2013. However, there was another glaring issue Klopp was still grappling with.

'I'm infinitely sorry to my team-mates, for you fans, and for all the staff. I know that I messed it up with the two mistakes and let you all down. I'd just like to turn back the time but that's not possible,' tearful goalkeeper Loris Karius posted on social media in the aftermath of the 3–1 defeat to Real Madrid in the 2018 Champions League final.

For the opening half-hour in Kyiv, Liverpool had more than held their own but then came the skulduggery and the implosion. A tearful Salah was forced off with a shoulder injury after being cynically slammed into the turf by Sergio Ramos. The Real Madrid captain struck again early in the second half when his stray elbow caught Karius in the head.

Moments later, the goalkeeper inexplicably rolled the ball straight into the path of Karim Benzema, who gleefully accepted the gift. Mané's equaliser briefly gave Liverpool hope but it was swiftly whipped away by the impact of substitute Gareth Bale. His sensational overhead kick restored the advantage and the Welshman settled proceedings with seven minutes left when his 30-yarder embarrassingly slipped through Karius' grasp.

Captain Jordan Henderson emerged from a scene of devastation in the dressing room to tell reporters: 'It was the worst feeling, but I believe in this team, I believe in this manager. We will be back in the Champions League final again.'

Four days after the final, Klopp received a call from Germany legend Franz Beckenbauer, who alerted him to the possibility that Karius may have been concussed by the blow from Ramos shortly before his first blunder of the night. This set in motion a bizarre chain of events that led to Karius, who by that stage was on holiday in America, being told to visit specialists at Boston's Massachusetts General Hospital.

Brain scans showed Karius had 'visual-spatial dysfunction', which can result in an inability to judge where objects are. Out of 30 markers for concussion, Liverpool said test results showed he had 26 of them. 'What the rest of the world is making of it, I don't care,' insisted Klopp, who branded Ramos 'a brutal wrestler'. 'We don't use it as an excuse, we use it as an explanation.'

Karius' confidence was shot to bits and he never played in a competitive game for the club again. Behind the scenes, Liverpool had been working on a replacement long before the Champions League final. Goalkeeper coach John Achterberg had followed Alisson Becker's development closely since being alerted to his potential by former Liverpool goalkeeper Alexander Doni in 2013 and had compiled an extensive dossier on the Roma No. 1.

'When we played against Ali in a pre-season friendly in the United States in 2016, I told Jurgen: "This is the one I was telling you about." I kept watching and writing reports on every game he played. I spoke to all the recruitment guys about him,' Achterberg said.

'There was a meeting in January 2018 with Ali's agent when we said how highly we rated him. That summer, we were going to sign midfielder Nabil Fekir from Lyon for £62 million, but the club backed out because he had a bad knee.

'If the Fekir deal had gone through, would we have had the money to sign Ali? Things certainly turned out for the best. I told the boss that Ali was the one. We needed to move quick in mid-July because we knew Thibaut Courtois was leaving Chelsea (to join Real Madrid) and they needed a replacement.'

Initially quoted £90 million by Roma, Edwards negotiated a £65 million deal for Alisson. He proved to be the final piece of the jigsaw. In his first season at Anfield, the Brazilian won the Premier

League Golden Glove for most clean sheets (21) and was crowned goalkeeper of the year by both UEFA and FIFA.

Alisson's stunning save to deny Napoli's Arkadiusz Milik deep into stoppage time during the final Champions League group game at Anfield in December 2018 proved to be one of the most pivotal moments of Klopp's reign.

If Milik had scored, Liverpool would have been dumped out of Europe. 'It was a lifesaver. If I'd known Ali was this good, I'd have paid double,' joked Klopp, who walked around the training ground singing '*All you need is Al-i-sson Beck-er*' to the tune of Queen's 'Radio Ga Ga'.

Liverpool marched on to the final in Madrid after an historic comeback against Barcelona in the second leg of the semi-final. They looked doomed after losing the first leg in the Nou Camp 3–0 and they had to face Lionel Messi and co at Anfield without the injured duo of Salah and Firmino.

In the pre-game meeting at the city's Hope Street Hotel, Klopp told his squad: 'The world outside is saying it is not possible. And let's be honest, it is probably impossible. But because it's you, we have a chance.'

What followed was arguably the greatest night Anfield has ever hosted. Divock Origi pulled one back before Wijnaldum's quick double early in the second half wiped out the deficit. Then, with 11 minutes to go, Alexander-Arnold took the most famous corner in Liverpool's history. His quick thinking with the delivery was accompanied by a clinical finish from Origi.

Despite winning their last nine Premier League games in that 2018/19 season and achieving a then club record haul of 97 points with just one defeat, Klopp's 'mentality monsters' missed out on the title by a point to Manchester City.

However, on a balmy night against Tottenham in Madrid they finally took the leap from nearly men to winners. 'Let's talk about six, baby,' Klopp beamed after Salah's early penalty and Origi's drilled finish late on sealed the club's sixth European Cup. 'Did you ever see a team like this, fighting, with no fuel in the tank? They suffer for me. They deserve it more than anybody.'

Around 750,000 supporters lined the streets of Liverpool for the victory parade the day after with Klopp declaring: 'If you could've put all the emotions, all the excitement, all the love in the air that day and bottled it up, the world would be a better place.'

It acted as a springboard to more success. Liverpool lifted both the UEFA Super Cup and the Club World Cup in 2019/20 before ending the painful 30-year wait for a 19th top-flight league title. In taking 79 points out of the first 81 on offer, Klopp's side blew their rivals away.

Some 25 points clear with nine games to go, they were on the cusp of glory when the season was suspended in March due to the Covid-19 pandemic. The players assembled in the canteen at Melwood when Klopp told them: 'Don't worry about football for now. You are the best team in England and the most worthy champions there has ever been.' He described football as 'the most important of the least important things in life' and urged them to focus on taking care of their families.

Their triumph was belatedly confirmed in late June after Manchester City lost to Chelsea. Players and staff celebrated together at Formby Hall, but the trophy-lift took place in a largely deserted Anfield and there was no parade. Not being able to share that eagerly-anticipated moment with the supporters hurt Klopp. Champions with seven games to spare, Liverpool finished on 99 points.

Having scaled such heights, they fell quickly. For a team that fed off the emotional energy in the stands, playing behind closed doors was a hard, soulless slog. Klopp also had to deal with the personal heartache of losing his mother Elizabeth and not being able to travel home to Germany for the funeral due to travel restrictions.

Liverpool had brought in Diogo Jota and Thiago to boost their title defence, but it unravelled due to an unprecedented centre-back crisis after Van Dijk, Joe Gomez and Matip all suffered season-ending injuries. Playing Henderson and Fabinho in the backline didn't work as it weakened the midfield. Having gone 68 home league matches unbeaten, they suffered six successive home league defeats – their most in a single campaign at Anfield since 1953/54.

Klopp ultimately turned to rookie defenders Nat Phillips and Rhys Williams to help salvage their top-four hopes. Remarkably, they took 26 points out of the last 30 on offer to finish third in 2020/21. The highlight of the run-in was Alisson's 95th minute headed winner at West Bromwich Albion as he became the first goalkeeper to score a competitive goal in the club's 129-year history. After being mobbed by his team-mates, he pointed to the heavens in tribute to his father José, who had tragically drowned in Brazil three months earlier. 'I'm sure he is celebrating with God at his side,' Alisson said.

Buoyed by the return of Van Dijk, and the shrewd signings of Ibrahima Konaté and Luis Díaz, Liverpool were soon back competing for the biggest prizes in 2021/22.

Klopp was an innovator. Having recruited Thomas Gronnemark as a specialist throw-in coach and brought in renowned big-wave surfer Sebastian Steudtner to teach the players breathing techniques, he enlisted the help of German neuroscientists from Neuro11 to do 'brain training' to improve output from dead-ball situations. Dr Niklas Hausler and Patrick Hantschke attached electrodes to the players' heads to measure brain activity and help them get 'in the zone' by reaching their optimal mental state.

Both the League Cup and FA Cup finals were won on penalties against Chelsea at Wembley with Liverpool scoring 17 of their 18 spot-kicks across the two shootouts. Quadruple talk gathered pace but Liverpool missed out on the Premier League and the Champions League by the finest of margins.

Once again the title race went down to the final day but Manchester City's late fightback from 2–0 down to beat Aston Villa 3–2 ensured they finished a point clear. Liverpool ended up on 92 points – the third time in the space of four seasons they had broken the 90-point barrier, but they had just one title to show for it.

Six days later, there was more anguish as they lost a Champions League final they really should have won against Real Madrid in Paris. The showpiece occasion was blighted by the chaos outside the stadium due to the organisational failings of UEFA and the French police, who resorted to using tear gas indiscriminately. Supporters found themselves crushed in dangerous bottlenecks and attacked by local gangs.

On the field, Liverpool were thwarted by the heroics of Real Madrid goalkeeper Thibaut Courtois and Vinicius Junior's goal after Alexander-Arnold was caught out at the back post. 'Where's next year's final? Istanbul. Book the hotel,' Klopp said defiantly post-match. Considering his side had netted a club record 147 goals in all competitions in 2021/22, it was a crazy statistic that across the three major finals they failed to score once – despite having 61 shots with an xG (expected goals) figure of 5.7.

With Mané joining Bayern Munich for £35 million and Firmino preparing to leave on the expiry of his contract in 2023, the front-line evolved. They broke their transfer record to seal a £85 million deal for Benfica's Darwin Núñez and Cody Gakpo followed from PSV Eindhoven for £44 million the following January.

However, Klopp overestimated what some loyal servants had left in the tank after an energy-sapping 63-game campaign. The 2022/23 season was bleak as an ageing midfield was repeatedly out-run and out-fought, and injuries cut deep. As the defeats stacked up, the manager became increasingly tetchy in his dealings with the media. Morale in the squad nosedived. 'I can't remember a worse game in my career,' was Klopp's assessment of a 3–0 reverse at the hands of Brighton as the problems kept stacking up.

The tactical tweak of moving Alexander-Arnold into the centre when Liverpool were in possession sparked a late revival, but it was in vain as they trailed home fifth and lost their status among Europe's elite.

There had been upheaval off the field with sporting director Edwards leaving in 2022 and his successor Julian Ward stepped down after just one year in the role. Some colleagues wondered if the manager would follow suit given the strain of such a difficult campaign.

But Klopp felt a big responsibility to stick around and oversee the major changes that were needed. James Milner, Naby Keita, Firmino and Alex Oxlade-Chamberlain all left as free agents, while Henderson and Fabinho were lured away by the riches on offer from the Saudi Pro League.

With the midfield department rebuilt with the signings of Alexis Mac Allister, Dominik Szoboszlai, Wataru Endo and Ryan Gravenberch in the summer of 2023, Klopp coined the phrase 'Liverpool 2.0' as a new chapter opened.

From the outside, Klopp looked refreshed as Liverpool clicked back into gear, but behind the scenes, the reality was very different.

Staff had first noticed that he was struggling under the weight of the job during the club's training camp in Dubai in December 2022. With Edwards gone, Ward serving his notice and FSG president Mike Gordon having taken a step back as the owners considered the possibility of selling the club, Klopp was increasingly isolated.

'That whole period was incredibly difficult,' recalls one senior Anfield figure. 'The only pillar of stability throughout all that was Jurgen. He was so alone and he felt it in that moment. You could sense that it had taken a toll. Dubai was the first time when anyone could envisage Jurgen not being Liverpool manager anymore. It felt like the beginning of the end.

'The selfish thing, against a backdrop of such instability, would have been to step down in the summer of 2023, but Jurgen was selfless. He didn't want to leave the club without Champions League football and there was an element of knowing they could attract better players if he was still there. He oversaw the midfield rebuild, knowing deep down that it was for his successor. He went into 2023/24 thinking: "If this goes well then I can get out the right way, if this goes badly then I get out anyway as the club will need me out".'

As he sat in meetings in the autumn to discuss Liverpool's pre-season tour plans for America in 2024, Klopp was more certain than ever that he just didn't have it in him to go again. By November 2023 his mind was made up and he called Gordon to inform him of his decision to step down at the end of the season.

Klopp then invited his trusted assistants Lijnders and Krawietz over to his house in Formby on the same day for separate appointments to relay the news to them. 'I feel the same. We've given all we can,' Lijnders told him. Krawietz, who had worked alongside Klopp for more than 20 years, vowed: 'I'll support you in whatever you want to do.'

Gordon, FSG principal owner John W. Henry and Liverpool chairman Tom Werner subsequently tried to persuade Klopp to stay, but deep down they knew it was futile. They could see that having given so much for so long he needed a break.

His impending exit remained a closely guarded secret until 26 January 2024 when Klopp made his public announcement. He had wanted to leave it as late as possible, but keeping it quiet any longer wasn't an option. Liverpool needed to embark on a search for his successor and his staff needed to be able to make plans for the future.

The announcement of Klopp's exit was carefully choreographed that day. He told staff in the coaches' room upstairs at the AXA Training Centre followed at 10.30 a.m. by a meeting with the players in the dressing room. Six minutes later it was released on social media, accompanied by a 25-minute video he had filmed with the club website the previous day.

A sense of shock reverberated through the world of football. At 3 p.m., Klopp conducted an emotional press conference in a packed media room. 'My managerial skills are based on energy and emotion and that takes all of you,' Klopp said.

'If I cannot do it anymore, stop it. It was not my idea when I signed the new contract (in April 2022). I was 100 per cent convinced in that moment we would go until 2026. But I realise my resources are not endless. I'm not a young rabbit anymore.'

Liverpool were top of the Premier League table, in the final of the Carabao Cup, the last 16 of the Europa League and still in the FA Cup. During his short speech to the players, Klopp joked that his exit was partly their fault because Liverpool had reached such a high level so soon after the summer changes that he felt he could pass the baton on to someone else.

When Van Dijk's extra-time header secured League Cup glory against Chelsea at Wembley a month later, Klopp described it as 'easily the most special trophy I've ever won' given how youngsters such as Harvey Elliott, Conor Bradley, Jarell Quansah, Bobby Clark, James McConnell and Jayden Danns had stepped up with so many senior players out injured. 'The people created an atmosphere in the stadium that I'm not sure Wembley ever had before,' Klopp added. 'I loved to see the kids' eyes. Virgil's first trophy as skipper, I will never forget that.'

As Liverpool rode a wave of emotion, it looked like Klopp would get the dream farewell. But 'The Last Dance', as some players and staff called it – a reference to the hit Netflix series about Michael Jordan's triumphant final season with basketball's Chicago Bulls – ultimately involved too many missteps.

It started with a self-inflicted defeat to Manchester United in the FA Cup. Then came the error-strewn Europa League quarter-final exit at the hands of Atalanta. With eight Premier League games to play, Liverpool were masters of their own destiny – two points clear of Arsenal and three ahead of Manchester City.

But they took just 12 points out of the last 24 on offer and finished third. That sequence of results included the first Merseyside derby defeat at Goodison Park for 14 years, which prompted a dejected Klopp to issue an apology to supporters. He said he felt he had 'failed' by not getting the best out of players during the run-in, but circumstances had conspired against him – mental and physical fatigue, injuries, loss of confidence and key players lacking rhythm after regaining fitness. It wasn't the January announcement which had derailed them.

By the time Klopp came to say his goodbyes, the pressure was off and he was at ease with what he had achieved at Liverpool rather than preoccupied with what had eluded him.

'I'm completely at peace,' he told reporters in his final pre-match press conference. 'It was the absolute opposite of a waste of time. A decade in your life is a massive one. I will not forget a day in that time because I met the best people I ever met and I did it for the best club I could have imagined. I don't imagine that the club will need my help in the future but if the city needs me, I'm there.'

The trophy haul of Champions League, Premier League, Club World Cup, UEFA Super Cup, FA Cup and two League Cups didn't really do justice to what he had created.

Klopp harnessed the power of Anfield. He reconnected the club with both the city and its global fanbase. He didn't just restore Liverpool to greatness, he fought the fans' corner on everything from ticket prices to the doomed launch of the European Super League.

The Anfield legacy of the most transformative figure in the club's history since Bill Shankly in the 1960s was secure. It was some act to follow.

2

BACK TO THE FUTURE

'Michael Edwards is one of the most formidable executive talents in world football. He returns to us in a role with greater seniority than he held previously and with a wider remit.'

Mike Gordon

Liverpool didn't just need a new manager and backroom staff following Jurgen Klopp's decision to stand down at the end of the 2023/24 season.

As the Fenway Sports Group hierarchy looked to the future, they knew that an extensive overhaul of the executive structure was required.

With such longevity and success, Klopp had become increasingly influential across all areas of the club. Sporting director Michael Edwards left in the summer of 2022 after over a decade of service to Liverpool, insisting he needed to take a break from such a pressurised environment. Within 12 months, his successor Julian Ward, who had previously been Edwards' assistant, and director of research Ian Graham had also left.

Unable to find a suitable long-term replacement for Ward, FSG president Mike Gordon gave the job to Jorg Schmadtke on an interim basis in late May 2023. Gordon had previously held discussions with Eintracht Frankfurt's Markus Krosche and Monaco's Paul Mitchell over the vacancy, but decided not to pursue either candidate.

Schmadtke, who was recommended to Gordon by Klopp's agent Marc Kosicke, was tempted out of retirement a few months after calling time on a four-and-a-half year spell as sporting director at Bundesliga side Wolfsburg. The former Fortuna Dusseldorf goalkeeper had previously enjoyed stints in similar positions in his homeland at Alemannia Aachen, Hannover 96 and FC Koln.

His appointment was only for one season, and it was felt that having a German speaker would be helpful given that RB Leipzig's Dominik Szoboszlai and Bayern Munich's Ryan Gravenberch were among Liverpool's top targets.

When Schmadtke publicly described himself as 'Klopp's assistant' and a 'service provider' as he negotiated transfer deals in the summer of 2023, it underlined how the balance of power had shifted from the dynamic that previously existed at the top of the club.

It was something Klopp touched on during his farewell night with supporters at the city's M&S Bank Arena in late May 2024 when he said: 'Now there will be changes. Different people responsible for different things is probably the right way. It's not that I wanted to do it like that [have so much responsibility]. It just developed in that direction with lots ending up on my desk.'

A new era at Anfield involved pressing the reset button. FSG weren't looking for a manager who would have the same kind of all-encompassing remit as Klopp. They weren't attempting to replace the irreplaceable. Instead they wanted a head coach who could focus his energy on training and developing players as they created a number of new senior roles to take care of other duties.

Klopp handing in his notice in November 2023 and then making the news public two months later meant the owners had time on their side. The plan was to build a new executive structure with a clear chain of command before Klopp's successor was appointed.

Gordon knew exactly who he wanted to mastermind that process. His first phone call was to Edwards but the response was: 'Thanks, but no thanks.' Edwards was adamant that he had no desire to return to his previous role as sporting director. He didn't want to go back to dealing with agents and negotiating transfer deals. He was enjoying more family time with wife Emily and their children, and the slower pace of life working as a consultant for Ludonautics, the sports advisory analytics business launched by his former Liverpool colleague Graham.

He had turned down around a dozen clubs from across Europe since leaving Anfield, including lucrative approaches from Premier League rivals Manchester United and Chelsea to run their football operations. The Glazers had approached Edwards prior to selling a 27.7 per cent stake in United to INEOS in early 2024.

Edwards initially told Gordon he didn't think going back would be right either for Liverpool or for him, saying: 'You wouldn't be getting the best version of me.' He explained that he needed to be stimulated, he needed a fresh challenge. His next job had to be different.

Gordon refused to admit defeat and together with principal owner John W. Henry and chairman Tom Werner set about putting together alternative proposals in a bid to pique his interest.

'There was no firm Plan B,' says one senior FSG source. 'John, Tom and Mike always believed that until Michael signed on the dotted line with someone else, they had a chance and that they had a duty to stick in there and do everything they could. They threw the kitchen sink at him and persistence eventually paid off.'

In early March 2024, a deal was struck following discussions in Boston after Edwards attended the MIT Sloan Sports Analytics Conference in Massachusetts. He was appointed as FSG's first CEO of football.

Edwards succeeded Gordon as FSG's day-to-day decision-maker on all football matters. Reporting to the FSG Board, he was given responsibility for overseeing Liverpool's budget and strategy. He was also tasked with identifying, buying and subsequently running another European club with FSG committed to embarking on a multi-club model.

'Michael Edwards is one of the most formidable executive talents in world football. He returns to us in a role with greater seniority than he held previously and with a wider remit,' Gordon said.

'It was clear when we initially reached out to Michael that a broader scope would be a key motivating factor for any potential return to the industry … As an organisation we constantly strive for improvement in our football operation, whether that be identifying fresh opportunities externally or areas for enhancement internally, and there is no better person to lead that ongoing process.'

Edwards said he was 'humbled by the desire and persistence FSG showed in wanting to work with me again' as he added: 'This is not something that I take for granted, given their track record across sport and business. It was vital for me that if I did return it had to be with renewed vigour and energy. One of the biggest factors in my decision is the commitment to acquire and oversee an additional club, growing this area of their organisation. I believe that to remain competitive, investment and expansion of the current football portfolio is necessary.'

Graham lost a consultant as Edwards stepped down from his role with Ludonautics. 'It was great fun working together again for that period in a start-up environment,' he said. 'I kept saying to Michael: "You're going to go back into club football, aren't you?" I'd say: "Surely Chelsea and United have called you?" And he was like: "Yeah, I might have spoken to them but it's not happening."

'I didn't believe him because I didn't think he would be able to resist it, but he said he'd had enough of that. Running recruitment, as well as all the other departments at the training ground, is really stressful. The reason he went back in the end was because FSG offered him something new and exciting. It gave him responsibilities he didn't have as sporting director so I could see the attraction.

'John, Mike and Tom see football in the same way Michael does. They demand high standards with no stone left unturned and Michael had proved over an extended period previously that he lives up to those standards. There's a natural fit.'

Boston-based Gordon had long since been looking to reduce his involvement with Liverpool. Having overseen the football operation for FSG since 2013, he felt the timing was right with Klopp's exit. In an email sent to all club staff, Gordon wrote: 'I do not hand over these responsibilities lightly and I know there is no one more capable than Michael to shoulder them.'

A month earlier FSG had brought Theo Epstein back into the fold as a senior advisor for their Major League Baseball team, the Boston Red Sox. During a nine-year spell as general manager, Epstein had guided the Red Sox to World Series glory in 2004 and 2007.

Edwards had a similarly impressive body of work at Liverpool having recruited a title-winning side. Senior FSG figures talked about 'going back to the future', with the return of trusted executives on both sides of the Atlantic with proven track records of success and sound decision-making handed broader, more expansive roles.

Damien Comolli didn't last long at Liverpool. Initially brought in from French club Saint-Etienne in November 2010 as FSG's first senior appointment following their takeover of the club, he was made director of football strategy before being promoted to the role of director of football.

Comolli was sacked in March 2012 for perceived mistakes in the transfer market, and the mishandling of a race row involving striker Luis Suárez and Manchester United's Patrice Evra. However, one telling contribution he did make was recruiting Edwards, who first arrived at Anfield from Tottenham as head of performance and analysis in November 2011.

'I wanted to create an analytics department and I wanted someone with both a football background and an analytics background,' Comolli told *The Athletic* in 2020. 'The most difficult thing when you are dealing with data is to be able to make sense of the data but more importantly, to translate the data to the coaches or the players in a way they can make sense out of it so it's useful to them.

'I actually asked one of the data providers who was working in the Premier League at the time. I said: "I'm looking for this type of guy. Who is the best one?". One of them told me Michael Edwards at Tottenham. Everyone thought I had worked with Michael at Tottenham but that's not the case.

'I called Michael, I explained to him the position I was looking to create, we had a couple of meetings and he took the job. He's a very bright guy. We didn't work together for a long time but when I left I told him: "You are going to take over". He said: "No way." I told him I was sure he would be given more responsibility and become sporting director at some point. Then Brendan Rodgers came in and said he would never work with a sporting director, blah, blah blah. I always thought Michael would have to wait a while and then they would recreate that position later on.'

Edwards' rise to becoming one of the most highly respected executives in world football was a remarkable one. The son of a lorry driver, he grew up in the Hampshire market town of Fareham and dreamed of becoming a professional footballer.

The right-back earned a two-year apprenticeship at Peterborough United in England's third tier and played for their reserves but was released at the age of 18 without making a first-team appearance.

Edwards enrolled at the University of Sheffield and got a degree in business management and informatics before returning south to embark on a career as a secondary school teacher. He missed the buzz of being involved in football and a meeting at a service station close to the M1 in 2003 offered an appealing route back in.

Prozone, the football data company, had secured a contract with Premier League club Portsmouth and they needed an analyst. Edwards had been recommended to Prozone's business development manager Barry McNeill by Simon Wilson, one of his former Peterborough team-mates.

Portsmouth manager Harry Redknapp was initially sceptical about the benefits of a stats-oriented approach. In Edwards' early days at the south coast club, Redknapp once asked him why he couldn't get anything out of a CD-ROM filled with player data. It turned out that he had put it into his car's CD player.

However, Redknapp soon came to appreciate the value of Edwards' input as Portsmouth went on to win the FA Cup in 2008. It was telling that when Redknapp moved on to Tottenham Hotspur, he took Edwards with him as head of performance analysis.

At Liverpool, Edwards quickly earned the trust of FSG president Gordon as he was promoted to technical director in 2015 and then sporting director 12 months later.

Not everyone was convinced about his methods. Experienced scout Mel Johnson, who was relieved of his duties in 2014, complained after his exit that the sport was 'not played on a computer', adding: 'Some of these IT guys have come straight out of university and landed jobs at top clubs, despite having no football background whatsoever.'

Manager Brendan Rodgers saw Edwards' growing influence as a threat to his authority and their relationship became increasingly strained. An article in the *Daily Mail* newspaper shortly after Rodgers was sacked in October 2015 dismissed Edwards as a 'laptop guru'. It didn't age well.

The perception of Edwards walking around the training ground armed with spreadsheets was always far removed from the reality. Those who worked alongside him at that time say his great strength was combining the insight gained from groundbreaking data analysis with old school scouting methods and character references. He wasn't a regular at matches at Anfield because he felt his time was better spent on the road watching potential targets and speaking to those who knew them best to build a complete picture.

Edwards recommended to FSG that Klopp was the compelling candidate to take over in 2015 from a three-man shortlist which also included Carlo Ancelotti and Eddie Howe.

Having been used to working with a sporting director at Borussia Dortmund, Klopp embraced Edwards' input to a much greater extent than Rodgers. He liked the fact that Edwards was forthright and always spoke his mind. 'It is a very good relationship,' Klopp told reporters in 2019. 'He is a very thoughtful person. We don't always have to have the same opinion from the first second of a conversation, but we finish pretty much all our talks with the same opinion or similar opinions.'

Together they built a team which led Liverpool to Champions League, Club World Cup and Premier League glory. Spectacular successes in the transfer market made FSG's self-sustaining business model work.

Edwards proved himself to be the shrewdest of negotiators. Holding out for £142 million from Barcelona for Philippe Coutinho midway through the 2017/18 season effectively paid for the signings of Virgil van Dijk and Alisson.

Coutinho had cost Liverpool just £8.5 million from Inter Milan five years earlier. Edwards had a clause written into the deal with Barcelona which stipulated that the Catalan club would have to pay a €100 million premium if they wanted to sign another Liverpool player over the next two years.

Concerned that Real Madrid might try to lure away Mohamed Salah, Roberto Firmino or Sadio Mané in their prime, Edwards got all three tied down to new contracts with no release clauses. Edwards had pushed hard for the signings of all three attackers, who had been plucked from Roma, Hoffenheim and Southampton respectively for a combined total of £103 million. They repaid that outlay many times over.

Edwards secured bumper fees for unwanted fringe stars with the £8 million Hull City paid for midfielder Kevin Stewart covering Liverpool's initial outlay for Andy Robertson, who moved in the opposite direction and blossomed into one of the best left-backs in Europe. Jordon Ibe and Brad Smith went to Bournemouth for a combined total of £21 million, while Danny Ward moved to Leicester City for £12.5 million, Mamadou Sakho to Crystal Palace for £26 million, and Danny Ings to Southampton for £20 million.

When Liverpool won the Premier League title in 2019/20, their net spend of £92 million covering the previous five years was lower than every top-flight club at that time apart from Crystal Palace, Sheffield United, Southampton and Norwich City. For context, Manchester City's net spend during that period was £506 million and Manchester United's was £378 million.

It's no wonder that when Liverpool were confirmed as champions that June following Manchester City's defeat at Chelsea, the first congratulatory message chairman Tom Werner sent from his mobile phone was to the sporting director.

Edwards always shunned the media and stayed out of the limelight. He didn't even have a Wikipedia page during his first spell on Merseyside and for a long time the only photograph of him circulating online was from a fundraising page ahead of running the Manchester Half Marathon. Operating under the radar was exactly how he liked it.

When Klopp invited staff onto the podium to join in the cele-brations after the Champions League final triumph in Madrid in 2019, Edwards stayed out of the way, taking pictures of the jubilant Liverpool supporters and consoling his former colleagues from Tottenham.

Edwards was instrumental in the club's move from their historic Melwood training base to a new £50 million facility in Kirkby in late 2020 and strengthened ties between the senior set-up and the academy.

When Emre Can wanted a new contract with a release clause, Edwards refused to budge as he felt it would have set a dangerous precedent and allowed him to leave on a free transfer. Georginio Wijnaldum, one of the pillars of the 2019/20 title-winning team, also left when his deal expired after not getting the kind of offer he wanted. It was ruthless but Edwards' judgement was proved right given how Wijnaldum's fortunes subsequently declined.

FSG respected how he was able to ignore the outside noise and take the emotion out of the decision-making process. There was a clamour to sign an alternative to Van Dijk after Liverpool's initial pursuit of the Southampton defender collapsed in the summer of 2017 amid accusations of an illegal approach, but Edwards insisted they would weather the storm and wait until the following January to get their man.

Edwards was never a 'yes' man. He could be blunt and combative. At times there was friction amid some heated discussions with Klopp. 'They were never mates, but they were also never enemies. That creative tension worked,' was how one senior club figure describes it.

When they couldn't agree, it was left to Gordon to refine the arguments and have the final word. The decision to give captain Jordan Henderson a new four-year contract at the age of 31 in August 2021 – something Klopp pushed hard for – was a bone of contention.

Three months later, however, when Edwards announced his intention to stand down once his contract expired at the end of the 2021–22 season, there was no ill feeling. He simply felt it was time to pass on the baton.

'I had always planned to cap my time at the club to a maximum of 10 years,' he wrote in an open letter to supporters. 'I've loved working here, but I am a big believer in change. It's good for the individual and, in a work setting, good for the employer too. Over my time here, we have changed so many things (hopefully for the better) but someone new brings a different perspective, new ideas and can hopefully build on (or change) the things that have been put in place beforehand. With the new training ground complete, many of the core players committed to the club through long-term contracts and some of the hard work translated into trophies, it's time for me to move on.'

Julian Ward, who had been promoted to assistant sporting director in December 2020, was the obvious choice as Edwards' successor. He had risen through the ranks after joining Liverpool from Manchester City in 2012 as their scouting manager for Spain and Portugal. Three years later, he had been appointed loan pathways and football partnerships manager, with the owners delighted at how he had strategically used the loan system to increase the value of youngsters like Harry Wilson, Rhian Brewster and Marko Grujic.

There had been a gradual handover of duties during Edwards' final season, with Ward pivotal as Liverpool beat Tottenham to the signing of Luis Díaz from Porto in the January window of 2021/22.

That summer Ward agreed a club record £85 million deal with Benfica for Darwin Núñez – a transfer largely driven by Klopp after the Uruguayan striker had impressed in a Champions League quarter-final against Liverpool. Given how different Núñez's profile was compared to the long-serving Roberto Firmino, it felt like a shift away from the club's data-led approach and he struggled to live up to that hefty price tag.

'My questions about Núñez were: "Are we going to change our style or formation for him? Is he a good enough player that it might be worth making those changes to our approach?" It was something we had resisted for many years,' explains then director of research Ian Graham.

'We wanted to go into each signing with our eyes open so we knew exactly the player we were going to get. I wanted to make sure that everyone knew what a big change it was and that we were comfortable with that.

'We always had a list of "great players but not for Liverpool". Defensive full-backs, targetmen, crossing wingers, we just didn't play in that style, but it didn't stop them from being good players. With Núñez, there wasn't much difference between him and the style we played, but there was a difference.

'I wouldn't say that the data said no to Núñez. It said we can sign him but he's a proper No. 9 and we hadn't played with one of those since 2015/16. It was more: "Are we sure we're going to make the best use of him?" If you're spending a large amount of money on a player then he has to start. Núñez had played brilliantly against Liverpool in the Champions League. That has an effect on people and didn't do him any harm in becoming a Liverpool player.'

Ward also bought Fabio Carvalho and Calvin Ramsay, sold Sadio Mané to Bayern Munich and helped end the uncertainty over Salah's future as he penned a new contract. However, it wasn't all plain sailing: a midfield injury crisis led to a panicked deadline day loan deal for Juventus' Arthur Melo, who wasn't fit and played just 13 minutes of first-team football all season.

Liverpool struggled on the field and in November 2022 Ward informed FSG that he would be leaving the club at the end of the season after just one year as sporting director because he needed a break. The news came just weeks after it emerged that FSG were considering a possible full sale of Liverpool with Gordon taking a step back to oversee the process. US banks Goldman Sachs and Morgan Stanley were tasked with sounding out interest from investors.

'We're exploring a sale, but there's no urgency, no time frame for us, and as far as I'm concerned, it's business as usual,' Liverpool chairman Tom Werner told the *Boston Globe*. 'One outcome could be our continued stewardship for quite a while.'

Senior Liverpool officials viewed it as 'a fishing expedition'. 'There was never any clearing of the decks, it felt like it was more a case of testing the market,' one said. 'And if you want to sell a slice of the cake for the best possible price, it makes sense to establish what the whole cake is worth.'

Within a few months it was clear that FSG would only be selling a minority stake and Gordon returned to his duties. In September 2023, a deal was struck with New York-based sports investment firm Dynasty Equity. Sources close to the deal said it was worth between $100 million and $200 million – a stake of around three to four per cent.

The sense of turmoil with Ward departing at the end of the 2022/23 campaign was heightened by the fact that Graham had also handed in his notice, with Will Spearman promoted internally to replace him. In the space of a year, Liverpool lost Edwards, Ward and Graham, who boasted more than 30 years of loyal service and expertise between them.

'I can't speak for Michael or Julian but for me personally I felt like I was overdue a change,' Graham said. 'I'd worked there for 11 years. I'd built it up from just me to a data department of eight really good people. We had built a brilliant set of tools and analysis. I'd achieved what I wanted to achieve.

'I'm not going to pretend that everything was always harmony and light at Liverpool. Of course we had arguments, of course there were big egos there and I include myself in that. It's difficult to keep the momentum going for 11 years when you're having passionate arguments.

'We all want the same thing. We all want the club to succeed but we have got different ideas. It's hard to keep that going and sooner or later you get burnt out. I thought I could continue longer than Michael could but after another nine months or so I thought: "I can see now what Michael was saying when he said it was time for a rest".'

With Michael Edwards refreshed and energised after accepting the role of FSG CEO of football in March 2024, he immediately appointed Richard Hughes as the club's new sporting director. The position had been vacant since the departure of Jorg Schmadtke at the end of the January transfer window.

Two decades earlier Hughes had played his part in ending the Gérard Houllier era at Liverpool as he scored the winner for Portsmouth in an FA Cup fifth round replay at Fratton Park. Now the former Scotland international, who was serving his notice as technical director at Bournemouth, was entrusted with helping to launch a new chapter at Anfield.

'I am incredibly proud to be offered this opportunity,' Hughes said. 'Liverpool FC is a unique club and I'm grateful to be given a chance to serve it in this capacity. People rightly talk about the rich history this organisation can boast, but it is the present and future which really excites me. I am fully aware of the expectations and responsibilities that come with taking this position.'

Edwards held a long-standing desire to work with Hughes again, holding him in the highest esteem having watched his career and reputation blossom. The connection between the pair stretched back more than 20 years to their days together as analyst and player respectively at Portsmouth.

Back then, Hughes was part of a group of senior players, including Eddie Howe and Gary O'Neil, who were frequent visitors to the analysts' room as they requested data and video clips from Edwards to study. The Glasgow-born midfielder captained the club and was regarded as the voice of reason in the dressing room who others looked up to.

Impressed by how Hughes articulated his views on different styles and formations, as well as opposition players' strengths and weaknesses, Edwards always assumed he would go down the coaching route when he retired from playing.

However, Howe, who was manager of Bournemouth when Hughes hung up his boots in 2014, convinced him to join the club's recruitment staff and he was elevated to the role of technical director two years later.

Hughes was integral to Bournemouth punching well above their weight in the years that followed as they finished ninth, 12th and 14th in the top-flight. Relegated to the Championship in 2020, they returned to the Premier League two years later and stayed there with 15th and 12th-placed finishes.

Edwards admired their recruitment record as they snapped up young talents like Tyrone Mings, Lewis Cook, David Brooks, Lloyd Kelly, Philip Billing, Aaron Ramsdale, Nathan Ake and Dominic Solanke. Liverpool themselves had extensively scouted Brooks and Kelly.

Mings was bought for £8 million and sold to Aston Villa for £26.5 million, while Ramsdale cost £800,000 and subsequently moved to Sheffield United for £18.5 million. Hughes had increasingly operated in the European market with two of his more recent eye-catching recommendations being Dynamo Kyiv's Illya Zabarnyi and AZ Alkmaar's Milos Kerkez. The value of Antoine

Semenyo, a £10 million buy from second tier Bristol City, also rocketed.

However, it wasn't just the deals Hughes did get over the line that commanded Edwards' respect. He was aware that the Liverpool trio Joe Gomez, Andy Robertson and Harvey Elliott had all been targeted by Bournemouth shortly before moving to Anfield. Hughes had also tried to sign Virgil van Dijk prior to the Dutchman leaving Celtic for Southampton in 2015.

What it proved to Edwards was that although Hughes had been hampered by circumstances at times as he came up against bigger clubs with deeper pockets and greater pulling power, the data-driven identification process was highly effective.

Born in Glasgow and the second eldest of four boys, Hughes spent his childhood in the Italian city of Milan. His father Kevin, a devoted Celtic fan, worked for the publisher Longman Italia and distributed books for Italians learning English as a foreign language in schools.

Hughes was a regular at San Siro as he grew up watching Arrigo Sacchi's legendary AC Milan team, who lifted the European Cup in 1989 and 1990. He watched in awe at the brilliance of Marco van Basten, Ruud Gullit, Franco Baresi and Paolo Maldini. Kevin would encourage him to study Maldini's positioning and how he organised those around him.

At the age of 10, Hughes' performances for his junior club caught the eye of AC Milan scouts but nerves got the better of him when he attended training at their academy. A year later, Atalanta came calling and that proved a much better fit – less pressure, fewer youngsters and a greater focus on individual development. By the time he reached the Under-19s, he was a promising holding midfielder and his coach was Cesare Prandelli, who went on to manage Fiorentina and Italy. Hughes regards him as the greatest mentor he ever had.

Having followed the British school curriculum at Milan's Sir James Henderson School, he finished his education a year ahead of his Italian peers at Atalanta and, not yet able to turn professional, he had a big decision to make.

With his 18th birthday approaching and a two-year contract offer from Arsenal on the table, he opted to head for London. When Atalanta were relegated from Serie A in 1998 and friends from his youth team were swiftly promoted to the senior ranks, he wondered if he had been too hasty in leaving. But after joining Bournemouth from Arsenal, his own professional career took off and he never looked back. His two playing spells at Bournemouth were separated by a nine-year stint at Portsmouth.

His time in Italy shaped him both as a footballer and a man. The tactical nous and reading of the game learned during his seven years in the esteemed Atalanta academy enabled him to hold his own against faster, stronger and more technically gifted opponents.

His passion and knowledge of Serie A – coupled with being able to speak the language fluently and the network of contacts he built up – also proved a big asset after turning his attention to recruitment. Edwards tapped into Hughes' expertise before pulling off the cherished signings of Mohamed Salah and Alisson from Roma, and the pair later did business when Solanke was sold to Bournemouth for £24 million.

As for the managers, Edwards believed Hughes had been brave to replace Scott Parker with O'Neil in August 2022 and even braver to bring in former Rayo Vallecano boss Andoni Iraola the following June. O'Neil was a mutual friend but business was business and Iraola had proved to be an inspired appointment.

Given Hughes' record on the south coast and how he had stood out among his peers at Premier League meetings, Edwards was surprised that FSG hadn't targeted him as a possible successor to Ward prior to the stop-gap appointment of Schmadtke. During his work as an advisor for the consultancy firm Ludonautics, Edwards had told several leading European clubs that Hughes should be on their radar.

When Hughes handed in his notice at Bournemouth after the end of the summer transfer window in 2023, it represented a considerable leap of faith. He was ready for a change but he didn't have another job lined up. 'I promise you, you won't be out of work in 12 months' time,' Edwards reassured him. But neither Edwards nor Hughes knew exactly where that work would be.

Edwards reasoned that by then he would either be running the football operations at a top club and would appoint Hughes as his sporting director or one of the many European clubs who regularly asked for his advice would turn to Hughes instead. Roma and AC Milan were among them.

After agreeing to become FSG CEO of football, Edwards' first call was to Hughes. 'It's Liverpool. Are you coming?,' he said bluntly. The answer was an emphatic yes. Edwards explained that while he would be responsible for the budget, he intended to stay out of the way and vowed to empower Hughes in the decision-making process.

'I've known Richard for half of my life in a professional and personal capacity and he is absolutely someone who embodies the best values of Liverpool FC. I trust him completely,' Edwards said when Hughes' appointment was confirmed in March 2024.

'He has outstanding judgement and a track record of making smart decisions which benefit the organisations he represents. Both Richard and I are aware of the weight of responsibility that comes with working in this capacity for a club such as this. The fact he is excited and energised by the challenge ahead is important.

'It is clear to everyone that Jurgen will leave a legacy to build upon and in Richard we have the right person to make the key decisions and offer the leadership to take us forward into a bright future. As one very successful chapter will come to a close for Liverpool in the summer, the objective of everyone here is for another one to begin – and with Richard I am confident we have the right person in position for us to achieve this aim.'

Hughes was given overall responsibility for the coaching, recruitment, medical and sports science operations, along with the administrative and facilities management at the Kirkby training complex.

To support him in his duties, Edwards brought back David Woodfine as assistant sporting director. Woodfine had been Liverpool's director of loan management prior to his departure at the end of the 2022/23 season. He had first worked alongside Edwards and Hughes at Portsmouth where he was a performance analyst between 2005 and 2010.

Woodfine initially joined Liverpool in 2014 as scouting and recruitment coordinator and went on to become head of football projects and scouting operations three years later before taking on responsibility for the loans in 2020.

Edwards' rebuild of the football executive structure continued apace with three more strategic senior appointments. The most striking of which was the return of Ward to the fold as FSG's technical director – a year after stepping down as Liverpool's sporting director. During his sabbatical, Ward had turned down the chance to become Ajax technical director and snubbed an approach from co-owners INEOS to help them turn around the fortunes of Manchester United.

However, the chance to work with Edwards again, combined with the scale and ambition of FSG's plans for the future, convinced Ward to accept the opportunity. He was tasked with overseeing player development across FSG's football operations, including oversight of the academy, loans and establishing a new football innovation department. It was also agreed that Ward would preside over the management of football operations at any club added to FSG's stable.

Ward had previously left on good terms, with the owners appreciating that he stayed on beyond his official departure date to complete the signing of Alexis Mac Allister from Brighton for £35 million in June 2023 having put in so much groundwork to win the battle for the Argentina midfielder's signature. He had also negotiated the £44 million deal with Ajax for Cody Gakpo the previous January. Crucially, FSG knew from experience that the Edwards-Ward double act worked.

Hans Leitert, who had been a goalkeeping scouting consultant at Liverpool since 2018, was promoted to FSG head of global goalkeeping and tasked with the appointment and development of goalkeeper coaches, as well as implementing a data-driven scouting system having previously done likewise for the Red Bull Group.

Another newly created role, FSG director of football development, was filled by Pedro Marques, who made the move after stepping down as Benfica's technical director after six years.

Regarded by Edwards and Ward as an industry leading expert in player development, career pathways, coaching methodologies and performance analysis, Marques had also previously had spells at Sporting Lisbon, Manchester City and City Football Group, where he was the global lead of football performance across their multi-club structure. Ward knew Marques from his own stint at City where he was their South American scouting strategist between 2010 and 2021.

At Benfica, Marques had overseen a youth structure comprising of 39 age-group teams and around 600 players across six sites. He had helped build an environment where exciting young talents such as Ruben Dias, Joao Felix, Goncalo Ramos, Antonio Silva and Joao Neves flourished and made the step up to the Portuguese club's first team.

In May 2019, Marques had received a call from Liverpool asking for his help ahead of the 2019 Champions League final against Tottenham in Madrid. They wanted him to take Benfica's B team to the club's training camp in Marbella for a practice match where they would set up tactically like Mauricio Pochettino's side and he duly obliged. Klopp came to regard it as a crucial part of Liverpool's preparations en route to winning a sixth European Cup. Five years later, Edwards and Ward viewed it as a real coup to secure Marques' services on a permanent basis.

There were significant additions to Liverpool's recruitment department too with Craig McKee and Mark Burchill following Hughes from Bournemouth to Merseyside. McKee was appointed head of scouting operations with Burchill made head of technical scouting, an approach to player evaluation which uses data science and technology to supplement traditional scouting methods.

The club's long-serving director of scouting and recruitment Dave Fallows had initially considered stepping down at the end of the Klopp era, but after talks with Edwards and Hughes it was decided he would stay on until the end of the calendar year to help with the transition. Chief scout Barry Hunter, who like Fallows had joined Liverpool in 2012, remained in position.

Matt Newberry, who had impressed as head of senior academy recruitment and then head of loan management, was subsequently promoted to director of global talent as Liverpool targeted more of the kind of deals that saw them sign gifted teenagers such as Trey Nyoni from Leicester City and Rio Ngumoha from Chelsea. The English market had become increasingly important for Premier League clubs since post-Brexit regulations came into force which meant they couldn't sign anyone under the age of 18 from overseas.

FSG set up an office in the affluent Greater Manchester town of Altrincham for Edwards, Ward and Marques to work out of when they weren't on the road. The idea was that it was close enough to Liverpool's Kirkby training base – about 45 minutes by car – but sufficiently far away to give Hughes space to develop relationships and put his own stamp on the job. Edwards only visited the AXA Training Centre about once a month during the season.

The lines of communication were clear. Edwards would report to the FSG board, Hughes and Ward would both report to Edwards, Marques would report to Ward, and Liverpool's first head coach as opposed to manager would report to the sporting director.

Hughes' official start date was 1 June, but it was unthinkable that the work could wait until then given his bulging in-tray. The summer transfer window was on the horizon and the key trio of Mohamed Salah, Virgil van Dijk and Trent Alexander-Arnold were about to enter the final 12 months of their current deals.

But the first task for Hughes and, arguably the most daunting, was recruiting Klopp's successor. Edwards would be there to offer support along the way, but Hughes would lead the process of identifying the best candidate.

The outgoing manager vowed to do everything he could to assist with the transition. Edwards had messaged Klopp to inform him about his new role after agreeing to return to the FSG fold and asked if they could meet up.

Klopp invited Edwards to his mansion house on Victoria Road in Formby and they talked for three hours about football. 'I want this to work,' Klopp told him. 'I want what comes after me to be a success. You can pick up the phone any time, night or day. I'm here to help and if staying out of the way helps then I'll do that as well. I'll be as involved as you want.'

The German coach went through the squad player by player giving his assessment of where he felt they were at. Edwards went away and told colleagues that he regarded the conversation as 'priceless'.

Klopp subsequently met Hughes to answer all the questions he had about the current personnel and where improvements could be made. Internally, it was described as 'the golden handover'.

'No playing politics from Jurgen, just very humble,' says one senior club figure. Klopp's opinion wasn't sought by either Edwards or Hughes on the pursuit of a new head coach but when he was informed about who would be taking over ahead of the news breaking publicly, he told them: 'Smart choice! Good guy and I love how his team plays football.'

3

THE BERGKAMP OF BERGENTHEIM

'Arne was a real No. 10. He could read a game so well. He was always thinking two steps ahead. With both his parents being teachers, he was disciplined with a real work ethic. He had a football brain which convinced me he would go on to become an excellent coach.'

Ben Hendriks

The peaceful village of Bergentheim in the far east of the Netherlands is just five miles from the border with Germany.

Situated on the edge of the Dutch Bible Belt, with a population of around 3,500, it's surrounded by countryside and the Almelo-De Haandrik Canal passes through. It boasts two churches, a public swimming pool, a small shopping precinct and a bar-restaurant called Veenlust offering locals a wide range of schnitzels.

The village is also home to Sportpark Moscou, the headquarters for the flourishing football club VV Bergentheim, who run 27 youth and senior teams across four pitches with some 750 members in total.

This is where Arne Slot spent his formative years. He had a tough act to follow. His father Arend was widely regarded as the best player the club had ever produced. Arend didn't make the grade professionally but was part of the Dutch amateur national team.

There's only one framed portrait of a Slot on the wall in the VV Bergentheim boardroom and that honour belongs to Arend, who also served the club with distinction as manager before being made an honorary member. Arend was also a former headmaster of the local school, and gained a reputation for being a strict disciplinarian who could be unapologetically blunt and forthright with his views.

Bert Snippe used to play alongside Arne's father. 'Arend was a No. 10 who made a lot of goals,' he told *The Athletic*. 'He was also a very good coach with a strong personality. Whatever he said was right!

'From a very young age, Arne would sit beside his dad on the bench for every match. He would see close up how his dad did it. Always learning and observing. Then at half-time Arne would go into the dressing room to listen to what was being said. The manager we see today, the story starts with Bergentheim. It all comes back to his father.'

Snippe has a newspaper cutting from the now-defunct *De Zwolse Courant* from 1988 with the headline: 'A week to remember – Bergentheim kids at KVNB centre.' At the age of nine, Arne's promise with a ball at his feet was recognised when he was selected to take part in a nationwide four-a-side tournament 80 miles away in Zeist at the headquarters of the Dutch football federation. They finished third and were pictured receiving a clock as their prize. Snippe remembers Arne, who had thick brown hair, as being 'the thinker' of the team.

Jan Ophof, who was a page boy when Arend married local kindergarten teacher Fennie in 1971, was Arne's first age-group coach for VV Bergentheim. 'My role was to train the boys aged 10 to 12,' he says. 'Arne was only nine but his father told him: "You are a good player, you can play a level higher."

'One evening this boy appeared in the dressing room: "Hello, I'm Arne, I'm here to train with you and I will work hard." We trained for an hour and he was our best player. It was as if he had the ball on a string. Arne was very intelligent for his age. He would come up to me and say: "Coach, can we do this? Can we do that?" He wasn't tall, he wasn't fast, but he knew where to pass, where to move.'

In their distinctive dark green kit, the children were taught to be relentless on the field, even if that meant infuriating opposition coaches like when Arne scored 12 times in a 22-goal demolition of a team from the nearby town of Ommen.

'The only problem for us was that if his father was at the side of the pitch, Arne looked more to his father than us,' adds Ophof. 'His father was the first-team coach. But he coached Arne too. We'd say to Arne: "Why are you walking over there, Arne?" And he would say: "Yeah, but my father wants to speak to me." I'm very proud of Arne. The whole village is proud of him. When will we ever say again that a boy from Bergentheim has done what Arne has?'

Ophof is among a group of members who pushed for Sportpark Moscou to be renamed in Arne's honour given his achievements as a manager, but the board of directors rejected the proposal.

Bergentheim is conservative and deeply religious – far removed both physically and culturally from the liberalism of the Dutch capital, Amsterdam. No football is played in the village on Sundays and there was a backlash in early 2025 when the local supermarket started opening on what had always been a day of rest and worship.

As well as being reluctant to put anyone on a pedestal or attract unwanted media attention, the directors pointed to the fact that Arne didn't ever represent Bergentheim's first team, having left at the age of 12 to join the academy at PEC Zwolle, his first professional club.

One scout, who had been watching the youngster's development with growing interest, grandly described him as 'the Bergkamp of Bergentheim'. At Zwolle, 25 miles west, he kicked on impressively in the youth ranks with his father constantly encouraging him to knuckle down and make the most of his ability.

Ben Hendriks pulls up a seat in the bar area of the plush Bilderberg Grand Hotel Wientjes. 'I am a man of Zwolle,' he proudly announces with a hearty chuckle. Hendriks was also the manager who gave Slot his first taste of senior action at the age of 16 in familiar surroundings.

'We had a big sponsor, a bread company, who also sponsored Bergentheim, so we went there for a pre-season game,' he recalls. 'Even with Arne being so young, I thought it would be a good idea to let him play with it being against his home village and I made him captain for the day. After the game, the experienced guys, who didn't know him so well, all said: "He's unbelievable for 16."

'Arne was a real No. 10. He could read a game so well. He was always thinking two steps ahead. With both his parents being teachers, he was disciplined with a real work ethic. He was a good passer. He let other players – better players – play, which is also a quality. He had a football brain which convinced me he would go on to become an excellent coach.

'I know Arne's father and he was a big influence on him growing up. But Arne also created the right mentality himself. Every morning he would cycle from Bergentheim to Marienberg and then get the train to Zwolle, where he would get picked up and attend a school behind the stadium and train before going back home again. There was total commitment. After that friendly match, he went back to the youth team before establishing himself in the first team after I'd gone. I knew Arne would be top.'

Having played for Feyenoord and Ajax, Jan Everse's playing career was prematurely ended by an ankle injury at the age of 26. The former Netherlands international turned his attention to coaching and in 1996 he was tasked with reviving the fortunes of second-tier Zwolle after back-to-back 14th-placed league finishes. 'They were rubbish, the football was so bad,' says Everse.

Slot's talent was clear to the new manager but he was hampered both by injuries and what Everse regarded to be a lack of contribution out of possession.

'Arne was a technical player with a good vision of the game and an excellent passer. He was always convinced of his own qualities. He never doubted – that's good because if you don't believe in yourself, you will never succeed.

'But sometimes he would only get 20 or 30 minutes. He was curious about why he was not playing more. I would say to him: "Arne, you are my best player. But the problem is, every time you play, your direct opponent is also the best player from the other team. I cannot afford that. When we lose the ball, you do nothing. We cannot rely on our qualities when we have the ball. It's not enough in modern football".'

Everse explained to Slot that he needed to be more aggressive in terms of pressing to win back possession. 'You have to run more, you have to defend, if you only touch the ball 15 times in a game, you do not have a value for my team.'

The message gradually got through. Slot trained harder, lost weight, spent more time in the gym to build up his strength, and his career blossomed. He started to appreciate how a team could only function as a cohesive unit if everyone was carrying out their role effectively. The attacking midfielder top scored for Zwolle with 18 goals in 1998/99 and achieved that feat again with 12 in 2001/02 as he helped them win promotion to the Eredivisie.

It proved to be a parting gift. Slot secured a move to top-flight NAC Breda under manager Henk ten Cate where he played alongside Edwin de Graaf. 'Some players you can see are going to be coaches,' De Graaf told *The Athletic*.

'Arne would ask the coaches why they were using certain tactics. And in the dressing room, he would talk to the group about a way of pressing or defending. He would ask: "Why were we doing it this way? Would it be better to do it this way?" He would make suggestions to his coaches. But he would do it in such a good way. He wouldn't do it with an attitude. He would ask: "What do you think about this?" He would also very quickly see what the opponents were doing.'

It was at Breda where Slot got his only taste of major European competition as a player when they were hammered 6–0 on aggregate by Newcastle United in the first round of the UEFA Cup in 2003/04. Former Morocco international Nourdin Boukhari, who had arrived on loan from Ajax, was struck by Slot's 'dry sense of humour' and 'tactical understanding', as well as his knowledge of the game which came to the fore on squad quiz nights.

In the summer of 2007, Slot joined Sparta Rotterdam where he soon struck up a close friendship with fellow new-signing Sander Westerveld. The former Liverpool goalkeeper had been part of Gérard Houllier's treble-winning team at Anfield six years earlier.

'Arne was 28, I was 32, we're both from the east of Holland and we clicked straightaway. From the first day we had such a good connection,' says Westerveld.

'I just needed a club for six months after leaving Almeria in Spain and Sparta came in for me as their keeper was injured. I was planning on going to Japan or the US, but I ended up staying at Sparta all season.

'Arne was like a lazy No. 10 – the guy who provides the final pass. He had great technique and vision in terms of through balls. He could pass the ball, see the options, delay and then speed up the game when he needed to. He was very tactical. It wouldn't take him long in a game to establish what the situation was.

'He was like the right hand of the coach on the field. With some players, you just know that they are cut out for management. I had the same feeling with Frank de Boer and Phillip Cocu. Arne was the guy at Sparta who would start the discussions with the coach at half-time. He knew exactly what had gone wrong. He was good at critically analysing and seeing opportunities. He didn't just point out problems, he came up with answers. I loved having Arne as a team-mate because he could do the talking. We had some great discussions over tactics.

'Arne used to call me "legend" because of the trophies I'd won at Liverpool. After I left Sparta, we kept in touch and used we meet up to play golf together. He would always start a message with "Hey legend …" When he achieved such success as a manager at Feyenoord I messaged him to say: "You're the legend now!"'

Slot's professional playing career ended where it started: he rejoined Zwolle initially on loan in 2009 before the move was made permanent 12 months later. Always thinking outside the box, he made headlines with his innovation.

'Have you seen what Arne used to do sometimes from the kick-off? People here used to laugh about it,' says Hendriks. 'He would flick the ball up and then *zuuuuut*! (gestures like a rocket taking off). He would shoot it up to heaven.'

Hendriks takes out his phone and finds a clip on YouTube from 2010 of Slot receiving possession inside the centre circle and hammering it into the air as team-mates charge forward in hot pursuit.

'It was about catching out the opponent,' he explains. 'Sometimes they might have the sun in their eyes and couldn't control it. Other times it was his way of saying: "Here you go, we'd like to have the second ball". Arne was always thinking. When he was sleeping, he was thinking about football. He always had a football brain and was very good at making people believe in themselves.

'When he had his testimonial game, Arne asked me and his father to be the managers when Zwolle played against the all-stars from Arne's career. Jaap Stam played in that game too. It was clear Arne would become a coach. He was always talking about Pep Guardiola and would study the games when Pep was coach of Barcelona.'

After helping Zwolle win promotion back to the Dutch top-flight in 2011/12, Slot retired a year later. Shortly before hanging up his boots in 2013, he came up against a Groningen side with a promising young centre-back called Virgil van Dijk.

Having told the club's directors he wanted to start coaching at the highest level possible, he was given a struggling Zwolle Under-14s side to work with. There had been a big turnover of players and early on they suffered some chastening defeats.

Defender Max Leeflang, who was part of that squad, told *The Athletic* in 2024: 'When you went onto the pitch, he wanted you to do everything good and when you made a mistake, you heard it every time. If you play one bad ball, he stopped the session and would say: "Next one has to be good". You'd think: "Come on, it's only one bad ball, just one mistake …". It is only when you are older you realise that these are the standards. We started winning. Then again, again, and again. Suddenly, everyone was talking about us: "How is this possible? The players are so bad …". The difference was Arne Slot. It was unbelievable.'

The youngsters would train from 8.30 a.m. until 10 a.m. before attending school lessons at the club's Centre for Sports and Education. Slot would then conduct a video analysis session with them. 'Before Arne, there was no video work at Zwolle,' adds Leeflang. 'I had never seen it. For everyone, it was new. I would ask myself: "Why are we doing this?" It was weird. But then we'd see the results and realise that it helped.'

Those who behaved badly at school weren't allowed to train. Slot knew that few of the boys would make it as professionals and reinforced that their education had to come first. There was a strong emphasis on fitness with weekly weigh-ins. Anyone who was heavier than the week before wasn't selected for the weekend.

Slot would set them up in a 4-3-3 formation but 'always wanted a fourth player in midfield' in possession which meant either the right-back or right-sided centre-back pushing up into the middle. 'At the time, the right-back at elite clubs would play high and wide but Arne was ahead of other coaches in his thinking,' says centre-back Leeflang, who also became captain.

'Arne wanted me to dribble forward with it. As soon as the striker approached, I would then have to play the ball and move, creating another angle. He wanted you to invite pressure from the opponent because that pulls the player out of position and creates space for you to play in. He would always say: "Don't play the ball back, always play forward." When I was 14, my dad used to say: "Listen to Arne, he's so good." I used to say: "Nah, there are so many good trainers …" Now I realise I was very wrong. He was the best. I have had other coaches with long professional careers behind them. They had played 500 matches but Arne was way better than them. The difference was so big.'

Hendriks, who was back working for Zwolle as a scout, recalls how Slot was impatient: 'After one season with the Under-14s, he wanted the next step. He wanted to be assistant for the first team. But the technical director said that wouldn't be possible so Arne said: "Okay so I'll have to leave." He went to SC Cambuur. Everyone was crazy about him there.'

SC Cambuur is based in the city of Leeuwarden, 65 miles north of Zwolle. Slot joined the top-flight club where he became No. 2 to manager Henk de Jong. 'Don't be a grey mouse,' was De Jong's opening bit of advice to Slot, which meant he needed to stand out. He didn't need to worry on that front.

Slot was buzzing with ideas as he used his extensive collection of video clips from Guardiola's Barcelona and Bayern Munich sides to illustrate his tactical points. He urged De Jong to reduce the number of high crosses Cambuur were delivering from wide areas because the data showed how ineffective they were.

During his time at Cambuur, Slot reached out to Pep Lijnders, who was part of Jurgen Klopp's coaching staff at Liverpool. Lijnders had initially joined Liverpool from Porto as Under-16s coach in 2014 before being promoted to the senior set-up by Brendan Rodgers a year later. Klopp retained his services as first-team development coach and later elevated him to assistant manager.

'Arne contacted me out of the blue to ask if we could meet up and talk about coaching,' says Lijnders. 'When I was back in Holland, he drove from one end of the country to the other – from Leeuwarden to my house down in the south.

'We sat in my winter garden and had a really nice talk. We exchanged some ideas and I answered a lot of questions. He had so much enthusiasm. We stayed in contact over the years that followed. We have a lot of similar ideas. He's a good guy who I always enjoy speaking to.'

It was at Cambuur where Slot first worked alongside Sipke Hulshoff. They clicked immediately. Hulshoff initially joined on a one-year internship to complete his UEFA Pro Licence, but after a brief spell in Qatar he returned as a permanent first-team coach.

When Rob Maas was dismissed in October 2016, Slot and Hulshoff were appointed as interim managers and then their services were retained for the rest of the season. Slot organised a supporters' evening to educate supporters about the playing philosophy and spoke for hours about their tactical approach.

The upturn in fortunes was significant as the second-tier side finished third in the league and reached the semi-finals of the Dutch Cup for the first time in their history, knocking out Ajax and Utrecht along the way, before losing on penalties to AZ Alkmaar.

'The way of playing and training was innovative and fun,' says Harm Zeinstra, who was Cambuur's goalkeeper. 'High energy, high intensity. They raised the bar. Arne and Sipke really complemented each other. No training session was similar to the last one. There were always different exercises.'

The painful end to that season left a lasting impression on Slot. His Cambuur side faced MVV Maastricht in the promotion play-offs and after a 1–1 draw away in the first leg, they were 1–0 up deep into the second half at home. Slot took a forward off and switched from his usual four-man defence to a back five to try to protect their narrow advantage, but they conceded two late goals and were dumped out. He vowed that he would never make fearful choices again and always play on the front foot.

Slot left Cambuur to join top-flight AZ and spent two years as assistant to John van den Brom before succeeding him as manager in the summer of 2019. AZ technical director Max Huiberts described Slot as 'eager to learn, innovative and very ambitious'.

'We always searched for young, new coaches,' Van den Brom told *The Athletic* in 2024. 'Arne was an interesting coach because he wanted to develop. What was nice for me is that he always thought in an attacking way. His focus was how can we make it clear to the players how we want to play? We used a lot of videos of Manchester City and Bayern – he was crazy about Guardiola. How his teams create space, how they attack.'

Slot's debut season as a permanent head coach was remarkable but ultimately bittersweet. His first speech to the players left a lasting impression.

'Everybody had chills because of the way he came across when he addressed us all,' recalls AZ striker Myron Boadu. 'It was a big moment for us. Even though we already knew him, we felt like this guy was going to be special and that this was the start of something. When he became the head coach, he came to my house with a No. 9 jersey. He talked with me and my parents and told me how much confidence he had in me, but that when he gives me this shirt, there's also a lot of responsibility that comes with it. He asked me if I wanted it and of course I said yes.'

Boadu, a graduate of the club's academy, had been on the periphery of the squad the previous season, scoring just three goals, but Slot unlocked his potential as he netted 20 times in 39 games in 2019/20. 'Sometimes we banged heads because he wanted me to do a lot more than just score goals,' he adds. 'He told me that I had to start the press and help the team defend. The way he motivated me was unbelievable. We would talk man to man and he'd tell me that I would feel disappointed at the end of my career if I didn't give everything. I'll never forget the things he said to me. His tactics were unbelievable. Everything we talked about during the week would happen in the game.'

Having changed both the culture and the playing style, Slot masterminded an unexpected title challenge. AZ stunned the heavyweights of Dutch football as they won 3–0 at Feyenoord and 4–0 at PSV Eindhoven. When they triumphed 2–0 away to Ajax at the start of March 2020, they moved level on points with the Amsterdam giants at the top of the Eredivisie.

With their fearless and aggressive approach, AZ had momentum behind them as they started to dream of just the third domestic title in their history. However, concern about the Covid-19 global pandemic was growing. The players were told not to shake hands with their opponents either before or after what turned into a 4–0 thrashing of ADO Den Haag the following weekend.

There were nine games to go when the Eredivisie was suspended and then eventually cancelled with Ajax ahead of AZ only on goal difference. For the first time ever, the Dutch title wasn't awarded.

Slot could at least console himself with the fact that his reputation as one of the best young coaches in Europe was blossoming. Hendriks, who had given Slot his first taste of senior football at Zwolle, encouraged high-profile agent Mino Raiola to start representing him. After Raiola's death in 2022, Rafaela Pimenta took control of the agency and became Slot's agent.

'Mino was a very good friend of mine,' says Hendriks. 'He asked: "How's Arne?" I said: "You have to take him, I guarantee that he's going to the very top." They worked together for a couple of years and then Rafaela was busy with Arne. It all worked out well.'

Slot's reign at AZ ended abruptly in December 2020. His team had made an unbeaten start to the campaign domestically and had claimed the impressive scalp of Napoli in the Europa League group stage. However, he was sacked after AZ discovered that he had been holding secret talks with Feyenoord about succeeding veteran manager Dick Advocaat the following summer. 'At AZ we want a head coach for the group who is fully focused on AZ,' said Huiberts bluntly. Slot's record of 2.11 points per league game was the best in the club's history.

'You always want to leave by the front door,' says Van den Brom. 'So it wasn't good for Arne and it wasn't good for the club.'

Slot spent his unplanned sabbatical playing golf and plotting how to revive the fortunes of Feyenoord, who finished in a distant fifth place in 2020/21, 29 points behind champions Ajax. The style of football under Advocaat was dull and uninspiring.

'When Arne joined Feyenoord in the summer of 2021 they sold their best player, Steven Berghuis, to Ajax and they didn't have lots of money to spend,' recalls Westerveld. 'Everyone said it would be difficult for him to make an impact there. AZ had actually finished higher in the table, but he saw a lot of potential in the Feyenoord squad and wanted to take on the challenge.'

In one of Slot's first team meetings at Feyenoord, he showed his players an array of clips from the Champions League final between Chelsea and Manchester City in Porto a few weeks earlier which was settled by Kai Havertz's goal. He wanted to illustrate the defensive work of the forwards on both teams to explain why the game had produced so few clear-cut chances.

After his first competitive game in charge, a Europa Conference League qualifier away to Kosovan side SF Drita, Slot sat down next to midfielder Orkun Kokcu on the flight home and explained that he needed to see more from him. No longer would he simply be able to create and let his team-mates do his running for him. He needed to improve his pace over the first few yards. The Turkey international took it on board, enlisted the services of a physical trainer, installed a gym in his home, and was given exercises to stimulate that development. Slot regularly texted him messages of encouragement and Kokcu's influence on the team grew considerably.

Feyenoord finished third in Slot's first season in charge and reached the final of the Europa Conference League, where they were narrowly beaten 1–0 by José Mourinho's Roma. Slot was awarded the Rinus Michels award for the best coach in the Eredivisie.

The players bought into his methods because they could see the results. In training before playing Marseille in the Europa Conference League semi-finals, he told his midfielders they needed to keep delivering lofted long passes out to the wingers in behind the defence. Slot had spotted a weakness in the French team's set-up and two goals in their subsequent 3–2 victory came via that route.

There was an exodus in the summer of 2022. With their players in high demand, Feyenoord sold off some of their biggest assets. Their 23-goal top scorer Luis Sinisterra joined Leeds United, Tyrell

Malacia went to Manchester United, Marcos Senesi signed for Bournemouth and Fredrik Aursnes moved to Benfica. Reiss Nelson returned to Arsenal after the end of his loan spell, while Guus Til, who had been on loan from Spartak Moscow, joined PSV.

Feyenoord received around €70 million in transfer fees and reinvested only €30 million as they embarked on a major overhaul of the squad which brought the average age down to just over 23 years of age.

Among the new arrivals was young striker Santiago Gimenez for €6 million from Mexican club Cruz Azul, who top scored with 23 goals in his debut campaign in Holland. 'When I first came to Feyenoord, it was difficult for me, it was a big step but Arne helped me a lot,' Gimenez told *The Athletic*. 'He gave me confidence, he pushed me to be better. He is the complete coach. Arne loves to attack and that attack makes you strong in defence.'

Slovakian defender David Hancko was signed from Sparta Prague, while winger Igor Paixao was recruited from Brazilian club Coritiba. Aursnes, who was bought for €450,000 and sold for €13 million, was replaced in midfield by Mats Wieffer from Dutch second tier club Excelsior for €600,000. Wieffer's development was such that within 12 months he was a full Netherlands international.

Despite such a turbulent summer, Feyenoord went on to blow their rivals away in 2022/23. A stunning 26-game unbeaten league run saw Slot become only the second Feyenoord coach this century to win the title. They also reached the semi-finals of the Dutch Cup and the quarter-finals of the Europa League.

'I spent a week behind the scenes shadowing Arne just before they became champions,' reveals former Liverpool striker and Feyenoord legend Dirk Kuyt. 'He's a manager who likes to help younger coaches like me and it says a lot about the type of person he is that he's willing to share his thoughts and vision so openly.

It was a fascinating experience in terms of the drills and how he prepares his team. Arne loves the game and thinks about football 24/7. That passion shines through when he speaks. He's always studying other teams and thinking about how his team can evolve.

'He knows exactly what he wants – attractive, attacking football. He likes to play an aggressive defence, high intensity, with the game played in the opponent's half. What struck me about Arne was his ability to make the players believe in what he believes in. I talked to some of them when I was there and they all spoke so highly about him. They loved how he organises the training sessions and how he gets his ideas across. He's an excellent communicator and man manager.

'Arne effectively had to build a new side going into his second season in the job. People doubted the new players who arrived and said he would need time to get things right, but he proved them all wrong. Outperforming Ajax and PSV to become champions was unbelievable because nobody expected that at the start of the season.'

Everse, who had managed Slot at Zwolle, watched on in admiration. 'He brought Ajax football to Rotterdam, which is more of a working-class city. He changed Feyenoord's mentality by his demands. Arne is better than me at managing the emotions of the team. Perhaps I was too critical, too cynical. Arne is a diplomat. He is very smart. He always first counts to 10. He is like a priest.'

The playing and training availability of the squad reached 90 per cent in each of Slot's first two seasons at Feyenoord. He worked closely with the club's data and fitness staff to ensure that players weren't overworked. He believed in the science and empowered the experts around him.

If Feyenoord were playing at 9 p.m., Slot would message the players to make it clear they should not be asleep at that time the night before the game to avoid their natural body clock leaving them feeling sluggish at kick-off.

When Slot and his staff decided that Marcus Pedersen needed to show more aggression on the field, they arranged for the Norwegian full-back to have kickboxing lessons at a local gym. To make recovery days more exciting, they would split the squad into groups to compete in a quiz for €50 while on the exercise bikes. Screen time on mobile phones was monitored and players were given individual pre-match plans, including meditation, visualisation using an iPad, and breathing exercises.

Performance methods were complemented by a DNA project led by Ruben Peeters, the joint head of performance, with samples of urine, stools, saliva and sweat taken from the players several times per season to reduce time lost to injuries. 'We are taking an inner selfie of the players, their digestion, gut health and how sport-specific genes are working together,' Peeters told *The Athletic* in 2023. 'Because we can do all the things you have heard about with regards to lifestyle, movement, or visualisation, but if the inside is not working at 100 per cent, then the impact of the external training sessions will not be good enough.'

Sports psychologist Dan Abrahams was recruited to help add another element to the club's high performance mindset. Feyenoord hadn't won away to Ajax since 2005, but together they overcame that mental block, culminating in a 3–2 win at the Johan Cruyff Arena in March 2023 en route to clinching the title.

'We broke it down into three words – dominant, relentless and brave. We called it a shared mental model,' says Abrahams. 'It was built on the philosophy that your most powerful psychologists are your players. You want to help them influence each other.

'Arne had a real passion for individual development. More than I'd ever experienced before. The players were surprised how much time he and his staff spent breaking down their game. He's a details person but he's also got a classic Dutch chilled-out side to him. There's a humbleness and ability to get on with people.'

Slot had been reunited at Feyenoord with Hulshoff, who was initially brought in to manage the Under-21s before later being promoted to assistant coach. Hulshoff, who led training sessions with Slot only jumping in when necessary, also conducted opposition analysis and helped present post-match debriefs. The No. 2's expertise was further recognised when national team boss Ronald Koeman added him to his Netherlands staff.

When the video analysts put selections of clips together for players to watch, Slot asked them to ensure that most of them were positive, especially the final one so that the session ended with them feeling good about themselves.

Matt Wade, who was Feyenoord's head of sporting strategy, was struck by how Slot operated 'very democratically but always retaining control'. He said: 'Arne was quite introverted but very rule based and principled which meant everyone knew where they stood. Him not being paranoid allowed freedom for specialists to operate.'

Slot riled Mourinho before the first leg of the Europa League quarter-final against Roma in April 2023 when he told reporters he preferred watching Guardiola's Manchester City or Luciano Spalletti's Napoli due to their more expansive brand of football. After Roma had triumphed 4–2 on aggregate, Mourinho launched into a furious tirade at Slot in the tunnel, telling him he should watch his team play more regularly. Slot just laughed and said: 'I'll watch what I want.'

Feyenoord chief executive Dennis te Kloese promised Slot the club would install a padel court if he delivered the Dutch title and was true to his word.

Two days after an emphatic 3–0 victory over Go Ahead Eagles had sparked wild scenes of celebration at De Kuip in May 2023,

Slot's parents Arend and Fennie granted a rare interview to respected Dutch journalist Vincent de Vries from *De Stentor* newspaper at their home in the village of Bergentheim.

De Vries discovered that a young Arne had attached a Feyenoord sticker to the window of the bedroom he shared with his brother Jakko. It was still there more than 30 years later.

'Sometimes I really have to pinch myself,' said a tearful Fennie. 'I still remember well when Arne appeared on television for the first time. We were all ready for it at home. We kept all the newspaper cuttings for a long time. We don't cut anything out anymore. It's become too much. I'm so proud of him. I'm also proud of Edwin, Jakko and Gerlinde, my three other children. But what Arne has achieved is so special – something almost magical.'

The couple posed for pictures looking through family photo albums and holding up a replica of the championship trophy. 'How he lets them play – that's football as you want to see it. Beautiful and well groomed,' Arend said. 'He never thought he would become a coach of a top club. "Dad, I'm not an international," he always said. Friends from Rotterdam have already warned us that for the next four or five years, Arne won't be able to walk through the city without a wig.'

In the more reserved surroundings of Bergentheim, Fennie was taken aback by the number of people who came up to congratulate her when she visited the local supermarket. A woman in her eighties who lived nearby turned up at their front door to hand over a bouquet of flowers.

Arend's mind wandered back to those days when he was the manager at Sportpark Moscou with Arne sitting alongside him, listening intently. 'Because my wife wanted some time for herself on Saturdays, I often took the boys with me,' he said. 'They were in the dressing room at every match briefing. How quietly Arne sat there in the corner, watching everything. I sometimes said: "Don't you want to play outside, boy?" No, he wanted to experience everything. He was six or seven. The way Arne talked about football at a young age was quite unique. He knew so much about it. It's funny, Arne used to be "the son of", now I'm "the father of the Feyenoord trainer".'

The transformation Slot had masterminded at Feyenoord ensured that he became one of the most coveted coaches in Europe. Interest from Premier League clubs Crystal Palace and Leeds United was turned down before both Chelsea and Tottenham approached his representatives in the spring of 2023. He had to give presentations to outline his tactical approach.

Tottenham thought they had persuaded him to move to north London to succeed Antonio Conte and Feyenoord had started drawing up a list of potential replacements. However, Slot surprised everyone by deciding to stay put and Ange Postecoglou was subsequently appointed by Tottenham instead.

Slot later told Dutch media that 'not going to Spurs was 99 per cent a family decision'. He would regularly commute between Rotterdam and the house in Zwolle, 90 miles away, that he shared with wife Mirjam and their children Isa and Joep. In late May 2023, he signed a new contract at Feyenoord which removed a release clause which stated his services could be acquired for a fixed sum of €5 million in the summer of 2024.

'I'm not done here yet,' Slot said after penning a deal until 2026. 'We have had a wonderful season with Feyenoord, with the championship as a wonderful reward for all the hard work that has been put in, but I really want to continue building. After the summer, an adventure awaits in the Champions League and there is a national title to defend. Enough to look forward to, so I am proud to be and remain Feyenoord's trainer in Rotterdam.'

Te Kloese dismissed stories in the UK media that Feyenoord had effectively priced Slot out of a move to Tottenham by demanding too much in compensation. However, the club CEO knew that they would need to prepare for his inevitable departure.

'Circumstances also played a role,' Te Kloese told *The Athletic* in 2023. 'Family circumstances, but also Feyenoord are in the Champions League. After the celebrations when we won the title – the scenes at the city hall, how many people turned up – [and] the emotion poured into it, you get a feeling this is a real big club. If you take everything into account, you recognise what you have here is not so bad.

'With a nice contract, with a supportive staff, people who all have the best interests for the club in mind – then to convince somebody to step out of that is not an easy thing. And I think at some point, probably when everything settled down, he also made up his mind that by doing well here, hopefully doing well next year also would open doors. And there's no secret in that there's a lot of interest in him. There's a lot of people looking at him and he's highly regarded.'

His stock continued to rise. Despite losing Kokcu to Benfica and registering another positive net spend, Feyenoord accumulated 84 points in 2023/24 – two more than when they landed the title the previous campaign. However, they finished second because they had the misfortune of being up against Peter Bosz's resurgent PSV side, who suffered just one defeat and ended up seven points clear.

Slot's first experience of managing in the Champions League ended with two wins out of six against Atlético Madrid, Lazio and Celtic, before dropping into the Europa League where they were beaten by Roma on penalties.

He secured a second trophy in three seasons when Feyenoord beat NEC Nijmegen 1–0 in the Dutch Cup final in April 2024. Three days later the news broke that Liverpool had opened talks with Feyenoord over compensation, after deciding to appoint Slot as Jurgen Klopp's successor.

'Sometimes in life, opportunities come along and you have to listen,' Slot told reporters after a 5–0 thrashing of Zwolle – the club where he started and finished his playing career. 'I have made that choice for myself. In the next days or weeks, you will see the announcement.'

The De Kuip crowd had serenaded him with a chant of '*Stand up for Arne Slot*'. He was leaving with their blessing and appreciation.

4

GOING DUTCH

'The playing style and philosophy attracted us to Arne, based on subjective footballing opinion and data as well. In all the metrics, Arne's Feyenoord team came out really well. The way they played real front-foot, attacking football, playing with intelligence and passion — attributes we welcome here at Liverpool.'

Richard Hughes

After Jurgen Klopp announced his decision to stand down, Xabi Alonso was immediately regarded as the favourite to take over at Anfield.

The former Spain midfielder ticked a lot of boxes. He had a close bond with Liverpool going back to his illustrious playing days on Merseyside between 2004 and 2009. He had been part of Rafael Benítez's side who had pulled off the 'Miracle of Istanbul' with their historic fightback against AC Milan in the 2005 Champions League final and was adored by the club's supporters.

Alonso had also enjoyed a flying start to his managerial career. In the space of 18 months he had taken Bayer Leverkusen from second-bottom in the Bundesliga to the brink of their first top-flight title.

There was some glowing praise from Klopp as speculation about Alonso's future cranked up. 'The next generation is already there and I would say Xabi is a standout in that department,' Klopp said. 'The football he is playing, the teams he sets up, the transfers he did, it is absolutely exceptional.'

However, despite all the focus on Alonso externally, Fenway Sports Group CEO of football Michael Edwards and Liverpool sporting director Richard Hughes had an open mind as the process of identifying the ideal successor got underway.

'FSG had a fundamental belief that Michael was the man to lead the transition from one era to another. Michael had a fundamental belief that Richard had to be the sporting director, but no-one had a fundamental belief about who the new head coach should be,' explains one senior club figure.

Liverpool's director of research Will Spearman and his data department were tasked with assessing the suitability of a wide range of candidates. Character references were sought to compile extensive dossiers.

Newcastle United manager Eddie Howe, Ipswich Town's Kieran McKenna, Tottenham boss Ange Postecoglou and Aston Villa's Unai Emery all scored highly on the club's data model. The claims of Roberto De Zerbi, Julian Nagelsmann, Andoni Iraola, Sebastian Hoeness, Michel and Paulo Fonseca were also discussed, but they were never seriously in the frame.

Athletic Bilbao head coach Ernesto Valverde, who had ended their 40-year wait for silverware by lifting the Copa del Rey, was greatly admired. He boasted a wealth of experience with his previous managerial roles including spells at Espanyol, Olympiakos, Valencia and Barcelona. Valverde had previously been discussed internally as the kind of figure they would turn to if Klopp ever left mid-season.

However, in the spring of 2024, it was soon established that three candidates stood out from the rest – Alonso, Arne Slot and Ruben Amorim.

Hughes had a good relationship with Alonso's agent Inaki Ibanez, who also represented Bournemouth boss Iraola. Given the job he was doing at Leverkusen and the groundswell of opinion for him, it was an avenue they had to explore but it quickly became apparent that Alonso wasn't going to be available in the summer of 2024.

During informal discussions, Hughes was informed that Alonso would be staying put for a further 12 months. He had persuaded players to remain at Leverkusen based on his own commitment and wouldn't backtrack for anyone. In late March there was official confirmation.

'My job is not over here,' Alonso told the German media. 'Putting everything together, I've taken this important decision. I am convinced it's the right one. This is my first full season as a manager. I still have a lot of things to prove and to experience. Right now, I have a situation where I feel really stable and happy. This is the right place for me to develop as a coach.'

There were no face to face talks with Liverpool and he was never offered the job. Alonso, who had also attracted interest from Bayern Munich, went on to lead Leverkusen to a league and cup double in Germany as they went through the entire season unbeaten domestically. Their only defeat in 2023/24 came at the hands of Atalanta in the Europa League final. Alonso was true to his word as he stayed for one more season before accepting the opportunity to succeed Carlo Ancelotti at another of his former clubs, Real Madrid.

During his Liverpool reign, Klopp would regularly ask his trusted No. 2 Pep Lijnders about the possibility of succeeding him one day. Promoting from within would have been a throwback to the famous Anfield Bootroom days when iconic manager Bill Shankly was followed by Bob Paisley and Joe Fagan. Lijnders was keen to launch a managerial career of his own, but a phone call from FSG president Mike Gordon in February 2024 confirmed that he wasn't in the mix.

'When Jurgen made his mind up, I was quite clear that it was also the right time for me to make my own way,' Lijnders said. 'I really felt we should end the project together. I was ready for a new experience. I also felt that the team needed something new. Mike called me and said: "Pep, we really considered you, but I think it's fair for you that we don't put you after Jurgen." Mike is a good guy. He knew as well. It was best for everyone for the future.'

After turning down interest from Portuguese club Porto and Championship outfit Stoke City, Lijnders accepted the role of head coach of Red Bull Salzburg in May 2024 and appointed Klopp's first-team development coach Vitor Matos as his assistant. However, within seven months Lijnders was sacked with Salzburg sitting fifth in the Austrian Bundesliga, having also lost five out of six games in the Champions League.

Liverpool set out certain criteria that needed to be met. They wanted a head coach with a distinct identity in terms of his brand of football – attacking, dynamic, high energy and possession-based. It needed to be someone capable of harnessing the power of Liverpool's fanbase like Klopp had done so effectively. A proven track record of developing players and keeping them fit was considered vital. Edwards and Hughes talked about making the right choice rather than the most popular one.

Spearman, a Harvard-educated physicist who spent five years as Liverpool's lead data scientist before succeeding Ian Graham as director of research in 2023, had been working on an algorithm that evaluated coaching performance across more than a dozen different metrics.

Slot's name kept on appearing at the top. 'Head and shoulders above the rest,' says one senior figure involved in the process. Edwards and Hughes had already discussed the merits of the Dutchman at length, but they hadn't expected the data to provide such an emphatic recommendation.

One of the metrics was 'points above expectation'. It underlined how Slot had Feyenoord punching well above their weight given the greater resources enjoyed by rivals PSV Eindhoven and Ajax. Another metric was 'player improvement' which assessed how someone's output on the field had changed during a coach's tenure by also examining how they performed both before and after. Again, Slot was at the summit.

Hughes had watched a lot of Slot's team in his role as Bournemouth's technical director. He signed Argentine defender Marcos Senesi from Feyenoord in 2022 and scouted others such as Marcus Pedersen, Quilindschy Hartman, and Luis Sinisterra, who ended up joining Bournemouth after a spell at Leeds United. Hughes had joked to other members of Bournemouth's recruitment department that they needed to stop suggesting members of the Feyenoord squad as suitable targets. 'It's not about the players, it's about the coach and his system,' he told them.

As for Edwards, he was a long-term admirer. A Liverpool staff member received a phone call from him in May 2023. Edwards, who was in his gym at home, had seen a report on Sky Sports News that Tottenham Hotspur were close to appointing Slot as their new head coach. 'That's a really smart appointment,' Edwards said. 'Daniel Levy has made a good decision there.' When Slot subsequently turned the London club down and decided to stay at Feyenoord, Edwards knew that he was destined for bigger things. All the data he had access to in his role as a consultant for Ludonautics reaffirmed that belief.

After Alonso publicly ruled himself out of contention, the name most persistently linked with Liverpool in the media was Sporting Lisbon coach Amorim, who was about to clinch his second Primeira Liga title with the Portuguese giants.

Amorim was a serious contender and boasted the best record in terms of player availability. However, that was partly attributed to him working in a less intense league. There was plenty to admire but Edwards and Hughes had doubts whether his preference for a three-man defence would suit the squad he would be inheriting at Anfield. There were also concerns that his slower, less dynamic style of play might fail to energise supporters.

Hughes held talks with Amorim in Lisbon but the Sporting boss was subsequently informed that Liverpool were going in a different direction. Slot was always the preferred candidate. They loved how his football connected with the emotional fanbase at Feyenoord, they felt it wasn't too much of a change from Klopp's approach and they knew he was well versed in working in a sporting director model. Having established via his agent Rafaela Pimenta that he was open to discussing the vacancy, Hughes was tasked with travelling to Holland to secure his services.

A meeting was arranged at Slot's plush townhouse overlooking the canal in Zwolle on 9 April. That morning Sky Germany inaccurately reported that Amorim had verbally agreed a three-year contract to take over at Anfield.

It was a source of some frustration for Liverpool because they didn't want Slot to wrongly think the job had been offered to anyone else, but it also provided them with a smokescreen about what was actually going on. Edwards liked the fact that they were operating under the radar as it meant they were unlikely to encounter any late competition for Slot's services.

Amorim set the record straight himself two days later when he told reporters: 'There's been no interview with any club, no agreement with any club.' A fortnight later the Portuguese coach was publicly apologising for holding talks with West Ham United about the possibility of succeeding David Moyes, admitting it was 'disrespectful'.

Amorim arrived in the Premier League seven months later when he was appointed manager of struggling Manchester United. He endured a dismal start to life in England as United limped home in 15th place – their worst finish since 1974/75 – and failed to qualify for European competition after losing the Europa League final to Tottenham.

'Why me?' asked Slot in his initial meeting with Hughes. Armed with a 60-page dossier packed full of data, character references and details about the player development and tactical approach which had delivered such success in Rotterdam, Hughes delivered a compelling case and succeeded where Tottenham had failed 12 months earlier. Similar in age and temperament, there was an instant rapport between the duo.

'I had a very good relationship from the start with Richard, which is one of the reasons I loved to join the club,' explained Slot. He had made it clear to his representative Pimenta after Liverpool's initial approach that he had no interest in taking part in a beauty parade and Hughes reassured him on that front.

'There was never one second of a doubt and that had largely to do with the fact why they wanted me and how they tried to convince me to come,' Slot said. 'I didn't have to open my laptop one time to show them what I did or how I worked. They knew everything about me. Richard knew many games and many of the assessments I'd made during games, the changes I'd made in tactics.

'Journalists in Holland wrote wrongly that I was one of the three or four candidates, but from the start it was clear to me. I told my agent that if I am one of three I am not interested. I'm only interested if they want me as the only one, because I didn't want to go into another summer where I had to do all these kinds of meetings and then waiting, waiting, waiting. My time at Feyenoord was too good. That's why I had no doubts because they were so clear that Liverpool wanted to have me and they knew everything about me.'

A couple of months before leaving Feyenoord, Slot had received a call from FSG technical director Julian Ward asking if he could pay a visit to Rotterdam during his travels through Europe as he was gathering information about how certain clubs operate. They knew each other from the years Ward was previously responsible for overseeing Liverpool's loans department.

Slot came to realise that Ward had been speaking to staff about what he was like to work with. It was all part of the club's mission to leave no stone unturned as they did their homework on him. 'What's he like around the building? What's he like in training? How does he treat his staff? How do his staff treat other staff?' were some of the questions posed. 'Respectful, honest, innovative, great communicator, straightforward, football obsessive, workaholic,' were among the responses.

Keen to avoid creating any unwanted distractions before Feyenoord's Dutch Cup final showdown against NEC Nijmegen on 21 April, Slot was clear that nothing could be sorted out until after that date. He had been stung by previous criticism when approaches from other clubs had leaked into the public domain.

Liverpool abided by his wishes and waited until after that 1–0 triumph before opening talks with the Dutch club over compensation. It was only on 24 April that the news broke in the UK that Slot was the chosen one. Slot had explained to Hughes that it was important to him that he left 'through the front door', with Feyenoord paid a fair compensation fee. A compromise figure of around €11 million was agreed between the clubs before Slot penned a three-year contract at Anfield.

There was a sense of bafflement internally when Sky Sports pundit Gary Neville wrongly claimed that Slot had been Liverpool's 'third choice' for the job after Alonso and Amorim. The reality was that Edwards and Hughes had landed exactly who they wanted after a thorough process analysing all the evidence in front of them.

The initial reaction among the fanbase was mixed. Some viewed it as a gamble given that Slot was still relatively inexperienced in managerial terms and hadn't previously worked outside his homeland. He had just one season of Champions League football under his belt.

Dutch coaches didn't have a great record in England. Ten of them had previously tried and failed to land the Premier League title. Out of that group, just four – Ruud Gullit and Guus Hiddink at Chelsea, and Louis van Gaal and Erik ten Hag at Manchester United – had lifted the FA Cup.

Ten Hag had won three Eredivisie titles in the space of four seasons and taken Ajax to the semi-finals of the Champions League, but he hadn't lived up to the hype at Old Trafford. By the summer of 2024 he was beleaguered and clinging on to his job. However, those who knew Slot best were always confident he would buck the trend.

'Arne had turned down moves to the Premier League previously because he didn't feel those projects were right,' says former Feyenoord and Liverpool striker Dirk Kuyt. 'He had been waiting for the right step to take. He wasn't in a rush. It had to be something he really believed in. The doubters all said: "He's never trained a foreign team before" but then Jurgen hadn't coached outside of Germany before he came to Liverpool and look what he achieved. Van Gaal once said: "When you're ready, you're ready." It doesn't matter what age you are or how much experience you have – it's about your qualities.

'You can't really compare Feyenoord with the size of Liverpool but Arne was used to dealing with pressure and high expectations in Rotterdam. When faced with difficult situations, when results didn't work out, when faced with tough questions from the media, he always stayed in control and stuck to his principles and the vision of how he wanted to play.'

Former Zwolle manager Ben Hendriks, who had given Slot his first taste of senior football as a teenager, said: 'The biggest difference between Arne and Ten Hag is communication. It's where Ten

Hag really struggled in England, but with Arne it's one of his big strengths.

'Arne explains everything so clearly that both the players and the journalists all know what he means and that's very important. You make a mistake with your words then the journalists kill you! It also helped that Klopp was so positive about Arne coming in and told the fans: "Believe in this guy, he's going to be fantastic." Arne was also very respectful about Klopp. It was a smooth handover.'

With their children Joep and Isa still in full-time education and preparing for exams, Slot and his wife Mirjam took the decision not to relocate their family to the UK. Slot initially moved into an apartment and then a house in Cheshire on his own. However, over the course of the season they visited regularly and he returned home to Zwolle when gaps in the schedule allowed.

'I drank some coffee with Arne when he was here in Zwolle in November,' adds Hendriks. 'He can walk around the streets here, no problem. Nobody asks for photos. They might just shout: "Hey Arne!" And he'll wave back. Arne is loyal. We're in regular contact on WhatsApp. I messaged to say: "I remember giving you your debut when you were 16, I'm very proud of you." A minute later, he replied: "Thank you Ben, it was a long time ago, but that was where it all started for me." Becoming Liverpool manager didn't change him. He's still grounded.'

There were five weeks between Arne Slot's official start date of 1 June 2024 and his unveiling in front of the world's media at the AXA Training Centre.

The delay was a deliberate ploy to put some distance between Jurgen Klopp's emotion-fuelled goodbye and the dawn of a new era. Slot had spent the time not only watching Liverpool matches from the previous season but also studying footage from training sessions. He had spoken to his predecessor on the phone about the squad he was inheriting with Klopp telling him he had got 'the best job in the world'.

Confident, relaxed and genuine, Slot comfortably dealt with everything that came his way as he answered questions from reporters at his unveiling. There were no headline-grabbing soundbites, no bold promises, but he struck the perfect balance between being respectful to the past and backing himself to repay the faith shown in him.

'Big shoes to fill, but you can also look at it as inheriting a squad and a team which has a winning culture,' Slot said. 'One of the reasons to come here is I do feel we have a really good squad. As a manager, you want to work at a club with good players, with the opportunity to win something. The past has shown there is a possibility for Liverpool to win some trophies. I look at being a successor to someone who was successful as ideal. I like to work with players and like to develop them but I like to win as well, and at this club there is an opportunity to do that.'

He also shrugged off the significance of being Liverpool's first head coach rather than manager. 'For me, it's not a change, I worked at Feyenoord and all my former clubs like this, always. There are not many clubs in the world where one person decides everything. It's a collaboration between people. That's how I like to work.'

Sitting alongside Slot, sporting director Richard Hughes explained why Slot was the outstanding candidate. 'The playing style and philosophy attracted us to Arne, based on subjective footballing opinion and data as well. In all the metrics, Arne's Feyenoord team came out really well. The way they played real front-foot, attacking football, playing with intelligence and passion – attributes we welcome here at Liverpool. It fits very well with the squad we have. There is a duty here to play the type of football where you're trying to grab games by the scruff of the neck. It's not going to be a hugely different approach to what has been so successful in the past and we hope to emulate that again.'

The prospect of following in the footsteps of an icon simply didn't faze Slot. It was something that former Liverpool goalkeeper Sander Westerveld, who had been friends with Slot since their days as team-mates at Sparta Rotterdam 17 years earlier, had discussed with him.

'I told him this is not the same as when Sir Alex Ferguson left Manchester United, who had an old team that needed to be rebuilt and then they fell away,' says Westerveld.

'Klopp had rebuilt the midfield the year before and there were a lot of talented young players at Liverpool with the potential to keep developing. Klopp had left the club in a very good state. Usually when you take over at a big club it's because the team is bad and big changes are needed. I told Arne the base was there to work from and he agreed. There was nothing to fear. I told everyone I knew that this was going to be the perfect fit.'

Another attraction for Liverpool when it came to appointing Slot was that he had few demands regarding the appointment of backroom staff.

Slot only brought assistant coach Sipke Hulshoff and lead physical performance coach Ruben Peeters with him from Feyenoord. Hulshoff resigned from his role working alongside Ronald Koeman with the Netherlands squad prior to the European Championships so he would be available for the start of pre-season training.

'Sipke is really important for Arne. He's his right hand,' adds Westerveld. 'He knows exactly what Arne wants and you can see that when you watch the training sessions. They share the same beliefs in terms of how the game should be played. Arne stands watching with Sipke more hands on.

'As for Ruben, he's the reason why Arne's record in terms of keeping players fit at Feyenoord was so good. He trusts Ruben completely when it comes to the workload of players. Arne is the leader, the problem solver, but he surrounds himself with good people.'

Slot had initially intended to also bring coach Etienne Reijnen with him from Feyenoord but he couldn't get a work permit. As a result Slot turned to fellow Dutchman and former Everton midfielder John Heitinga, who had Premier League coaching experience from his time on David Moyes' staff at West Ham United.

Aaron Briggs was recruited as first-team individual development coach having filled a variety of analyst and coaching roles for Manchester City, Monaco and Wolfsburg. Liverpool advertised for a specialist set-piece coach but after being unable to find a compelling candidate that responsibility was given to Briggs.

Edwards and Hughes were keen to ensure that Slot didn't just assemble his own people. They wanted him to be challenged with fresh ideas and there was no pushback. For example, they felt that it was important that Briggs' role was a club appointment given his work with the club's most gifted youngsters.

Fabian Otte, another club appointment, was headhunted from the USA national team set-up as the new head of first-team goalkeeper coaching to work alongside Claudio Taffarel, whose bond with Liverpool No. 1 Alisson Becker ensured he was the only coach retained from Klopp's reign.

It was telling during Slot's unveiling that when the conversation turned to transfers he repeatedly talked up the talent already at his disposal. Rather than demanding signings to put his own stamp on the team, he favoured a process of evolution rather than revolution. The Dutchman shared the belief of Edwards and Hughes that the squad was strong and that development would largely come from within through work on the training pitch.

There was also a sense that with so much change off the field with a new football executive structure, new head coach and new backroom staff, stability among the playing ranks would prove to be beneficial.

'For me, it's clear that we have inherited a good team,' Slot said. 'The longer a team plays together, if there's a good head coach, then normally you will see things improve. I'm fortunate in going to a club where not many transfers go out of the club. At Feyenoord, it was almost normal that eight, nine, 10 players left the club after every season, so it is more difficult for a manager to get progress. But here I am expecting Richard to keep most of our players and from there we can only build.'

At the start of the summer transfer window, recruitment discussions internally were centred on two positions – an attacker and a holding midfielder. Slot wanted a sixth senior forward to complement Mohamed Salah, Diogo Jota, Luis Díaz, Darwin Núñez and Cody Gakpo so he could rotate his options.

With Newcastle United needing to raise funds by the end of June to satisfy the Premier League's profitability and sustainability rules (PSR), which limit clubs to losses of no more than £105 million over a rolling three-year period, they agreed to sell England winger Anthony Gordon to Liverpool for £75 million. Gordon was a boyhood Liverpool fan who had been released by the club's academy at the age of 11 before joining neighbours Everton.

Joe Gomez, who was Liverpool's longest serving player having arrived from Charlton Athletic in 2015, was all set to move in the opposite direction for £45 million following positive talks with manager Eddie Howe. They were two separate deals but each dependent on the other. Newcastle had initially targeted fellow centre-back Jarell Quansah but were informed that he wasn't for sale.

Discussions were so advanced that enquiries were made with the England camp about holding medicals for both Gomez and Gordon during the European Championship in Germany.

However, at the eleventh hour, Newcastle pulled the plug when the £35 million sale of Elliot Anderson to Nottingham Forest and Yankuba Minteh's £30 million move to Brighton & Hove Albion gave them the cash they needed to avoid a potential points deduction without offloading one of their biggest assets.

Gomez ended up staying put and made 17 appearances (11 starts) in all competitions before a hamstring injury wrecked the second half of the 2024/25 season for him.

Asked how close he had come to joining Newcastle the previous summer after producing a dominant display in Liverpool's Champions League win over Girona in December, Gomez told reporters: 'Yeah, it was definitely for real. But I know how blessed I am to be here. I don't take that for granted. It is the best club in the world in my eyes and [after the transfer didn't happen] it was quickly a case of adapting and getting right back into the swing of things. It was quickly put to bed. I believe things happen for a reason.'

Liverpool registered their interest in young Lille centre-back Leny Yoro but didn't take it any further when it became clear that he wanted guarantees about playing time. They viewed him as a long-term project and Yoro subsequently joined Manchester United for £69 million.

The experienced trio of Joel Matip, Thiago and Adrian had all left at the end of the Klopp era. However, Matip had already been effectively replaced by the emergence of academy graduate Quansah, while Thiago had played a grand total of just five minutes across 2023/24 due to injury. Vitezslav Jaros had returned from a productive loan spell in Austria at Sturm Graz to take over from Adrian as the third-choice goalkeeper.

Liverpool were in the market for a holding midfielder but the profile they were looking at changed following the handover from Klopp to Slot. Rather than a 'destroyer' type No. 6 to break up

play, Slot wanted someone more technically gifted and press resist-
ant, who could operate in tight spaces, pick the right pass under
pressure and provide more control.

They set their sights on Real Sociedad's Martin Zubimendi, who
had just helped Spain triumph at Euro 2024 with victory over
England in the final. A delegation were dispatched to San Sebastian
where Liverpool were assured that Zubimendi, who had previously
snubbed interest from Bayern Munich, Barcelona and Arsenal, was
ready to cut his ties with the Basque club he had first joined at the
age of 12.

His release clause of €60 million (£51 million) would have to be
paid in one instalment, but Liverpool's owners gave the deal the
green light. They knew that trying to negotiate a lower fee would
be fruitless given Sociedad's reluctance to sell.

Everything was agreed with the player but when Liverpool
formally approached Sociedad in early August, the landscape
shifted. His hopes of a fond farewell were dashed when Sociedad
cranked up the pressure by informing him that he would have to
trigger the clause himself – effectively forcing his way out.

Zubimendi started to have second thoughts. The longer he spent
pondering his future, the more Liverpool feared the worst.
Zubimendi simply wasn't prepared to tarnish his legacy at his
boyhood club so the move collapsed.

Slot put a brave face on it. 'Zubimendi decided not to come so
we go forward with the ones we have. We're in a good place,' he
told reporters.

It wasn't the first time Liverpool had been thwarted in their
pursuit of a holding midfielder. Two years earlier they had missed
out on Aurelien Tchouameni, who opted to sign for Real Madrid
after leaving Monaco. In the summer of 2023 they had tried and
failed to land Brighton's Moises Caicedo and Southampton's
Romeo Lavia, who both ended up at Chelsea instead.

Wataru Endo had exceeded expectations during Klopp's final season – clocking up 43 appearances in all competitions after arriving for a modest £16 million fee from Bundesliga outfit Stuttgart. However, the Japan captain clearly wasn't the long-term answer as a No 6. and looked ill-suited to Slot's possession-based approach.

The sense of dismay among a section of the fanbase when Liverpool were turned down by Zubimendi intensified when it emerged that the club weren't going to pursue a Plan B.

Hughes and Slot were in agreement that there wasn't a suitable alternative available on the market. The only holding midfielder they regarded as better than Zubimendi was Manchester City's Rodri and he was unobtainable. Paris Saint-Germain's Manuel Ugarte was among the other options Liverpool were offered but dismissed prior to the Uruguayan completing a £42 million move to Manchester United late in the window.

The club's stance was that there was no point signing someone inferior to what they already had. Slot had informed Hughes that he saw Ryan Gravenberch's best position as being a No. 6 so that was where the bar was set.

Rewind two years and Liverpool's data had showed that the three best young midfielders in the world were Jude Bellingham, Tchouameni and Gravenberch. Bellingham and Tchouameni had gone to Real Madrid for a combined £200 million, while Gravenberch had joined Liverpool for a modest £34 million in 2023 after an unhappy spell at Bayern Munich. At the start of the 2024/25 season, the Dutchman was still only 22 and the potential was clear.

'What happened with Zubimendi was stressful but it also showed the value of good decision making,' says one senior club figure.

'If you panic in those situations, you can fuck yourself. It took some big balls to just sit tight. Richard Hughes got a lot of stick but there was nothing that we would have done differently. We pursued the best around, got a yes from the player and then he changed his mind at the last minute. Sticking with what we had after that was unpopular at the time but it proved to be spot on.'

Liverpool were the only Premier League club not to make a signing before the season started and it was late August before they belatedly did some business.

It was all about succession planning when they agreed a £29 million fee with Valencia for goalkeeper Giorgi Mamardashvili. Liverpool had been monitoring the Georgia international's development for a number of years with a collection of positive scouting reports backed up by the data analysis.

With interest in him growing following his eye-catching performances at Euro 2024, they knew it was unlikely he would still be available in 12 months. As a result Hughes did the deal but agreed that Mamardashvili would remain with the Spanish outfit for one final season before joining Liverpool in the summer of 2025.

Alisson, who had reaffirmed his commitment to the cause in the face of lucrative offers from the Saudi Pro League, was fully aware of the club's plan before they stepped up their pursuit of Mamardashvili. Liverpool knew that back-up keeper Caoimhin Kelleher was likely to leave in 2025 with the Republic of Ireland international desperate to finally emerge from Alisson's shadow and become a No. 1 himself.

The academy was boosted by the signing of England youth international Rio Ngumoha from Chelsea, but the only new senior addition to Slot's squad for the 2024/25 season was Italy forward Federico Chiesa, who had been frozen out at Juventus by coach Thiago Motta. Down to the final year of his contract and available for an initial fee of just £10 million, Liverpool regarded it as low risk with a potentially big upside.

Chiesa had been valued at around £80 million before injuries – most significantly a ruptured anterior cruciate ligament in 2022 – dented his progress. When the player learned about Liverpool's interest, he called his father Enrico, the former Italy striker who scored at Anfield against the Czech Republic in Euro 96, for advice. 'Go!' he told his son. 'It's the best choice for your career.'

The former Fiorentina attacker was welcomed with open arms but struggled to make an impact on Merseyside as he was hampered by both fitness and form. He clocked up just 104 minutes of Premier League football in 2024/25.

With the sale of fringe players Fabio Carvalho (Brentford), Sepp van den Berg (Brentford) and Bobby Clark (Salzburg) generating up to £62 million, Hughes returned a healthy profit on Liverpool's transfer dealings in the summer of 2024.

It was impressive work but externally a debate raged over whether the owners had backed Slot sufficiently in terms of investing in the squad. It had been a familiar theme during Klopp's reign and something he had been quizzed about during his farewell night at the city's M&S Bank Arena in late May.

'Can anyone imagine Liverpool as the club with endless money?' Klopp said. 'Kylian Mbappé comes here, Jude Bellingham comes here, Erling Haaland comes here. It is not us. People can judge me for the finals I lost, no problem. I couldn't care less. We won what we won and we did it the Liverpool way. That's how I see it.

'The owners are good people. We had hard conversations and other clubs didn't do what we did in the same time. We built two new stands and a new state-of-the-art training ground. Somewhere else the grass is always greener. We have owners who feel responsible for the club. Are they the best in the world? I can't say, I don't know the others – but they worked really hard to ensure we were successful. I felt supported. If others make of it that if I'd been supported more we would have won more, I have no clue. We did it as well as we could and I'm fine with it.'

Liverpool's net spend throughout the Klopp era, which had yielded seven major trophies, was around £340 million. That figure was dwarfed by the net spends of the other members of the so-called Premier League's 'big six' over the same period – Manchester United (£890 million), Chelsea (£841 million), Arsenal (£700 million), Manchester City (£690 million) and Tottenham (£510 million).

Only Manchester City, who had twice beaten Klopp's side to the title by a single point, had been more successful than Liverpool in terms of silverware won between 2015 and 2024, but when Klopp departed, City still had more than 100 charges hanging over them for alleged breaches of the Premier League's financial fair-play rules. 'If you organise a bus parade, I am in. How long it takes I don't care,' joked Klopp when asked about the possibility of being reassigned those titles.

What had changed significantly at Liverpool over the course of Klopp's tenure had been the size of the club's wage bill. It had shot up a remarkable 86 per cent from £208 million to £386 million per year between 2018 and 2024. Only City (£413 million) were spending more on salaries in the Premier League when Slot took over.

Making FSG's self-sustaining business model work had involved some tough decisions recruitment-wise. 'You can't spend it twice,' is one of the owners' mantras. Without the riches of a nation state behind them, Liverpool couldn't afford expensive mistakes in the market or to stockpile players. There had been a strong emphasis on bringing through youngsters from their academy.

But what they had recognised was that if you want to retain elite players then you have to suitably reward them. As a result Liverpool had become a final destination for world-class talent during Klopp's reign rather than a stepping stone to other European giants.

Liverpool had out-performed Manchester United commercially in 2023/24 for the first time in the Premier League era with revenues of £308 million compared to £303 million. It was also the first time that commercial income had been more than half of Liverpool's total annual revenue (£614 million). The club's expanding global appeal was underlined by the signing of lucrative multi-year sponsorship deals with American blue-chip brands such as Google Pixel, Peloton, UPS and Orion Innovation.

It was a world away from the early years of Klopp's tenure when Liverpool ended a partnership with Russia-owned gaming firm 1xBet, which had its UK licence suspended after reports of its website hosting betting on cock-fighting and using pornography to encourage gambling. A deal with coconut water brand Chaokoh wasn't renewed amid allegations of animal cruelty by the Thai company, who denied illegally capturing monkeys and using them to pick the fruits.

By the time Slot took over, Liverpool had more than 80 staff working on commercial partnerships, divided between offices in Liverpool, London, New York, Boston, Singapore, Hong Kong and Japan. They had become the first Premier League club to reach 10 million YouTube subscribers and had the most social media engagements (1.5 billion) in 2023/24. For context, there were 61.3 million engagements when Liverpool won the Carabao Cup in Klopp's last season compared to 12.7 million when the Kansas City Chiefs won the Super Bowl earlier the same month.

Matchday revenue had been transformed by the £200 million invested in redeveloping both the Main Stand and the Anfield Road Stand to increase the capacity from around 44,000 to 61,000. 'Why would you ever leave here?' asked FSG principal owner John W. Henry on his first visit to the stadium after the takeover in

2010. Despite the numerous hurdles, they had found a way to retain the history and tradition while also modernising Anfield, like they had done at Fenway Park, home of Major League Baseball's Boston Red Sox.

Liverpool CEO Billy Hogan was convinced that the foundations were strong enough to handle the seismic departure of someone as influential as Klopp.

'When you go back to 2010 when FSG acquired Liverpool, if you look at where the club was at that point and where we are today, it's night and day in terms of the size and strength of the organisation,' he told *The Athletic* in 2024.

'We're incredibly proud of that transformation and the success we had over Jurgen's nine years at the helm. Now we're entering a new era and we're excited about that. As Mike Gordon said when Michael Edwards rejoined, nobody better understands the responsibility and necessity to deliver for Liverpool in terms of the sporting operations side. He's got tremendous history and success doing that.

'We've now got a structure in place with people leading Liverpool through this transition. It's about making the best possible decisions for the club and it doesn't change the strategy we're operating under, which is to be run sustainably as an organisation and make sure we are competing for trophies on an annual basis.'

Wary of the fact that Slot had been facing a barrage of questions from the media about the lack of transfer activity, Edwards and Hughes arranged a meeting with their head coach at his new home in Cheshire in August 2024. It coincided with the draw for the revamped league phase of the Champions League which they watched together.

They wanted to reinforce why Liverpool had largely opted to keep their powder dry in the market. Initially, the search for a new head coach had consumed them and with time tight they didn't have the usual body of work heading into a transfer window. They didn't want to make snap judgements and end up with buyer's remorse.

But more importantly, they explained that they had a lot of faith in the existing squad and believed that with his coaching acumen he could help elevate those players to the next level. Slot reassured them that he was fully on board with the club's approach.

With an eye on the longer-term, Hughes set about revamping the club's scouting network in terms of how they gathered and recorded information, with four new regional European scouting jobs created. With the help of his assistant David Woodfine, he also reorganised departments at the AXA Training Centre and sought to improve the levels of cooperation and understanding between them.

There was a redesign of the offices upstairs with a move away from one big coaches' room with more space opened up for one-to-one meetings and a focus on greater collaboration with analysts. From Hughes' perspective, it was about creating the best possible environment to empower experts in their particular field.

Before the 2024/25 campaign got underway, Opta's Supercomputer, which uses an algorithm created by the sports analytics company Stats Perform, simulated all the matches 10,000 times to forecast where each Premier League club would finish. They predicted that Liverpool had just a 5.1 per cent chance of winning the title. Reigning champions Manchester City (82.2 per cent) were expected to run away with it followed by Arsenal (12.2 per cent).

The target laid down by the owners for Slot was securing Champions League qualification which meant finishing in either the top four or five places depending on how English clubs fared in continental competition that season. Being outside of Europe's elite and missing out on that considerable windfall had been the main reason why the club had posted a hefty pre-tax loss of £57 million for 2023/24.

But the new coach already had his sights set considerably higher. 'Arne wasn't saying early on we should win the league, but he was saying we could,' says one senior club figure. 'He didn't want to put a limit on anything.'

5

OFF TO A FLYER

'It's probably the happiest I've been. As a style of play, it suits me. This now is more me. I can get on the ball more. Now the midfielders are going to be the heart of the team. We're not in a rush to attack. In the past, it was a bit too direct. Arne wants us to have all the ball and completely kill teams.'

Curtis Jones

Arne Slot couldn't wait to get started.

Among the changes Liverpool's new head coach introduced at the AXA Training Centre in July 2024 was bringing in an earlier report time of 9.15 a.m. The players were informed that kicking off the day by eating breakfast together in the canteen was compulsory.

The squad would no longer be staying at the city's Titanic Hotel the night before matches at Anfield as Slot felt they would benefit more from sleeping at home in their own beds before meeting up the following morning.

The club's state-of-the-art Kirkby base had undergone a summer makeover with the installation of a coffee bar just inside the players' entrance. It had been a long-standing idea of FSG's new CEO of football Michael Edwards, dating back to his tenure as Liverpool sporting director. He had been inspired by a similar set-up at clubs he had visited in Italy, including Roma. It quickly became a place for players to congregate and socialise both before and after training – fostering a greater sense of camaraderie and togetherness – as they enjoyed the company of popular barista Alex.

Training sessions were more structured, more tactical, more technical. Jurgen Klopp's approach had been all about the collective, but Slot favoured a more individualised way of working. Rondos designed to improve passing accuracy and quick decision-making became an established part of the sessions rather than simply a warm-up activity. Tricks and flicks were discouraged with Slot insisting: 'You wouldn't do it in a game so why do it in training?'

The biggest culture shock for the players early on was the sheer number of meetings they were asked to attend both before and after training. Slot, the son of two teachers, was on a mission to educate. He would rewatch every training session and provide feedback, along with coaches Sipke Hulshoff, John Heitinga and Aaron Briggs.

'It was like a new headmaster laying down a new way of doing things,' says one senior club figure. 'It was different and the players had to acclimatise to it. You had full team meetings, you had separate meetings for the defence, the midfield and the attack, and then you had the one-to-ones. The schedule was packed and it was a jolt to them. Arne was met with curiosity in pre-season but there was no resistance. That's testament to the elite culture that Jurgen had left behind. They all bought into it and embraced the learning.'

The sheer attention to detail was something the players hadn't experienced previously. Slot would always request from the analysts that a selection of video clips accentuated strengths as well as highlighting where he felt improvements could be made.

Pre-season wasn't ideal with so many star names reporting back late following their international commitments at the European Championship and the Copa América. Slot had just 11 days between getting his full squad together for the first time at Kirkby and the Premier League opener at newly promoted Ipswich Town.

However, one player who was on board from the start was Mohamed Salah. 'Phenomenal,' was the verdict of Liverpool's head of physical performance Conall Murtagh after the prolific Egyptian attacker finished top in the punishing six-minute race test at Kirkby, where players ran at maximum intensity around a large square.

Salah not only returned early for pre-season but, at the age of 32, looked in the shape of his life, having benefited greatly from an extended summer break. He had endured a difficult end to Klopp's reign as he struggled to regain rhythm following the hamstring injury he had suffered at the Africa Cup of Nations midway through the season and cut a disconsolate figure. He scored just twice in his final nine appearances of 2023/24 and there had been a public spat with Klopp on the touchline at West Ham United, which was followed by Salah's headline-grabbing message to the waiting media post-match: 'There's going to be fire today if I speak.'

Team-mates were struck by how happy and positive he seemed as a new era dawned. Slot knew he would be a massive asset but there was no treating him with kid gloves. During a one-to-one in July, Salah was shown clips from a warm-up where Slot felt Liverpool's global icon was going through the motions rather than really setting the tone for the youngsters who looked up to him.

Recalling that meeting in Slot's office, Salah told Sky Sports: 'Arne said: "Look at the second player after he sees you taking it easy, look at the third one." Then you see the whole line walking like me. He said: "That's your influence on the team." It was quite tricky in the beginning but after that you get used to him and how he talks to you and what he wants from you and then things become easier.

'We had a few honest conversations. He showed me a few clips and said: "With this Mo we can win everything, with this Mo we can't win much. I want to get the best out of you. I want this Mo to be available the whole season and for you to have your best years with me." I said: "Okay, let me know what you want from me and I will do it because I'm very professional." It wasn't so much challenging me, more showing what he wanted from me. He said: "If you want to add or change something then be open with me." A new manager coming in, giving me space and appreciation, letting me talk to him all the time about what I want to improve, what I want the team to do for me, what I want to do for the team, I think that's what I needed.'

Mutual respect abounded. 'I probably gave Mo 15 compliments during that same conversation and then showed him that warm-up,' Slot said as he provided some context to their exchange. 'I'm not so stupid to just say something like that out of the blue. If you want to bring a message across you have to say it in the right way. To be fair to Mo, in the six-minute runs they all had to do he was number one.'

Slot was similarly blunt with vice-captain Trent Alexander-Arnold after he reported back for club duty. 'In my opinion, in certain moments Trent could do a bit more, to say it mildly, and that's what we talked about,' Slot revealed. 'I said to him: "You are a much better defender than everybody tells you. Unfortunately, you don't show it all the time. That's why people sometimes say you are not." If Trent is at it, focused and concentrated, there are not many players that can go around him because he's fast, he's agile, he has a great mentality. But it's about showing that every single game, because in this world we are judged not only on the 34 games we do well, we are mainly judged on the four games we don't do so well.'

Alexander-Arnold took it on board and asked the new head coach to be his 'biggest critic' as they pored over clips and made subtle changes to his positioning to help the defensive side of his game. 'I said to him that I would like to be the defender that no-one wants to come up against in Europe. We agreed that he will be harsh on me,' Alexander-Arnold told reporters early in the season.

'If any time an attacker gets past me, he will call it out in meetings and say this cannot happen. We go through every game together and he highlights where he wants me to improve. It is really refreshing to have a manager who will help and guide and teach me how to be better as a player. I am someone who wants to learn, someone who wants to be the best and someone who strives to be the best ever.'

'Kill them with passes. Move it!' boomed Slot as he took training at Lincoln Financial Field, home of the NFL's Philadelphia Eagles, during Liverpool's pre-season tour of the United States. After whistling to stop the session, he gave some instructions to Kostas Tsimikas: 'Open your body and look for an inside run.' During one lengthy drill, 10 players tried to build attacks while being pressed by nine opponents. There was a strong emphasis on one and two-touch play.

After a fortnight in Kirkby, a youthful squad had headed across the Atlantic. Despite the absence of key personnel, it was striking how quickly the changes in playing style were embedded. Where Klopp had preached 'organised chaos', Slot wanted more control.

'I spoke about keeping the ball in some situations a bit longer than Jurgen's teams did in general, not always going for the pass that has a lot of risk, waiting a bit longer for the right moment,' Slot explained. 'But if we don't have the ball then we need to be really aggressive. We don't go to a low block. We're always there to press high.'

Slot implemented a 4-2-3-1 formation which effectively became 4-2-4 out of possession. He wanted a more patient build-up with underlapping full-backs and deep runs from his midfielders. He was keen to ensure there was greater protection for a backline which had conceded the first goal in 16 league matches in 2023/24.

Eyebrows were raised at just how effusive midfielder Curtis Jones was in his praise for the Dutchman prior to the first game of the tour against Real Betis in Pittsburgh. 'He's amazing. It's probably the happiest I've been,' Jones told the assembled media at the UPMC Rooney Sports Complex, the elite training facility of the Pittsburgh Steelers.

It was a big statement coming from an academy graduate who had broken into the senior ranks and made 133 appearances for his boyhood club during Klopp's reign. However, there was substance behind Jones' words. 'As a style of play, it suits me. This now is more me. I can get on the ball more. I came around a team who had world-class lads on the wing and up front. The centre-mids were always more like runners, more disciplined.

'Now the midfielders are going to be the heart of the team. In terms of our build-up, we have to be more calm and play more as a team. We're not in a rush to attack. We want to have the ball and just break teams down. In the past, it was kind of a rush. It was a bit too direct, it was up and down. Now Arne wants us to have all the ball and completely kill teams.'

Some interpreted it as a criticism of Klopp but Jones told *The Athletic*: 'It definitely wasn't a dig at Jurgen. I owe him so much. Jurgen changed me from a boy to a man. He was the man who made me understand so much.' Jones simply felt that his skillset was well suited to Slot's brand of football. As momentum grew over the course of the season, he wasn't shy referencing the fuss over his quotes and reminding staff at Kirkby that he had been the first to shout from the rooftops about the new head coach's ability.

After Dominik Szoboszlai's goal had secured a 1–0 victory over Real Betis in Pittsburgh, FSG president Mike Gordon met Slot for the first time at the team's base at the Fairmont Hotel. The owners had trusted the judgement of Michael Edwards and Richard Hughes when it came to appointing Klopp's successor. But Gordon swiftly appreciated why Slot had got the job as he was struck by his strategic thinking and concise nature. 'He's even better than I imagined,' was the feedback from Gordon to Edwards and Hughes.

Prior to beating Arsenal 2–1 in Philadelphia, the squad paid a visit to the city's iconic Rocky Steps and the famous Front Street boxing gym, featured in the film *Creed*, where they donned gloves and were put through their paces in the ring. There was also a team-bonding trip to watch the Phillies play the New York Yankees at Major League Baseball's Citizens Bank Park.

Former Liverpool goalkeeper Sander Westerveld, who was on the tour, said: 'I've got to be honest, I wondered how it would work when Arne walked into Liverpool and started telling someone like Mo Salah: "Right, you need to do this, this and this." Would Salah look at him and think: "Who is this guy? What do you know?"

'But any doubts I had disappeared during the time I spent in Philadelphia. I phoned Arne and he sorted out for me and my two boys to go and watch training. Afterwards I spoke with some of the players and they were like "wow" about the sessions he was putting on. They were so enthusiastic and in awe of him. He made such a positive impression on them from the start.'

A successful trip ended with a 3–0 hammering of Manchester United in Columbia, South Carolina which showcased Slot's impact in such a short space of time. 'Yeah, but I think the reason why this club hired me was that there's not so much difference between me and Jurgen,' Slot said modestly. 'I think there are a lot of similarities in terms of our playing styles so then it's not so difficult to adjust certain things. If you go from one particular playing style to another it's much harder. A lot of things could stay the same and that meant being able to really focus on what needed to be implemented. That's why I think it was quite fast that you could see certain things being different.'

The friendly against United was significant because it featured Ryan Gravenberch in the No. 6 role for the first time. The Netherlands international had endured a mixed first season at Liverpool following a £34 million move from Bayern Munich in the summer of 2023. There had been flashes of his undoubted quality in a more advanced position, but he lacked endurance and had struggled to hold down a regular place in Klopp's team. Seventeen of his 38 appearances in all competitions in 2023/24 had been off the bench. Slot knew that the youngster he had watched make the breakthrough at Ajax at the age of 16 was capable of much more.

The new head coach had made a series of phone calls in June to the players who were going to miss the opening stages of pre-season due to the Euros and the Copa América. Those chats were more than simply introductions, Slot got straight down to business and spelt out exactly what he wanted to see from them.

'During the first conversation I had with Arne, he said to me: "I want to try you as a No. 6," Gravenberch recalled. 'I played there against Manchester United in pre-season and after that game, he just put me there. I was like: "OK, let's do it."

'From that moment on, I played as a No. 6. The defensive part was maybe where there was a question mark. The attacking part was good but the defending part I had to learn in terms of the duels, sometimes not watching my man properly, I made a lot of steps with that.'

Slot had asked Gravenberch to cut short his time off so he could experiment in the final game of the tour against United. 'I was curious how he would do in that position,' Slot said. 'I really liked how comfortable he looked in that game. There was one moment where we played the ball to him, someone tried to press, and he used his body so well. We needed to find out in the opening few games if he was defensively strong enough and he definitely was. He had all the ingredients to play that position.'

Alexis Mac Allister had informed Slot during their first phone call that although he had no problem playing in the holding role, as he had done frequently under Klopp during the previous season, he felt he was better suited to operating with a No. 6 behind him. The Dutchman agreed with his World Cup winner.

The feeling of apprehension in the fanbase when Real Sociedad's Martin Zubimendi turned down a move to Anfield and Liverpool opted not to pursue an alternative, wasn't replicated internally because they could see Gravenberch growing in stature.

Slot had found the perfect solution, with the decision to play Gravenberch deeper proving inspired: he started all 34 Premier League matches prior to the title being wrapped up. He was deservedly crowned Premier League Young Player of the Year for the succession of elegant, composed and dominant performances he delivered.

'It was not easy to be honest. It might have looked it, but it was not,' he says. 'I'm not naturally a defensive midfielder. A lot of work went into it, not only from me, but also the coaches and the other players on the pitch. For example, Virgil (van Dijk), who helped me adapt to this role.'

Gravenberch was also indebted to assistant coach John Heitinga, who had been appointed as his mentor. They analysed a lot of clips together and did one-on-one sessions on the training field to iron out issues. An extensive strength and conditioning programme designed by the physical performance staff contributed to Gravenberch's improved duel success and ball retention rates, while he took advice from Van Dijk about rest and recovery between matches.

The first player Slot had called after his appointment at Liverpool was his captain. Van Dijk told him: 'No matter what you need, I am here for you. You can always call, always text me, any questions, whatever.' An instant rapport was established.

Slot explained to Van Dijk how he wanted him to take on extra responsibility for launching attacks. Rather than the No. 6 dropping deep or Alexander-Arnold inverting from right-back to collect possession from one of the centre-backs, Slot wanted Van Dijk to thread passes through the lines into midfield. The talismanic defender relished adding another string to his bow.

'The manager asked a lot of me but I like that,' Van Dijk said. 'He knows that I am very comfortable on the ball at the back. I have different weapons in my opinion. Obviously, I can play a 60 to 70-yard pass, but I am also comfortable breaking the lines and if you have players there that can be in the right position like we have, then it speeds things up and helps. It has been a big change for me because obviously over the years we played a certain way under Jurgen and very successfully, but I am enjoying it.'

The feeling was mutual. 'From the first session with Virgil, I was like "wow",' Slot said. 'He is the one who leads the team from start to finish so when I go out on the training ground and blow my whistle I will hear one player for sure and that's Virgil.'

With Van Dijk, Alexander-Arnold, Joe Gomez, Cody Gakpo, Luis Díaz, Darwin Núñez and Alisson all back on board, Slot could finally hold meetings with the full squad at Kirkby in the build-up to the final friendly against Sevilla and then the curtain-raiser at Ipswich.

'Arne basically said: "We finished third last season and now we want to finish above the other two",' says left-back Andy Robertson. 'It was clear in his mind that he was coming to win trophies, not just to be happy with the top four. He tried to get as many ideas across as quickly as possible and we jumped on board. We knew that him and his staff watched back absolutely everything so you had to be on it every day otherwise you'd get picked out.'

French defender Ibrahima Konaté recalls Slot showing the squad data from the previous season to highlight areas where the bar needed to be raised. One was how susceptible they had been to counter-attacks after losing possession.

'Just before we started the season he showed us why we didn't win the league the year before, some details, and he said if we change that and improve on that we have a big chance to win the league,' Konaté said. 'He showed a lot of clips from training. He showed one player who didn't run well or stopped running and said: "He didn't run now. Why? Because I gave you a compliment?" He said the truth to everyone – Mo, Virgil, every player – if something was wrong. Everyone was like: "Oh, he looks at me every day. He looks at me every training session. I have to give two thousand per cent always".'

Slot kept emphasising the importance of players sprinting back to get behind the ball when opponents attacked. Hard graft was non-negotiable.

For Slot, long days at Kirkby frequently ended with a game of padel involving his backroom staff. Unless he had family visiting from the Netherlands, he would then take some food home to reheat for his dinner. If there wasn't a game on television, he would sometimes watch a show on Netflix with Dutch comedian Jochem Myjer a particular favourite. However, usually he would open his laptop and carry on analysing either that day's training session or an upcoming opponent before calling it a night. 'The life of a manager is not always as exciting as it seems,' he said.

* * *

Arne Slot's relaxed demeanour on the touchline belied the nerves he was feeling when Liverpool walked out at Ipswich's Portman Road on the opening weekend of the 2024/25 Premier League season.

'Not because it was my first game in charge of Liverpool, more that it was the first game of the season,' he told *The Athletic*. 'You never know exactly where you are. We had to go to Ipswich which was probably like an FA Cup final for them, being back in the Premier League after so many years outside it. There were fireworks, everyone was ready for it. Hot day, early kick-off. Plus not knowing what to expect because it was a different league for me.'

After a scrappy opening 45 minutes, Slot showed his ruthless streak. Unhappy with the number of challenges Liverpool had been losing, he replaced young centre-back Jarell Quansah with Konaté at the break. He sat down with Quansah at Kirkby the following day and explained his logic so no resentment lingered. Slot was keen to stress that it had been a collective issue rather than down to one individual.

However, it proved to be a pivotal moment for both defenders. Konaté, who had lost his way alarmingly towards the end of Klopp's reign, rediscovered his mojo and regained his status as a regular alongside Van Dijk. Quansah slipped down the pecking order and only made three more league starts all season before moving to Bayer Leverkusen in a £35 million deal in July 2025.

The substitution at Ipswich helped trigger the response Slot had demanded – having won just 42 per cent of duels in the first half, that figure jumped to 55 per cent after the interval. Victory was secured courtesy of two expertly crafted goals as Salah laid on the opener for Diogo Jota and then tucked away the second himself. Salah set a new Premier League record of nine goals on the opening weekend of a season – taking him clear of Frank Lampard, Wayne Rooney and Alan Shearer.

Eyebrows were raised when Slot headed straight down the tunnel after the final whistle at Portman Road rather than going across to acknowledge the travelling supporters, who had been used to Klopp marking such triumphs with a flurry of fist pumps.

'The funny thing is I mainly choose that if the players have done something special then I want them to get the credit for it,' Slot said. 'In Holland it's not common that a manager would always go over to the away end. Maybe only one or two do it, maybe no-one does it! I walked in that day feeling like the boys deserved the credit for the win. Then afterwards I heard for the first time: "This isn't normal in this country." So after that I started doing it of course in terms of thanking them. But even if you see me now, I still don't want to take the shine away from the players. They are ones who have worked so hard for 90 minutes to get a result and they should be the ones who get the main credit.'

Slot wanted his bond with the fanbase to grow organically through his brand of football rather than trying to force it with gestures. And after a comfortable home win over Brentford, he turbo-charged that process when Manchester United were swept aside 3–0 at Old Trafford at the start of September.

The sight of Liverpool winning there with such a swagger was symbolic given how Klopp's final season had imploded at the same venue with a 4–3 defeat in the quarter-finals of the FA Cup in March quickly followed by a damaging 2–2 draw in the Premier League.

'If you ask me: "What was the game where you probably won the players over?" I think it was this game against United because we changed some small details in the way we did our build-up,' Slot said.

'I said to them that United would be expecting Dominik Szoboszlai to play on the right. That they will have prepared all week for it, but he's going to play on the left and we're going to do this, this and this a bit different. Indeed exactly what I said happened. I think it was a day when the players thought: "Oh, what he's trying to tell us works." To win 3–0 at Old Trafford gave us the confidence that there was maybe something special ahead of us.'

Liverpool's game plan involved targeting Casemiro and exposing the space in behind United's full-backs, and it worked a treat as they pressed relentlessly to win back possession. The veteran Brazilian's pass was intercepted by Gravenberch in the build-up to the opener as Salah's cross was nodded home by Luis Díaz. Then Díaz hounded Casemiro before a one-two with Salah led to the Colombian firing home his second.

At half-time Slot was more interested in showing his players clips where they had given United a glimmer of hope – with Díaz slow to track back and Alexander-Arnold sloppy with his distribution.

It served to focus minds and early in the second half Mac Allister shrugged off Kobbie Mainoo and fed Szoboszlai, who created the third for Salah. There was still more than half an hour to play but rather than go for the jugular, Slot's side kept their shape and kept United at arm's length. The control and game management was refreshing with Gravenberch excelling.

As Slot's name boomed around Old Trafford, he raised a clenched fist in the direction of the travelling Kop. Not since George Kay 88 years earlier had a Liverpool boss won his first away league clash with United. Slot also became the first manager in the club's history to win his opening three league games in charge in the top-flight without conceding a goal.

'No, I don't,' said Slot in his typically matter-of-fact manner post-game when asked if he thought his first experience of the rivalry between the two biggest clubs in English football could have gone any better. 'Everything you want to see as a manager you saw in this game.'

* * *

The return to action after the September international break brought the first setback of the Slot era. Nottingham Forest won at Anfield for the first time since 1969 courtesy of Callum Hudson-Odoi's goal.

It was a flat and disjointed Liverpool performance as Nuno Espirito Santo's side sat deep and frustrated the hosts, who had 69 per cent possession and 34 touches inside Forest's box, but struggled to create clear cut chances with an expected goals (xG) of just 0.94. Van Dijk branded it 'unacceptable' as the skipper told reporters: 'We're so much better than we showed today.'

Externally, there was talk of Slot's honeymoon period being over, and whether the change to a slower build-up was contributing to a flatter atmosphere at home matches.

Behind the scenes, Slot remained calm. He knew that all the miles his players had clocked up on national team duty had contributed to such a lacklustre display. Luis Díaz and Alexis Mac Allister had only reported back to Kirkby two days earlier from South America. It was telling that in the games straight after the October and November international breaks both Díaz and Mac Allister started on the bench as lessons were learned.

There was no big inquest after the Forest defeat as attention shifted to the opening Champions League game away to AC Milan three days later. Slot had wondered how his players would handle the extra demands of Europe's elite club competition given that Klopp had heavily rotated against lesser opposition in the Europa League a year earlier.

When Christian Pulisic fired Milan ahead inside three minutes, the San Siro erupted, but Liverpool kept their heads amid the din and went on to take complete control. Briggs and analysts Dan Spearritt, Joel Bonner, Jansen Moreno and James French had helped to highlight how goalkeeper Mike Maignan was slow to come off his line from set-pieces and that weakness was exploited

by headers from Konaté and Van Dijk. Cody Gakpo, who benefited from being played in his favoured position on the left,
tormented Milan with his pace and power as he provided the assist
for Szoboszlai to make it 3–1.

'After losing to Forest and then going 1–0 down so early in
Milan, there was no sense of panic,' says one senior club figure.
'That was down to what Arne and his staff had created in such a
short space of time. The players all believed in the process. That
night in the San Siro was massive.'

It marked the start of a stunning 24-game unbeaten run in all
competitions which included 20 victories. Time and time again
Slot positively impacted the direction of games with intelligent
tactical switches or substitutions which paid off.

'Some managers are like: "This is my style and you have to do it
the whole game", but Arne adapts,' Salah said. 'He's adapting
somehow to how our opponents play, putting Dominik in different
positions, Macca in different positions. He doesn't have that ego
that [says]: "Okay, these are my tactics so it will work in the second
half." In my head that's very clever.'

Robertson added: 'Arne changes a lot of things on a game-to-game
basis depending on the opposition and what our team is. Our blue-
print under the previous regime was constant. If we did it 100 per
cent, most teams couldn't live with us. We're calmer on the ball now,
not as frantic, but the manager still wants us to be full of energy.'

Half-time team talks were short and sharp with the head coach's
messages backed up by video analysis and use of the tactics board.
He rarely raised his voice as he knew doing so too often would
reduce the impact of his words. During games Slot would turn and
say 'clip' to his analysts to indicate a phase of play he wanted to
show his players again.

Former Liverpool goalkeeper Sander Westerveld adds: 'Arne is a
problem solver. The first half is just Arne watching the game, the

second half is him reacting to what he's seen and coming up with ways to make it better. You saw it from day one away at Ipswich. Difficulties in the first half, second half a different game. He doesn't just stick to a game plan. He's flexible and when you're working with such quality players it's easier to get your messages across and change things.'

Díaz scored twice as Bournemouth were swept aside at Anfield and then Salah's penalty sealed a hard-fought 2–1 win over Wolves. Feet remained firmly on the ground with Slot making it clear in the away dressing room at Molineux how unhappy he was with Liverpool's failure to keep possession and control the closing stages.

Konaté, who had nodded in the opener against Wolves, assumed he had won the man of the match award after learning that Sky Sports wanted to speak to him. However, it soon dawned on the Frenchman that he had actually been summoned to hand the accolade over to Gravenberch.

'How is this possible? Today I scored and stopped one or two balls, and I didn't deserve it? What happened?' Konaté laughed. 'Congratulations my brother. Who decided? Gary Neville?!'

Slot bluntly summed up post-match why Konaté wasn't the recipient. 'Maybe he forgot that moment when we conceded a goal. To say the least it was avoidable,' he said regarding Konaté's moment of hesitation which had allowed Jorgen Strand Larsen to steal in and set up an equaliser for Rayan Ait-Nouri.

The trip to Crystal Palace, which was settled by Diogo Jota's drilled finish from Gakpo's low cross, included the worrying sight of Alisson limping off with a hamstring injury. With Caoimhin Kelleher having not travelled due to illness, rookie Vitezslav Jaros made his senior debut off the bench and pulled off a crucial late save to deny Eberechi Eze.

Having to do without Alisson for two months could have had serious consequences, but the impressive manner in which Kelleher stepped up to fill the void ensured that the Brazilian's absence simply wasn't a talking point.

Kelleher had been the subject of interest from Nottingham Forest in the summer of 2024 with the Republic of Ireland international keen to become a No. 1 after so long as Alisson's deputy, but Liverpool refused to sanction a sale.

It had been some journey for Kelleher, who arrived at Liverpool's academy from Ringmahon Rangers in his home city of Cork, Ireland in 2015. He had been a prolific striker at youth level before at the age of 14 he turned his hand to goalkeeping after Ringmahon's regular shot-stopper left the club. His dad, Ray, recommended the switch to his coach Eddie Harrington.

'An absolute stroke of fortune the way it all panned out,' admitted Kelleher. 'I had started doing a bit of training as a goalkeeper before the other lad quit, maybe with the idea in mind that in a year or so I might become a keeper. But I was never planning on becoming one that soon. Who knows, if I had waited another year, I might have left it too late to really create a career for myself. It's amazing to look back on how everything just seemed to fall into place perfectly.'

Kelleher won all four penalty shootouts he was involved in for Liverpool – more than any other keeper in the club's history. Famously, he scored Liverpool's 11th spot-kick in a remarkable shootout against Chelsea in the 2022 League Cup final at Wembley before opposite number Kepa Arrizabalaga blazed over the bar. He felt blessed to have served his apprenticeship under someone as elite as Alisson even if it did mean having to accept life as a back-up.

'The biggest things are his mentality and the way he is within games,' Kelleher explained. 'That's what you need to be the best. He's always very calm and composed. He never gets too high, he never gets too low. Goalkeeping is about making split-second decisions and he has that clarity you need to make good ones.'

Kelleher ended up making 20 appearances in all competitions in 2024/25, including 10 Premier League matches, before joining Brentford in a deal worth up to £18 million in early June 2025. He left with the appreciative applause of the Kop ringing in his ears.

Rival supporters had been consoling themselves with talk that Liverpool's lofty status had been helped by a kind run of early fixtures, but that discussion was well and truly silenced in late October. In the space of a week they beat Chelsea at home, won away to RB Leipzig in the Champions League and rallied to claim a gutsy draw at Arsenal.

Curtis Jones was the match-winner against Enzo Maresca's resurgent Chelsea side as the academy graduate produced one of the most complete performances of his Liverpool career. His girlfriend Saffie had given birth to their first child a few days earlier and his thumb-sucking celebration after scoring was a tribute to baby Giselle. He had spent the previous night in the spare room to ensure he was fully rested. 'It's the best thing ever,' Jones said post-match. 'I'm playing with a smile on my face. It's a different type of joy. She's a little dream.'

Defensively, he did brilliantly to snuff out the threat of England colleague Cole Palmer. Attacking-wise, he won the penalty which Salah converted and then after Nicolas Jackson had equalised, he darted into the box to steer Salah's inviting centre past Robert Sanchez. It was exactly the kind of deep run from midfield which Slot had been working on in training.

Darwin Núñez was the hero of the night at Leipzig in the Champions League, scoring the only goal as Liverpool registered six successive away wins at the start of a season: a first in their 132-year history. Winning 11 of their opening 12 matches in all competitions was also unprecedented.

'We should be proud because so many great teams have worn this shirt and so many great managers have been at the club, so to achieve something that hasn't been done before is almost impossible and always nice,' Slot said post-match in Germany. 'But there is something that is much nicer than records – and you know what I mean by that: trophies.'

The players had been surprised to learn that their pre-match walk close to the team hotel would take place in the company of lions, giraffes, elephants and hyenas at Leipzig Zoo. It was typical of the more relaxed nature to such trips in the new era.

At the Emirates four days later, Liverpool twice came from behind to earn a point against Arsenal thanks to goals from Van Dijk and Salah. Slot's bold triple substitution which saw Szoboszlai, Gakpo and Tsimikas introduced after the break swung the contest Liverpool's way after a torrid first half.

'We could prepare them a bit better for the second half with what we had seen in the first half,' Slot said. 'We took some more risk but the main thing was we put more energy into it. We pressed them more aggressively. We came back so strong in the second half.'

Liverpool's record against the other members of England's traditional 'big six' was much improved. In 2023/24, Liverpool had taken just 12 points out of a possible 30 from those games. Under Slot, that tally jumped to 21 points out of 30 and probably would have been higher but for the fact that they played Chelsea away and Arsenal at home after the title had already been won.

They had gone to the Emirates without the injured quintet of Alisson, Jota, Federico Chiesa, Harvey Elliott and Conor Bradley. However, across the season there was a significant upturn in player availability. It had been one of the elements of Slot's work at Feyenoord which had attracted him to Liverpool initially.

Injuries had heavily contributed to Klopp's final season unravelling. According to the trusted data-driven website Premier Injuries,

Liverpool suffered 35 time-loss injuries in 2023/24, which is defined as any injury that results in a player missing at least one competitive fixture. The total number of days lost was 1,383 and total of games missed was 156.

Under Slot, there were just 22 time-loss injuries in 2024/25, 764 days lost and 88 games missed, which represented a reduction of 44 per cent on the previous season. Only Nottingham Forest (673) lost fewer days to injuries across the top-flight.

It underlined why Slot had been so determined to bring Ruben Peeters with him from Feyenoord as lead physical performance coach. Peeters is a specialist in periodisation, which involves managing the intensity and volume of the demands placed on a player to optimise performance and minimise injury risk.

One of the biggest challenges for Liverpool when Peeters first arrived was how to integrate him into their existing medical and sports science structure, given how highly they regarded other senior figures such as Conall Murtagh, Lee Nobes and Chris Morgan.

Key to that process was Liverpool's director of medicine and performance Jonathan Power, a lifelong supporter of the club, who had grown up in the West Derby area of the city. Power had been working in Bermuda as a consultant in sport and exercise medicine prior to landing his dream job and returning to Merseyside initially as club doctor in 2023.

Power proved adept at ensuring the club tapped into Peeters' skillset without sidelining Murtagh, the head of physical performance, who Hughes had been told was 'a genius'. Morgan (head of performance physical therapy) and Nobes (head of rehab physiotherapy) were both given new titles in recognition of being 'best in class'.

More expertise was recruited in the form of physios Robin Sadler and David Breen. Sadler had previously been at Manchester City,

Derby County, Manchester United and Rangers, while Breen's background was largely in rugby union at Munster and Harlequins.

'How Ruben was integrated was absolutely crucial,' one senior club figure says. 'It's testament to both Arne and Jonathan Power that it was managed so well. There was a real sense of harmony and working together rather than any egos getting in the way.'

With Hughes as sporting director and Slot as head coach, the AXA Training Centre became a more relaxed and calmer place to work with a more collegiate way of operating. It was a different type of leadership and staff commented on how there was a freshness around the place with a less frenzied atmosphere.

Liverpool had needed Klopp in 2015. He had made the club elite again and created one of the greatest teams in the club's history. But the demands had left many feeling weary. It would be unfair to say that the AXA was an unhappy place previously but a lot of people were worn out having given so much of themselves. Suddenly, you had an injection of energy with new personnel not scarred by nearly a decade of carrying Liverpool on their back.

Whereas Klopp used to crank up the intensity of training in the build-up to matches, Slot eased off. Klopp's methods had yielded great success but it had involved pushing players to the limit physically. Inevitably, that meant at times they broke down and by the end of May 2024 they were running on empty. Players appreciated being given more days off by Slot to spend with their families and fully embraced the changes to the daily schedule at Kirkby.

Each morning started with the players filling out a wellness check questionnaire about how they were feeling, including details about the quality of their sleep. There were ice baths to 'wake up the body' with blood tests taken regularly. Yoga and medication took place before Slot's team meeting.

After that it was into the Green Room as they were put through a range of exercises designed to boost sharpness, mobility and balance before heading out on to the grass. GPS tracking was used to help ensure that a player's output in training was between 60 per cent and 40 per cent of what would be expected in a game.

The benefits were there for all to see. Salah, Van Dijk and Gravenberch were ever-present en route to winning the title – the first time that three Liverpool outfield players had started the opening 34 league games of a season since 1987/88.

Given all the effort that went into avoiding injuries, no wonder Slot dismissed suggestions that Liverpool had been fortunate in comparison to rivals Manchester City and Arsenal.

'If you think injuries are only a part of luck or bad luck then we've been lucky, but we try to believe in the fact that we try to prevent them from a certain way of working,' Slot said. 'That we don't have many injuries, I don't see that as luck. I see it as, first of all, top professionals – our players do everything to try to stay fit – and, second of all, great facilities and a great staff. You cannot go through a season in the Premier League, Champions League and all these cup competitions we play in this country without any injuries, it's more the amount of injuries that you hopefully try to prevent.'

6

THE POWER OF ANFIELD

'When things go against you, you have to show up.
Winners always do. Fortunately, we have a lot of winners
in our team. The crowd were incredible in the second half.
That's the loudest since I've been here.'

Arne Slot

As they trudged off the field at half-time, the Liverpool players were braced for a dressing-down.

They had endured a torrid opening 45 minutes at Anfield. Brighton & Hove Albion were firmly in control and led courtesy of Ferdi Kadioglu's sweet strike. Their advantage would have been greater but for the heroics of goalkeeper Caoimhin Kelleher.

Just to add to Arne Slot's problems, Ibrahima Konaté left the pitch wincing in pain at the break after his arm had been accidentally trodden on by captain Virgil van Dijk.

Arsenal had been beaten 1–0 at Newcastle United in the day's early kick-off and Premier League leaders Manchester City were trailing at Bournemouth. The sense of angst in the stands was unmistakeable – Liverpool were in serious danger of squandering a golden opportunity to take advantage.

Yet rather than vent his spleen in the dressing room, Slot kept his cool and succinctly explained what needed to change tactically to turn the contest around. With the use of video analysis, he showed how Brighton had been able to play through Liverpool's press far too easily. Long-serving defender Joe Gomez was informed that he would be replacing the injured Konaté.

'I don't think it helps to be 15 to 20 times angry at half-time over a season,' explained Slot. 'You have to save these moments for when it really matters. Nine out of 10 times I am only angry if I feel that there is no work rate. There was no need to be that day because the players had worked hard but the other team just did things differently to how we expected. That's why we were a little bit too late [in terms of our pressing].

'It was smarter to adjust things rather than be angry. I have the same approach with my children. If they don't work hard, I can be hard on them. But if they work hard and things don't go great at school or something else goes wrong then I will never be hard on them.'

The date of the Brighton game, 2 November 2024, came to be regarded internally at Liverpool as one of the most pivotal dates in the entire season.

On and off the pitch, Slot's side were a very different beast in the second half as the mood was transformed. They played with more aggression, urgency and intensity, and the home supporters responded by providing an inspirational soundtrack.

Slot threw caution to the wind with the introduction of Luis Díaz and Curtis Jones for Dominik Szoboszlai and Alexis Mac Allister shortly after the hour mark. It was effectively a four-pronged attack and within six minutes of that bold double substitution Liverpool had gone from 1–0 down to 2–1 up.

Cody Gakpo restored parity and then Díaz and Jones combined to tee up Mohamed Salah, who cut inside and unleashed a left-footed thunderbolt beyond Bart Verbruggen for the winner.

'I had only experienced the atmosphere on TV before and now I have experienced it in person,' Brighton manager Fabian Hurzeler said. 'It was loud and wild. We couldn't find solutions and the dominance of Liverpool grew bigger.'

This was the first time Slot truly felt the power of Anfield. Having won 48 per cent of duels before the interval and forced just one save, Liverpool won 70 per cent of duels after the break and had seven attempts on target.

Once in front, the head coach took off striker Darwin Núñez and brought on holding midfielder Wataru Endo to help protect their slender advantage. The reliable Japan captain only started one league match all season but embraced his bit-part role in helping to close out matches. Fourteen of his 20 league appearances in 2024/25 lasted 15 minutes or less.

As news filtered through that Manchester City's club record 32-game unbeaten Premier League run dating back 11 months had been ended by a shock 2–1 defeat at Bournemouth, the Kop delivered a booming rendition of '*Liverpool, Liverpool, top the league*' after the final whistle.

'It's the kind of win you need in a season if you want to be competitive,' Slot told reporters post-match. 'You can't always be the best team on the pitch from the first to the last second. When things go against you, you have to show up. Winners always do. Fortunately, we have a lot of winners in our team. The crowd were incredible in the second half. That's the loudest since I've been here. But I also told the players that the football we played in the first half, in the end you will get punished for playing like that somewhere.'

With both City and Arsenal stumbling, the door had opened for Liverpool and they charged right through it. Having hit the summit with victory over Brighton, it was a position Slot's side never relinquished.

After opening their Champions League campaign with wins over AC Milan, Bologna and RB Leipzig, Liverpool faced a step up in class when Bundesliga champions Bayer Leverkusen came to Anfield.

The build-up was dominated by talk of Xabi Alonso's return to Merseyside. 'At that time I was focused. I had a big feeling with my players,' was Alonso's response on the eve of the contest when asked whether taking over from Jurgen Klopp was ever a serious option for him.

Liverpool certainly had no regrets about how their managerial search had borne fruit, and Alonso felt the full force of the new era during a remarkable second-half demolition of the German double-winners.

Once again, a big tactical call from Slot paid off handsomely. Díaz had never previously started a game for Liverpool at centre-forward since his move from Porto in January 2022. The Colombian had always operated off the left wing but Slot opted to leave out Núñez and play Díaz through the middle.

Slot explained to his staff that Leverkusen's Jonathan Tah loved a physical battle and won most aerial duels. What the big centre-back was less fond of was facing a more elusive attacker who dropped off into space and then made runs from deeper areas.

With Díaz leading the line, it worked a treat. He left Anfield with the match ball signed by his team-mates safely tucked away under his arm after celebrating the first hat-trick of his professional career. It was also the first treble by a Liverpool player at home in Europe since Philippe Coutinho's treble against Spartak Moscow in 2017.

'I really enjoyed playing in that position,' Díaz told Amazon Prime. 'The manager makes it very clear exactly what he wants from us. It wasn't easy for him to come in and fill Jurgen Klopp's shoes, but things have gone so well. We have to keep it going.'

The contest had been goalless after an hour but finished 4–0 with Cody Gakpo heading home the second. Díaz ran the length of the pitch deep into stoppage time to complete his hat-trick by delivering a no-look finish to a blistering counter-attack.

'What I like until now is that we are able to keep producing this energy – and even go [to] a gear higher,' Slot purred. 'Some teams we've faced have had some difficulties with that intensity.'

Díaz was well on his way to enjoying the most productive season of his Liverpool career. Having netted 13 goals in all competitions in 2023/24 (one every 278 minutes), he contributed 17 in 2024/25 (one every 196 minutes).

Former Liverpool midfielder Alonso, whose name was chanted late on in the game by the Kop, was left to rue how his side had folded under pressure: 'I can explain many things, but I cannot control this atmosphere that is created. I know the feeling of the Liverpool players. That's an extra boost that they feel, "Okay, now is the moment, now they are behind us and now we go." To defend in those moments, it's not easy.'

The Leverkusen squad trained at Liverpool's AXA base the following day before flying back to Germany. The experience left a lasting impression on Leverkusen's Florian Wirtz and Jeremie Frimpong, who were blown away by the facilities. That trip to Merseyside contributed to their decision to move to Anfield when Liverpool pursued them the following summer.

Meanwhile, momentum was maintained by league wins over Aston Villa and Southampton before Slot's side embarked on a seismic week, with Real Madrid and Manchester City both visiting Anfield.

Liverpool had failed to beat Real Madrid in eight meetings over the previous 15 years. That miserable sequence included defeats under Klopp in both the 2018 and 2022 Champions League finals, but under Slot the curse was lifted in style.

Given the European champions' ongoing pursuit of Trent Alexander-Arnold, who was only on the bench after recovering from a hamstring injury, it was ironic that his deputy stole the show. Youngster Conor Bradley was handed the biggest test of his career and passed it with flying colours.

The fearless Northern Ireland international provided the moment that lit the fuse at Anfield. When Kylian Mbappé raced away from Alexis Mac Allister down the left, Liverpool were exposed but Bradley charged across and put in a crunching tackle just outside the penalty area. It was the epitome of perfect timing and controlled aggression.

As Mbappé was unceremoniously dumped on the turf and Bradley emerged triumphant with the ball at his feet, the home supporters roared their approval. Bradley went on to provide the assist for Mac Allister to sweep home the opening goal.

Mbappé's night went from bad to worse as Kelleher brilliantly kept out his spot-kick before Salah fired a penalty wide. Gakpo's header secured victory with Bradley given a standing ovation when he was substituted in the game's closing minutes.

'It's nice for Conor, his family, for us, but it's also very nice for the academy that a player who came through the ranks did so well,' Slot said. 'I'm totally not surprised by him doing so well because he showed this last season and this season in training sessions and games as well.'

With fellow graduates Jones and Kelleher also integral to beating Real Madrid, it was a proud night for academy director Alex Inglethorpe. Jones, who was involved in both goals and completed 55 of his 59 passes (93 per cent), was the pick of the England midfielders on display as he put Jude Bellingham in the shade.

As for Kelleher, the accomplished manner in which he continued to deputise for the injured Alisson ensured that the absence of Liverpool's No. 1 wasn't a talking point.

'I thought Caoimhin was getting a bit bored so I thought I might as well give my mate something to do,' joked Robertson, who had given away the penalty by bringing down Lucas Vazquez in the box. 'Thankfully, that mistake didn't get punished and we managed to dust it off and go again. Caoimhin has been sensational. A phenomenal keeper. "World class" gets thrown about quite often but I don't think it's wrong to say Caoimhin is up there. The biggest compliment you can pay him is that you can't tell that Alisson is missing – and Alisson is the best in the world.'

What meant everything to Inglethorpe was that Liverpool's academy products accounted for 18 per cent of the total league minutes played under Slot in the Premier League in 2024/25. That was a higher percentage than any other top-flight club with Manchester United (16.3 per cent) second and Chelsea (14.5 per cent) third.

'I've always wanted us to play our part and contribute,' said Inglethorpe, who joined Liverpool from Tottenham initially as Under-21s coach in 2012 before being promoted to the role of academy director two years later. 'When you win arguably the toughest competition in the world, and you do it with more academy minutes than any other club, I don't think it gets any better than that.

'Something else that's important to me is that we were sixth in terms of total academy spending across the Premier League so we haven't bought our way to doing this. We've been able to get results in a way that's prudent.'

Four days after beating Real Madrid, another statement triumph arrived when Liverpool piled on the misery for a wounded Manchester City, who suffered a fourth consecutive league defeat for the first time since 2008. City bemoaned the loss of Rodri to a serious knee injury but their problems ran much deeper. They looked tired and disjointed. The gulf between the teams in energy, quality, fluency and body language was stark.

Liverpool were sharper in all departments and swarmed all over Pep Guardiola's side. The shot count at the break was 10–1 but somehow the hosts only led courtesy of Gakpo's close-range finish.

Slot's game plan involved being more direct than usual as they sought to exploit the space behind City's overworked back line. He had also highlighted in a team meeting City's vulnerability when it came to hard and low deliveries across the face of goal. The fact that Salah brilliantly created the opener for Gakpo with exactly that kind of cross was immensely satisfying for the head coach and his staff.

The second half showcased Liverpool's structure and organisation as the tempo slowed but their control remained. City had 66 per cent possession after the interval but didn't muster a shot on target until after Salah's penalty had put the result beyond doubt. The Egyptian star celebrated by sitting on the advertising hoarding with his arms outstretched, basking in the adulation of Anfield.

City striker Erling Haaland had just 16 touches throughout as he was expertly shackled by Van Dijk and Joe Gomez, who didn't put a foot wrong after making his first Premier League start in his favoured centre-back role for 15 months.

Remarkably, the difference in expected goals (xG) between the teams was even greater than when Liverpool thrashed Manchester United 7–0 in March 2023. Back then it was 2.78 versus 0.82, against City it was 3.43 versus 0.83.

Senior players felt it was the most complete performance they had been part of against City and it meant that bit more to Slot given his long-standing admiration for Guardiola and his innovative methods. His mind wandered back to his early days on the coaching staff at Cambuur in his homeland when he would use clips of Guardiola's Barcelona and Bayern Munich sides to emphasise his points. Now he was going toe to toe with him and emerging triumphant.

What a week for Slot's parents Arend and Fennie, his brothers Edwin and Jakko, wife Mirjam and their children Isa and Joep to be over visiting from the Netherlands. As they watched on from

1. Jurgen Klopp's emotional farewell at Anfield after the game against
Wolverhampton Wanderers in May 2024, credit: Clive Brunskill / Getty Images

2. Arne Slot in action for Dutch club PEC Zwolle during his playing days in 2012, credit: VI Images / Getty Images

3. Arne Slot celebrates winning the 2022-23 Eredivisie title with Feyenoord, credit: Broer van den Boom / BSR Agency / Getty Images

4. Slot is introduced as the new Liverpool manager at the AXA Training Centre, Liverpool in July 2024, credit: Cameron Smith / Sportimage Ltd / Alamy Live News

5. Diogo Jota fires home the first goal of the new era against Ipswich Town at Portman Road in August 2024, credit: Marc Atkins / Getty Images

6. Mohamed Salah and his bow and arrow celebration in front of the away end after extending his remarkable scoring record against Manchester United at Old Trafford in September 2024, credit: Michael Regan / Getty Images

7. Cody Gakpo launches Liverpool's second-half fightback as they secure a precious victory over Brighton & Hove Albion at Anfield in November 2024, credit: Chris Stading / Andrew Orchard sports photography / Alamy

8. Luis Diaz celebrates on a memorable night for the Colombian attacker against Bayer Leverkusen in the Champions League, November 2024, as he scores the first hat-trick of his professional career, credit: Carl Recine / Getty Images

9. Conor Bradley dumps Kylian Mbappé on his backside with a crunching challenge during the win over Real Madrid in November 2024, credit: Justin Setterfield / Getty Images

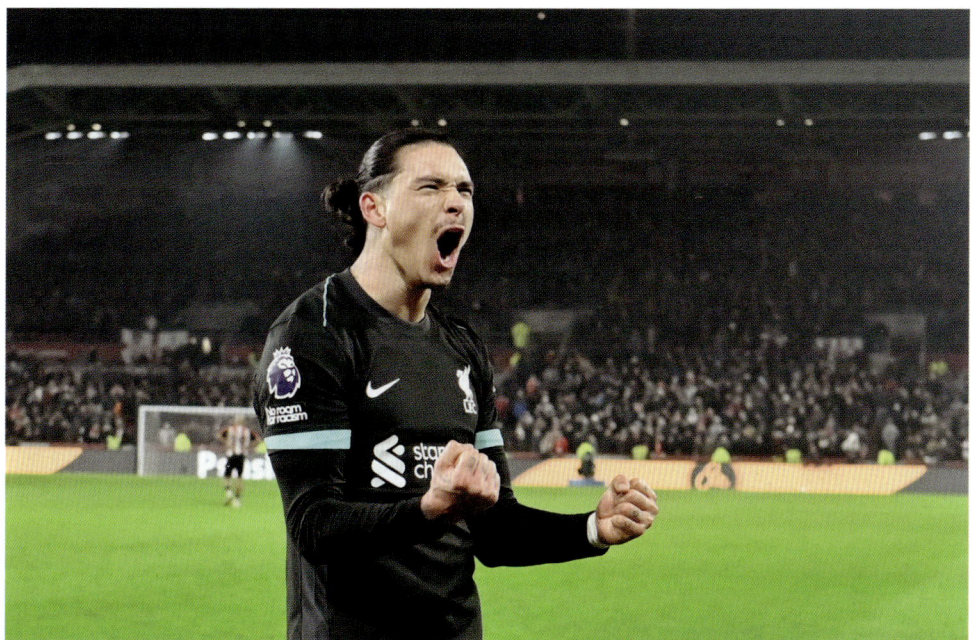

10. Darwin Nunez comes off the bench to score a dramatic late double in January's pivotal Premier League victory at Brentford, credit: Justin Tallis / AFP / Getty Images

11. Arne Slot angrily confronts referee Michael Oliver after a controversial final Merseyside derby at Goodison Park in February 2025, credit: Carl Recine / Getty Images

12. Dominik Szoboszlai lies shattered on the turf after the final whistle having helped Liverpool secure their first away league win over Manchester City for nearly a decade, credit: Via Associated Press / Alamy Stock Photo.

13. Liverpool players and staff celebrate together after the Premier League title was secured with the 5-1 thrashing of Tottenham in April 2025, credit: Kieran McManus / Shutterstock

14. Captain Virgil van Dijk lifts the trophy as Liverpool are crowned champions of England for the twentieth time, credit: Carl Recine / Getty Images

15. Virgil van Dijk and former player Alan Hansen with the Premier League trophy as they celebrate Liverpool being crowned champions at Anfield in May 2025, credit: MI News & Sport / Alamy Live News

16. Virgil van Dijk adds to the floral tributes at Anfield in memory of Diogo Jota and his brother Andre Silva after their tragic deaths in a car accident in July 2025, credit: Peter Powelle / PA / Shutterstock

the Main Stand, Slot looked up and blew kisses to them before heading down the tunnel.

In the home dressing room, Van Dijk was in charge of the music playlist, having encouraged contributions from his team-mates. One unlikely anthem in the march to glory was 'Sultans of Swing' by British rock band Dire Straits, which regularly blared out after cherished wins. Alisson is a big Dire Straits fan and another of their tracks, 'Walk of Life', also became a firm favourite.

Victory over City extended Liverpool's lead at the top of the Premier League to nine points – the biggest margin any club had enjoyed after 13 games since Manchester United in 1993/94. In the space of a month, Slot's side had swept aside the reigning champions of Germany, Spain and England by a combined score of 8–0.

'Playing against Real Madrid and Man City, teams that have been and are so good, with managers that have won so many trophies, it's always nice to come out in both situations as a winner,' Slot said.

'But the reason these teams won so many things is not that they won once or twice, they were able to win every three days. Winning once or twice, even against these big teams, is not enough to win anything at the end of the season. Let's not get carried away. It's all about consistency until the end of the season, keeping the players fit and playing with this much energy. There's a long way to go and so many challenges.'

It wasn't just the results which provided a lift but the manner in which they were achieved: by playing on the front foot. Privately, Slot told staff that he regarded that week of victories over Real Madrid and Man City as crucial in terms of fuelling belief and pushing Liverpool on.

Guardiola, who had lost four consecutive league matches for the first time in his managerial career, wasn't impressed with Anfield's expression of collective glee at his plight as they chanted '*You're getting sacked in the morning!'* during the closing stages of the game. He reacted by defiantly holding up six fingers – a nod to the number of Premier League titles he had won for City following his arrival from Bayern Munich in 2016.

'I didn't expect that at Anfield,' Guardiola said. 'I didn't expect it from the people from Liverpool, but it's fine. It's part of the game and I understand completely. We've had incredible battles together. I have a respect for them.'

Guardiola really shouldn't have been surprised. Liverpool had suffered at the hands of City in the modern era, particularly in the title races of 2018/19 and 2021/22 when they were agonisingly edged out on the final day by a solitary point. City being charged by the Premier League in February 2023 with more than 100 alleged breaches of financial fair play rules had added extra spice to the rivalry. The home fans were never going to hold back as they revelled in their rival's misfortune.

Van Dijk had walked out at Anfield prior to the City game holding the hand of a young boy who touched the hearts of millions around the world.

Isaac Kearney was born with a rare genetic disorder, Wolf-Hirschhorn syndrome, which means he develops at a slower rate than other children. It is caused by a missing section of chromosome four and as a toddler he had to undergo open heart surgery.

Liverpool had contacted the six-year-old's family as part of their Red Together initiative, which celebrates their diverse fanbase. Staff had seen videos on social media of him singing an array of Liverpool songs.

They arranged for Van Dijk and Salah to pay a surprise visit to Kirkby's Northwood Primary School where Isaac was playing the board game snakes and ladders.

'I'm looking for someone who is a big Liverpool fan and loves to play the guitar, I think his name is Isaac,' said Van Dijk as he approached him. The youngster's hand shot up and then when the Dutchman gave the nod for Salah to join him, Isaac nonchalantly replied, 'Hi Salah!'

Mum Melissa, dad Alan and their daughter Florence joined Isaac for the subsequent trip to the AXA Training Centre. They had been told that it was unlikely they would meet Slot given his hectic schedule, but he emerged from his office to high-five Isaac and chatted to him about his favourite players.

'Isaac was running around like he owned the place,' Melissa told *The Athletic*. 'We thought he might meet one or two more players, but it was the whole squad. He was just so happy and excited as he went around shouting the names of all the players. They were all so kind. Arne was so genuine and down to earth.'

Van Dijk and Salah presented Isaac with a full kit and invited him to be a mascot against Manchester City to mark the United Nations' International Day of Persons with Disabilities. Watching him kick a ball on the Anfield turf before kick-off was emotional for his parents given that they had once been told he might never be able to walk.

'We didn't think he was going to be able to do it on the day because he was a bit overwhelmed,' Alan said. 'But Virgil was absolutely incredible with him. In the tunnel, he really put him at ease. He's a class act. Liverpool is Isaac's life and brings him so much joy.'

When Liverpool released the 10-minute video on Christmas Day, it quickly went viral. Within a month it had been viewed more than 140 million times across the different platforms. For the rest of the season, Alan and Isaac had to leave home earlier to attend matches at Anfield because of the number of times the youngster was stopped for selfies on the way to the stadium.

* * *

Late night resurfacing work on the runway at Newcastle Airport meant Liverpool had to embark on the 180-mile journey home from St James' Park by coach. The mood was one of quiet contemplation after a rollercoaster night in the North East in early December.

Their lead at the top had been trimmed to seven points after Kelleher's rare misjudgement was punished by Fabian Schar's late equaliser in a thrilling 3–3 draw. A run of seven successive wins in all competitions ground to a halt.

Fatigue certainly played a part with a jaded Ryan Gravenberch taken off in the second half having played the full 90 minutes in the previous 18 Premier League and Champions League matches. It was the first time all season that an opponent had found a way to stop him running the show as he won just two out of seven duels.

'In the first half we had a lot of problems with their intensity and aggressiveness,' admitted Slot. 'They forced us into too many mistakes. It wasn't that difficult to be better in the second half and that's what we were. We dominated the second half. Being 3–2 up one minute before the end, it feels a disappointment to drop two points.'

It was the first time in Slot's reign that they had conceded three goals in a game and Newcastle's expected goals (xG) total of 2.09 was comfortably the highest Liverpool had allowed all season.

Twice, Liverpool trailed and each time Salah spearheaded the resurgence. The Egyptian forward created a goal for Jones and then scored two himself, with exquisite finishes. Alexander-Arnold's impact off the bench midway through the second half was considerable as he provided two assists. With Bradley injured and Slot managing Alexander-Arnold's game time, the head coach had initially started with Jarell Quansah as a makeshift right-back.

The following day Slot received an apology from broadcaster Amazon Prime after they had wrongly claimed that he had visited referee Andy Madley's room during the interval at St James' Park to complain about decisions. He accepted it as a genuine mistake.

With 70 mph winds battering Merseyside as Storm Darragh raged, Liverpool decided to get their squad together at the city's Titanic Hotel the night before what was supposed to be the final league derby at Goodison Park.

Given the treacherous conditions, there was plenty of relief when the players were informed at 8 a.m., some four and a half hours before kick-off, that it had been postponed due to concerns over fan safety. Buildings had been damaged and a number of roads were blocked due to fallen trees. Slot gave them the day off to spend with their families.

Internally, it was regarded as a blessing in disguise, given the unexpected breather it gave them during such a gruelling schedule. As well as a number of injury worries, Liverpool would also have been without Mac Allister in midfield due to suspension after he collected his fifth yellow card of the season against Newcastle. Playing in a gale and driving rain would have suited Everton given their more direct approach.

Liverpool's perfect record in the Champions League was extended with an unconvincing 1–0 victory away to Girona. Salah's penalty after Díaz had been brought down proved enough to secure the points, with Alisson pulling off some smart saves on his return to action after two months out.

However, the big talking point at the Girona game in Catalonia was the ongoing struggles of Núñez. Salah's red-hot form was masking the lack of output from Liverpool's erratic No. 9, who had scored just once in his previous 10 appearances and looked devoid of confidence.

During his 71 minutes on the field against Girona, the Uruguayan had just 16 touches, completed only four of his eight passes and won one out of four duels. Liverpool created four big chances, according to Opta, and he squandered two of them due to an alarming lack of composure.

'I think every striker all around the world has periods where every ball goes in, and sometimes he has a period when you try so hard but you're not able to score,' Slot said. 'The good thing is that we have many players who can score for us. I would have loved to see Darwin score because every striker wants and needs to score goals. That is why I kept him on for quite a long time.'

Slot had succeeded in reviving the fortunes of players such as Díaz, Konaté and Szoboszlai, who had lost their way towards the end of the Klopp era, but trying to iron out Núñez's rough edges proved beyond him.

Even with Jota sidelined for two months with a chest injury, Núñez couldn't secure a regular place in the side with Slot frequently turning to Díaz to play centrally instead.

The fans stuck by the most expensive signing in the club's history because they loved how he wore his heart on his sleeve. There was a desperation to see him succeed, but the patience of even his most avid supporters was increasingly tested.

With 15 goals in his first season at Anfield and then 18 in 2023/24, there was an expectation that he would become more prolific but it didn't happen. He ended up netting just seven times in 47 appearances (17 starts) in all competitions in the title-winning campaign.

Trying to get tactical instructions ingrained in Núñez was an issue for Slot and his staff. So too was trying to get him to control his emotions both in training sessions and in matches when things weren't going his way.

Núñez was popular in the dressing room but his adaptation to Premier League football hadn't been helped by the language barrier, as he was slow to learn English. He had also been affected by the abuse he had received on social media, and only belatedly took the advice of staff to avoid reading it.

There had been acts of petulance – like deleting Liverpool-related posts on his social media accounts and then failing to applaud Klopp during the guard of honour on the day he waved farewell to Anfield.

Núñez was dubbed Liverpool's 'agent of chaos'. He was a potential match-winner but just as likely to infuriate as he was to thrill. And for £85 million Liverpool needed him to be much more than just a useful impact sub off the bench.

Gomez actually came closer to scoring against Girona when he saw a header tipped over the bar. The long wait continued for Liverpool's longest-serving player to celebrate the first senior goal of his professional career. By the end of the season, only two players in the club's history had clocked up more appearances than Gomez's tally of 241 without ever scoring.

The former Charlton Athletic defender was closing in on ex-England international right-back Rob Jones, who played 243 times for Liverpool between 1991 and 1998. However, Gomez still had some way to eclipse Ephraim Longworth, who remarkably failed to find the net in 370 appearances for Liverpool between 1910 and 1928.

'I can't say I have got a celebration planned – it depends on the goal!' Gomez told reporters in Girona. 'But going up for corners is a big thing. That is one thing that has hindered me this whole time as I was never up for them so my odds have been boosted now.'

Picked ahead of Quansah to partner Van Dijk while Konaté was sidelined by a knee problem, Gomez enjoyed a run in the team throughout December having previously only started in the Carabao Cup under Slot.

'It's been great to learn how Arne wants us to play,' Gomez added. 'A lot of it is about how we can get three-v-twos around the pitch. Just because the pass is on, it doesn't mean you should play it, he tells us just wait on the ball a bit more. You just want to improve as a player and the coach is helping me and the rest of the boys do that. Arne is constantly reminding us that we cannot get complacent. The coaching staff and the gaffer's attention to detail is second to none. Even when we come in at half-time sometimes when things aren't going our way, the ability to adapt in certain situations and guide us in the right way is so good.'

That was certainly the case when in-form Fulham came to Anfield. Liverpool looked doomed when inside the opening 20 minutes they fell behind to Andreas Pereira's goal and had Andy Robertson sent off for bringing down Harry Wilson.

But Slot masterminded an unlikely salvage act. Rather than retreating after going a man down, the Dutchman changed to a back three and kept all his attacking players on the field. The ploy of Salah staying wide and then delivering to the far post led to Gakpo's equaliser from a diving header early in the second half.

After Rodrigo Muniz restored Fulham's advantage against the run of play, Slot replaced Alexander-Arnold with Jota, who joined what was effectively a front five in possession with Harvey Elliott, Núñez, Salah and Díaz. At times Gravenberch was patrolling the midfield single-handedly.

The sizeable gamble paid off as Jota, making his first appearance since October, calmly turned away from Jorge Cuenca and slotted past Bernd Leno. Despite being a man down for so long, Liverpool finished with more possession (61 per cent), more shots (16 v 12) and more touches in the opponents' box (35 v 15).

'Credit to them, it didn't feel like they had 10 men at all,' admitted Fulham left-back Antonee Robinson. 'They took a lot of risks pushing men high and they were rewarded for it. They piled the pressure on and were really positive.'

In the Sky Sports studio, pundit Jamie Carragher raved: 'The reason Liverpool got a point in this game is down to the manager. He's as good as any manager in the Premier League at spotting things on the pitch and changing things quickly.'

Robertson was as relieved as anyone that Liverpool took something from the contest following his early red card. Slot had plenty of sympathy for his left-back, who was still feeling the effects of a dangerous challenge from Issa Diop when a heavy touch led to him fouling Wilson.

It had been a difficult period for the Scotland captain with his status as the club's first-choice left-back coming under scrutiny for the first time since he had established himself at Liverpool after arriving from Hull City for £10 million in 2017.

Robertson's backstory was inspirational. He was released by his boyhood club Celtic at the age of 15 because they felt he was too small to make it at the top level. Three years later he was playing in the fourth tier of Scottish football for amateur club Queen's Park. He worked part-time for the Scottish FA, taking ticket bookings over the phone at Hampden Park in Glasgow and had a Christmas job on the tills at retailer Marks & Spencer. He considered signing up to a university course and pursuing an alternative career as a PE teacher.

'Life at this age is rubbish with no money,' he tweeted in 2012, aged 18. A year later his fortunes changed dramatically. He was snapped up by Scottish Premiership club Dundee United and then moved south of the border 12 months later to sign for Hull.

There were some raised eyebrows when Liverpool bought him, given he had just been part of a Hull side relegated from the Premier League with the worst defensive record in the top-flight.

Liverpool had initially intended to sign Roma left-back Emerson Palmieri but needed a Plan B after he ruptured his anterior cruciate ligament. The data department, led by then director of research Ian Graham, put forward Robertson as a suitable alternative.

'The promise with data analysis is we can find a player who has been overlooked for different reasons elsewhere,' Graham said. 'There were some disagreements internally and some doubts. We recommended Robertson as a really good attacking full-back but we weren't certain about his qualities as a defender. That made it difficult to give a 100 per cent recommendation. Jurgen Klopp solved that by saying he wanted his full-backs to attack and if there are defensive weaknesses we can solve that elsewhere with cover from midfield positions.'

Given the return Robertson gave Liverpool on their modest investment, he has to be regarded among the most shrewd signings of the Premier League era.

After a tricky opening few months at Anfield, Robertson deposed Spaniard Alberto Moreno as the club's regular left-back and earned the adoration of the Kop. With his combative defending and lung-bursting runs forward, Robertson was pivotal to all the glory secured during the Klopp era. He formed a lethal double act with close friend Alexander-Arnold as they provided the ammunition from wide areas. He also blossomed into a leader in the dressing room.

However, an ankle ligament injury he had carried through the Euros meant he missed most of Slot's first pre-season and was play-ing catch-up. He was fit by mid-August but some uncharacteristic errors crept into his game. Slot rotated him with Kostas Tsimikas, who ended up starting five Champions League and nine Premier League matches in 2024/25. There was a period when the pecking order became blurred.

Being left out hurt Robertson but he appreciated that Slot was always open and honest with him when it came to explaining his rationale behind team selection.

'I've got doubters for the first time in a long time,' Robertson told reporters following November's home win over Aston Villa. 'I am trying to prove people wrong again. I am a lot older and a lot wiser now than when I first came here. People can write me off all they want. But I will always try to keep working, keep improving.'

Critics pointed to how his assists had dried up. Having provided 26 in all competitions across the 2021/22 and 2022/23 seasons combined, he contributed just two in 2023/24 and by Christmas in 2024/25 his only assist was for Gakpo against Real Madrid. He finally ended a 13-month wait for a Premier League assist against Arsenal in May.

But it was far too simplistic to hold that up as proof that he was in serious decline. The role of the full-backs had changed under Slot, who preferred them to make underlapping runs rather than staying out on the touchline. Liverpool looked increasingly to their midfielders to provide creativity. The stats showed that Robertson was seeing less of the ball than previously and receiving it more centrally.

Even Alexander-Arnold, who had more licence to attack than Robertson, only provided seven assists in all competitions in 2024/25 – short of the numbers he had registered in 2021/22 (18), 2022/23 (10) and 2023/34 (nine).

With Robertson turning 31 in March 2025 and approaching the final year of his contract, Liverpool's recruitment staff had to start thinking about succession planning. There was plenty of speculation about Antonee Robinson after his eye-catching display for Fulham at Anfield, but the fact he was approaching the age of 28 meant the USA international didn't fit the bill.

Liverpool wanted someone younger with a decent amount of top-level experience but with the potential to develop further. Bournemouth's Milos Kerkez, who Liverpool sporting director

Richard Hughes knew well from his time on the south coast, was quickly installed as the preferred option.

Robertson won his battle with Tsimikas as the Scotsman once again made the left-back spot his own during the second half of the 2024/25 season. His performances in high-stakes games against Manchester City (away) and Paris Saint-Germain (home) were exceptional and he ended up playing 45 times in all competitions.

Slot's frustration with the officials against Fulham led to him being shown a third yellow card of the season, triggering a one-match touchline ban for the Carabao Cup victory at Southampton a week before Christmas. He spent that evening on the south coast sat in the stand alongside first-team tactical analyst Roderick van der Ham, who proved to be an important mid-season addition to the backroom staff after arriving from Slot's former Feyenoord.

It was the second booking of the season that Slot had received at Arsenal which really annoyed him. Unhappy with how Mikel Arteta's players were regularly breaking up the flow of the game by going down for medical treatment, he had turned to Konaté on the touchline and said: 'This is a fucking joke.' Fourth official Sam Barrott thought Slot had said: 'You are a fucking joke.' Barrott informed referee Anthony Taylor, who brandished the yellow card for dissent.

Liverpool ended 2024 with a real show of force. Tottenham, Leicester City and West Ham were dismantled by a combined score of 14–4.

Their previous trip to the Tottenham Hotspur Stadium in September 2023 had been engulfed in controversy. Díaz's finish had been incorrectly disallowed for offside after the VAR official Darren England mistakenly believed that the on-field decision had been to award the goal.

'Check complete, check complete. That's fine, perfect,' England had told referee Simon Hooper through his headset after watching the replay. Hooper responded: 'Well done boys. Good process.'

After Hooper restarted the game with a free-kick for the hosts rather than a kick-off, the penny finally dropped in the VAR room that Díaz had initially been flagged offside. Liverpool went on to concede a late winner through Joel Matip's own goal following red cards for both Jones and Jota. Klopp's call for the match to be replayed fell on deaf ears as Liverpool had to settle for a grovelling apology from referees' chief Howard Webb.

There was no such gnashing of teeth on their return to north London. Tottenham 3 Liverpool 6. The numbers were ridiculous: Liverpool had 24 shots, 12 on target, they created nine big chances, and their xG was 4.60. They were 5–1 up with half an hour to go when, understandably, a bit of complacency crept in.

Salah, who scored two and created two more, became the first Premier League player in history to reach double figures for both league goals and assists before Christmas in a season. Díaz struck twice with the midfield duo of Szoboszlai and Mac Allister also chipping in. Slot had talked to Szoboszlai about the importance of timing his runs to exploit Tottenham's high line and his athleticism proved invaluable. 'Maybe our best performance away from home,' Slot said. 'It was total dominance. We scored six and could have scored more.'

It was the seventh time in the Premier League era that Liverpool had been top on Christmas Day, but there were cautionary tales. Just once previously, in 2019/20, had they gone on to be crowned champions.

However, this time around they didn't need to worry about Manchester City breathing down their neck. An unexpected crisis at the Etihad, with six league defeats in the space of eight games, had already consigned Guardiola's side to also-rans. Arsenal looked more of a threat but they lacked a prolific frontman, were far too reliant on set-pieces and lost Bukayo Saka to a serious hamstring injury.

In contrast, the array of firepower Slot could call upon was underlined by the Boxing Day win over lowly Leicester City which was orchestrated by Gakpo – two years to the day since Liverpool agreed a £44 million deal to sign him from PSV Eindhoven.

Under Klopp, the Dutch attacker had been a jack of all trades, shifted from the wing to the centre and also deployed deeper. It wasn't conducive to him delivering consistently.

Slot told him he would be deployed solely off the left flank – where he had made his name for PSV – and Liverpool reaped the rewards. Having stunned Anfield by scoring early on through Jordan Ayew, Leicester were seconds away from going into the interval ahead when Gakpo cut inside and curled an unstoppable right-footer beyond Jakub Stolarczyk.

'It was crucial because that lifted us,' Slot said. 'It was not only helpful for us, but it also worked the opposite way for Leicester as they felt like: "Okay, now it's going to be tough." We expect our wingers to keep wide, to try to get them in one-v-one situations. Cody has done this really well. It's just nice to have so many options.'

Jones' close-range finish after the break was followed by Gakpo laying on Liverpool's third goal for Salah. With 18 goals in all competitions, Gakpo ended up being their most potent threat behind Salah. He had looked destined to score many more before an ankle problem hampered him in the second half of the season.

A 5–0 thrashing of West Ham United ensured that Liverpool finished the year a commanding eight points clear of second-placed Nottingham Forest with a game in hand. There was more history-making for Salah at the London Stadium as he set a new record for both scoring and assisting in eight Premier League games in the same season. By the end of the campaign he had managed it 11 times.

As 2025 dawned, Slot had won 23 of his 27 games in charge in all competitions. Memories of how this squad had faltered in the final months of the Klopp era were still too fresh for anyone at Anfield to start getting giddy.

But, internally, belief was growing that this time it would be different. It all felt much calmer and more sustainable than a year earlier when they had to regularly rely on energy-sapping late salvage acts to stay in the race until the spring.

Contract negotiations were dominating the news agenda with supporters craving some positive news on the protracted talks involving three of Liverpool's biggest stars.

7

MORE IN THAN OUT

'I had my best years here. I played eight years, hopefully it's going to be 10. I am very happy to be here. I signed the contract because I believe we can win a lot of big trophies together. Keep supporting us and we'll give it our best. Now I'm more in than out!'

Mohamed Salah

Aside from appointing Jurgen Klopp's successor, the biggest issue Richard Hughes inherited when he took over as sporting director was the contract situations surrounding Mohamed Salah, Virgil van Dijk and Trent Alexander-Arnold.

By the start of the 2024/25 season, Liverpool's most potent attacker, their inspirational skipper and supremely talented home-grown vice-captain had all entered the final 12 months of their deals. It was unprecedented and speculation about their futures was intensifying.

As the impasse dragged on into the new year and the possibility of losing them for nothing loomed large, the fear was that the uncertainty would have a detrimental impact on the team's fortunes. However, it didn't happen as the trio all made huge contributions to the Premier League title triumph.

That was testament to the professionalism of the players them-selves and also how Hughes went about his business. He led the process with FSG CEO of football Michael Edwards making it clear to him what the implications would be for the club's budget depending on who renewed and at what cost.

Hughes commanded the respect of the representatives involved during complex and protracted negotiations. It was appreciated in the dressing room how Arne Slot proved so adept at brushing off questions in press conferences about the contracts and avoided creating unwanted headlines. It helped that as head coach rather than manager Slot was more detached from the process than Jurgen Klopp would have been.

There were no club briefings, no details entering the public domain about what had been offered and what had been demanded in an attempt to win the PR battle. The Anfield hierarchy had taken the decision to keep their counsel throughout – even in the face of growing criticism about the perceived lack of progress.

'From the outset, Richard was determined to protect Arne,' says one senior club figure. 'He was adamant that he didn't want any politics around it.

'With a title up for grabs, Richard's stance was "no matter how messy this gets, we prioritise team unity". It was a brave decision because the longer it went on, Richard's competence was being questioned externally. But, internally, there was nothing but admiration for how he handled it. One of Michael's great strengths is that he doesn't give a shit about public opinion and his attitude was "we're exactly where we need to be". Anyone can sort out a new contract by giving someone what they want, but it was about finding solutions that worked for everyone.'

With Salah turning 33 and Van Dijk 34 in the summer of 2025, they were similar cases. Liverpool's owners had always been reluctant to hand out lucrative extensions to players in the twilight of their careers. Their logic was sound. You don't want to find yourself paying superstar wages to fading bit-part players.

A sporting director has to take the emotion out of the decision-making process. Forget what someone has already contributed, and consider what they still have left to offer for the seasons ahead and whether that money can be better spent elsewhere. There was no room for sentiment.

Georginio Wijnaldum and Roberto Firmino, two players adored by Liverpool supporters for the part they played in the Klopp era, had previously been allowed to leave as free agents in their early thirties after failing to agree new terms. Nothing that duo went on to achieve had cast those ruthless judgement calls in a bad light.

Sometimes change is crucial as a team evolves, but it's also a strength to recognise when exceptions to the rule are necessary. That was the case with Salah and Van Dijk, who both penned new two-year contracts in April 2025.

Salah was on the way to scoring 34 goals and providing 23 assists in 52 appearances in all competitions. The Egyptian attacker won a record-equalling third Football Writers' Association Footballer of the Year award and clinched both the Premier League Golden Boot and Playmaker accolades.

Van Dijk was the defensive rock on which Liverpool's title challenge was built as he delivered a succession of commanding performances. The Dutchman's leadership also made him a huge asset in terms of setting standards on and off the pitch.

There had always been a confidence internally that an agreement would be reached for Salah and Van Dijk to stay put. Both players had spoken publicly about their emotional bond with the club and the desire to enhance their Anfield legacy, but the financial package had to be right.

It suited Liverpool in many ways that the impasse continued into the spring, given that the duo played with a point to prove. Also by April, the club had nearly a full season of data to analyse which served to illustrate the heights the pair were still consistently reaching.

Alexander-Arnold was always a different story. At the age of 26, he was approaching his peak years and had Real Madrid pursuing him. Over the course of the season it became increasingly clear to Hughes that the academy graduate's head had been turned and he wouldn't be signing an extension.

The Spanish giants tried and failed to buy Alexander-Arnold for £20 million in the January window as Liverpool refused to countenance a sale while they were competing for silverware.

During the March international break, the England right-back informed Slot that he would be leaving when his contract expired in the summer. His decision was only made public after the title had been wrapped up. He faced an angry backlash from a section of the fanbase and was booed during a game against Arsenal, but emotions cooled somewhat and he ultimately got the Anfield send-off he had hoped for.

Having looked destined to depart as a free agent, there was a late twist when Real Madrid's determination to get him a month early so he could take part in the revamped Club World Cup in America allowed Liverpool to negotiate a fee of £8.4 million (€10 million).

The three high-profile contract sagas and how they were handled by those involved provided intriguing sub-plots throughout the narrative of the season.

'As you know, it's my last year at the club,' Salah told UK broadcaster Sky Sports after scoring once and providing two assists in Liverpool's emphatic 3–0 victory over Manchester United in September. 'I just want to enjoy it. I feel like I'm free to play football and we will see what can happen next year.'

Asked to clarify whether it could be his final appearance for the club at Old Trafford, where he boasted an incredible return of 10 goals in nine outings, the Egyptian replied: 'I was coming to the game thinking this could be the last time. Nobody at the club has spoken to me yet about contracts so I will play my last season and see at the end of the season. It's not up to me, it's up to the club.'

The interview set alarm bells ringing among the fanbase, but for Edwards and Hughes it was music to their ears. It was the first indication they had been given that Salah was interested in talks over a new contract.

They knew that to keep someone like Salah, who had endured a difficult end to the Klopp era, they needed to get the managerial appointment right. He wouldn't want to hang around unless he felt fulfilled in a team challenging for the biggest prizes. They viewed his comments at Old Trafford as a ringing endorsement of Slot, who had taken away some of his defensive duties so he could focus on wreaking havoc in the final third.

Two years earlier, Liverpool had rejected a bid of £150 million for Salah from Saudi Pro League club Al-Ittihad and were aware that interest from the Middle East remained strong, especially as the opportunity to sign him as a free agent opened up.

However, despite the eye-watering wages being offered in the Middle East, Anfield officials doubted whether he was prepared to turn his back on playing at the highest level in Europe. They also knew that he was happy and settled in the north-west of England with his wife Magi and their two young daughters.

The path to an agreement with Salah's representative Ramy Abbas, a Colombian lawyer, was far from straightforward. Abbas, who is based in the United Arab Emirates, prefers to do business face to face rather than on the phone. The note on his WhatsApp profile warns: 'Voice notes ignored. If you're late, I will leave.'

The first meeting between Hughes and Abbas took place in a restaurant in Dubai in late September, a few weeks after Salah's enlightening pitchside interview at Old Trafford. Abbas was impressed by Hughes and made it clear that his client wanted to stay at Anfield. But as they went their separate ways, Abbas was concerned that the club might not be prepared to maintain Salah's status as one of the world's highest paid players. His basic salary was around £400,000 per week with that figure enhanced by performance-related bonuses.

Salah felt the numbers he was delivering on the field continued to justify such an outlay and offered proof that he remained at the peak of his powers. He still retained hope of winning the Ballon d'Or having seen Lionel Messi, Cristiano Ronaldo, Luka Modric and Karim Benzema lift the prestigious trophy in their early to mid-thirties.

When Salah had previously renewed his contract in July 2022, Abbas had been so proud of the three-year deal that was eventually brokered that he helped Harvard Business School in America turn it into a case study. Back then, just a few weeks before putting pen to paper while on holiday on the Greek island of Mykonos, Salah had believed his future lay elsewhere given the sizeable gap between what he wanted and what was on the table. But then FSG president Mike Gordon broke the deadlock with an improved offer.

That had been an acrimonious saga at times with Salah giving interviews to Spanish publications where he talked about the possibility of moving to La Liga and described Barcelona and Real Madrid as 'top clubs'. Abbas used social media to crank up the pressure on the owners.

Prior to the 2022 Champions League final in Paris, Salah announced that he would be staying at Anfield for the final year of his contract even if an extension wasn't agreed. The message was clear – get it sorted or accept losing him for nothing. By that stage, Barcelona had registered their interest and sources close to the player claimed he hadn't ruled out joining another Premier League club if his contract expired.

Those levels of brinkmanship weren't replicated in 2024/25, but Salah wasn't shy to voice his frustration at times. There was a second meeting between Abbas and Hughes in Dubai in October, but the player's representative felt there was insufficient progress over how much Liverpool were willing to pay or how long they wanted him to stay. The wait for a formal opening offer continued into the following month.

On 24 November, after scoring twice in a 3–2 victory over Premier League strugglers Southampton, Salah decided to put the issue centre stage. He had just become only the third Liverpool player in history to score a century of goals for the club away from Anfield – following in the footsteps of Ian Rush and Roger Hunt.

Context is important. To say that Salah rarely speaks to the English written media would be an understatement. In his previous seven and a half years at Liverpool, he had stopped twice to answer questions in mixed zones after matches. The first time, in April 2018, he kept a promise to local reporters after reaching the 40-goal mark against Bournemouth in his record-breaking debut season at Anfield. Fourteen months later, he was holding court in Madrid after helping the club win the 2019 Champions League final against Tottenham Hotspur.

Hundreds of requests had been politely turned down over the years. As Salah walked out of St Mary's Stadium, it was bitterly cold, the wind was howling and he was greeted by the sound of dozens of admirers screaming his name. The smart money said he was going to board the waiting team bus without breaking stride.

However, he glanced to his right where I was one of four journalists waiting more in hope than expectation behind a metal barrier. I asked if he would be willing to give us a few minutes of his time. 'Is it going to be your questions or questions that the club wants you to ask me?' he inquired. 'Our questions,' I replied and he agreed to talk.

It was clear that Salah wanted to get something off his chest as the conversation soon turned to the ongoing uncertainty over his future.

'Well, we are almost in December and I haven't received any offers yet to stay in the club. I'm probably more out than in,' he said. 'I'm not going to retire soon, so I'm just playing, focusing on the season and I'm trying to win the Premier League and hopefully the Champions League. I'm disappointed, but we will see.'

Asked if he wanted to stay at Anfield beyond the summer of 2025, Salah added: 'I have been in the club for many years. There is no club like this. I love the fans. The fans love me. It is not in my hands or the fans' hands. I'm just doing my best because this is who I am and I try to give it all for myself and the club. The whole team has the chemistry now with the new manager. Hopefully we keep winning.'

Salah is a keen chess player and it was a calculated move rather than an impulsive one. He had initially planned to say something similar to Sky Sports post-game but they didn't ask him about his contract. Anfield legend turned TV pundit Jamie Carragher accused Salah of being 'selfish' for speaking out ahead of a huge week for the club with games against Real Madrid and Manchester City.

Slot used humour to try to defuse the situation: 'If I look at my line-ups then Mo is more in than out! I focus a bit more on what else Carragher said – Mo is one of the five best players Liverpool ever had and I completely agree with him, which is not an easy thing as there have been many great players at this club. I don't think it distracts Mo at all. Maybe it even brings the best out of him if you look at his performances until now.'

A banner appeared on the Kop featuring an image of Salah doing his bow and arrow goal celebration with the message: 'FSG. He fires a bow. Now give Mo his dough.' However, the argument 'just give him what he wants' didn't stand up to scrutiny at a time when Hughes was also negotiating with the representatives of Van Dijk and Alexander-Arnold.

Liverpool finally made Salah a formal offer in early December but there was no agreement. 'We are far away from that … nothing has really moved on,' he told Sky Sports after the 5–0 victory at West Ham United after Christmas. Before facing Manchester United in early January, he said: 'There is no progress.'

The day after scoring in the 2–2 draw against United, the choice of image that Salah posted on Instagram was telling. There he was stood over a free-kick alongside Alexander-Arnold with Van Dijk in the background. Asked for his take on the social media post, Carragher sought to turn the conversation in the studio away from Salah.

'I would say that Virgil van Dijk has come out of this whole situation this season as the captain of the club in a higher esteem: the way he has conducted himself, performances on the pitch, way he's led the team. He hasn't got involved in too much around this,' he said. 'He's come across as a real statesman in how he has handled it. He's been asked questions, he's knocked them away. Fingers crossed, he signs. The other two could maybe look at Virgil van Dijk and take a leaf out of his book.'

Responding to that clip on X and in doing so fuelling the news cycle, Salah posted: 'I'm starting to think you're obsessed with me.' The words were followed by a winking emoji and within a few days it had been viewed over 21 million times.

'I have got a Mo Salah obsession but I don't think it's the type of obsession he thinks it is,' replied Carragher on air. 'It's more of a footballing obsession and watching him in a red shirt. I come in, I get asked a question, I answer as diplomatically as I possibly could. I thought, "I'm not going to criticise Mo Salah or Trent, I'm going to rave about how Virgil van Dijk handled it." I get myself in all sorts of trouble again.'

From 1 January, foreign clubs were allowed to approach Salah over a possible summer move, but Abbas knew that the player's priority was to re-sign with Liverpool rather than pursue the riches on offer in Saudi Arabia.

Key for Salah was the relationship he had struck up with Slot and how he felt the Dutchman had helped to elevate his game through tactical expertise. Salah admired how Slot never made excuses about fixture scheduling or injuries and shared his own belief that Liverpool should be serial winners rather than regard themselves as plucky underdogs.

The longer the season went on, the more compelling the evidence in front of Edwards and Hughes that trying to replace Salah would not only be incredibly expensive but almost impossible. His pace may have dipped but he had added more strings to his bow with his creativity. His return of 0.48 assists per 90 minutes in the Premier League in 2024/25 was the best of his career. With 0.77 goals per 90, he hadn't been so prolific since 2017/18. Salah had more shots (130) than any other top-flight player and also created the most chances (86) from open play.

His durability was undeniable: he started all 38 league matches for the first time in his Liverpool career. Salah, who has spoken about wanting to keep playing until he's 40, put that availability record down to a strict regime which included daily yoga and meditation sessions, as well as a diet of fruit, vegetables, grilled fish, chicken and salad as he avoided processed foods. As well as a gym and a pool, his house was equipped with cryotherapy and hyperbaric chambers. Cryotherapy exposes your body to extremely cold temperatures to aid recovery, while hyperbaric therapy involves breathing pure oxygen in a pressurised environment to help heal damaged muscle tissue.

Over the course of the campaign, Salah leapfrogged Jermain Defoe, Robbie Fowler, Thierry Henry, Frank Lampard and Sergio Aguero to climb to fifth in the all-time list of Premier League goal scorers with 186. He also went above Billy Liddell and Gordon

Hodgson into third place in Liverpool's all-time list with 245 in all competitions, with only 1966 World Cup winner Roger Hunt (285) and former Wales striker Ian Rush (346) above him.

The fact that Salah was more tight-lipped when asked by TV broadcasters about his future in February and March was down to the fact that behind the scenes, negotiations between Hughes and Abbas were gathering pace. Ultimately, the numbers stacked up for both sides as he agreed similar terms to his existing deal.

On the evening of 10 April, the man nicknamed the 'Egyptian King' by supporters sat on a throne in the centre circle under the floodlights at Anfield as he filmed an announcement video for LFCTV. At 8 a.m. the following morning, the news broke that he had signed a deal until summer 2027. Salah explained that his daughter Makka was 'the happiest one in the family' because she didn't want to move away from her school friends.

'I had my best years here,' he said. 'I played eight years, hopefully it's going to be 10. I am very happy to be here. I signed the contract because I believe we can win a lot of big trophies together. Keep supporting us and we'll give it our best. Now I'm more in than out!'

Salah later revealed during an interview with Gary Neville for Sky Sports that at the start of the season he had thought there was just a '10 per cent' chance of him staying. 'We know the philosophy of the club. I'm not attacking them, I know how they dealt with their players over 30 in the past,' he said.

'I didn't expect that I'd stay. From January I think onwards, it was like "okay, things are getting better and better". It took us a while. I think the club was testing me to see if I could still provide or not!'

They were and the answer had been emphatic.

* * *

Liverpool had been tracking more than 30 centre-backs from across Europe over the course of the 2016–17 season. Aymeric Laporte, Kalidou Koulibaly and Jerome Boateng also made the shortlist, but Van Dijk was viewed by the club's recruitment staff as being in a class of his own.

The Netherlands defender was something of a late bloomer, having been overlooked by all the top clubs in his homeland before moving from mid-table Dutch outfit Groningen to Celtic and then Southampton.

Heading into the summer of 2017 there was serious competition for his signature from Manchester City and Chelsea, but Jurgen Klopp's pulling power came to the fore. During their discussions, he left Van Dijk in no doubt about his admiration for him and burning desire for them to work together. Liverpool legend Steven Gerrard and then captain Jordan Henderson also joined the charm offensive.

It did the trick. Van Dijk was won over and made it clear that his heart was set on Liverpool. However, Klopp's joy proved to be short-lived. Reports the pair had met in Blackpool and that the player was Anfield-bound infuriated Southampton as there had been no discussions between the clubs over a transfer fee.

Southampton complained to the Premier League and accused Liverpool of making an illegal approach. After a series of emergency meetings, FSG president Mike Gordon felt the club had no option but to issue an apology. A statement included the line: 'We have ended any interest in the player.'

The reality was very different. Edwards and Klopp ignored the clamour from a section of the fanbase to pursue a Plan B as they were convinced that Van Dijk would be worth the wait. Gordon worked hard behind the scenes to repair relations with Southampton chairman Ralph Krueger and, six months later than planned, Klopp got his man.

The £75 million fee, which shattered Liverpool's transfer record, made Van Dijk the most expensive defender in the world. When he headed home a late winner in front of the Kop on his debut against Everton in the FA Cup in January 2018, Klopp beamed: 'A fairytale in a world with not a lot of fairytales anymore.'

Commanding in the air, strong in the tackle, ice-cool with the ball at his feet and with an excellent range of passing, Van Dijk provided quality, composure, organisation and leadership. Liverpool fans took him to their hearts.

He was integral to all the glory that was achieved under Klopp. He fought back from the agony of a ruptured anterior cruciate ligament, inflicted by a crude challenge from Everton goalkeeper Jordan Pickford at Goodison Park in October 2020 which kept him out for 10 months. He made a mockery of claims that he would never be the same player again.

'They thought I was finished,' he declared after dramatically nodding home the only goal of the 2024 Carabao Cup final against Chelsea deep into extra time at Wembley. It was the first trophy he lifted as Liverpool captain after inheriting the armband from Jordan Henderson the previous summer.

His importance was such that Gordon contacted his agent Neil Fewings shortly after Klopp had publicly dropped his bombshell in January 2024 about stepping down as manager. It was made clear that the owners wanted Van Dijk to continue to be a leading light beyond the final year he had left on his contract. Van Dijk was delighted as he had no desire to move on.

However, as a new era dawned with Slot at the helm, it also made sense for all parties not to rush into an agreement and to see how the dynamic worked.

'I can say discussions are ongoing, but we will see what happens in the future,' Van Dijk told reporters after October's home victory over Chelsea. 'My full focus is on Liverpool, wanting to win games that are ahead of me and nothing else. What the future will bring I have no idea at the moment. I can only tell you that discussions have started.'

Slot's status as head coach rather than manager provided more space for Van Dijk's influence as skipper to grow around the training ground. He took a keen interest in the work of the medical, fitness, catering, coaching and analysis departments, while also providing support and advice to the younger members of the squad, who regard him as a role model. Like Henderson before him, when Van Dijk speaks, team-mates listen. With his private physio and chef, he showed others the way with his commitment to recovery as he headed straight for the ice bath post-match.

Whereas Klopp sought feedback from a leadership group consisting of five senior players, Slot largely turned just to his captain. Mutual respect abounded.

Despite knowing that his future would be a regular topic of conversation, Van Dijk still fronted up to the written media after every game – win, lose or draw. He understood the importance of setting the right tone and reinforcing key messages. As Liverpool's lead at the top of the Premier League table grew, there was no danger of Van Dijk letting anyone get carried away.

'I might get a glass of red wine tonight just to celebrate, me and my wife, but that's it,' he said after making his 300th appearance for the club in January's 4–1 victory over Ipswich Town. Sixty-four players had previously reached that milestone for the club but none could match his remarkable win percentage of 69.7 per cent. 'It shows I did quite well up until now. But it's down to everyone involved: the players, the managers, and the fans. It's a good stat to have. We will keep going.'

Over the course of the season there were regular face to face meetings between Hughes and Fewings as each sought to secure the best possible deal. Just like with Salah, Liverpool were relaxed about it dragging on into the final months of the campaign. There was interest from other elite European clubs about a possible free transfer, but Van Dijk's preference was always to stay put.

He emphatically dismissed premature reports in early March that he had already agreed an extension. 'Genuinely, I don't even know what will happen next year. If anyone says they do know, they are lying to your face,' he said. Yet within a few weeks a break-through had been achieved with Van Dijk admitting in early April there had been 'progress'.

By then Van Dijk was on the brink of captaining Liverpool to the Premier League title and the idea of losing him was inconceivable. He attempted more passes (2,921) than any other top-flight player in 2024/25 with an accuracy of 92 per cent. That included a league high 975 forward passes with an 80 per cent success rate. His total of 294 successful passes into the attacking third put him way ahead of his peers and underlined his importance to building attacks.

Among players to contest at least 200 duels, only Nottingham Forest's Nikola Milenkovic (70 per cent) had a higher success rate than Van Dijk (69 per cent). Among those to contest at least 100 aerial duels, only Everton's James Tarkowski (75 per cent) ranked above Van Dijk (72 per cent).

Van Dijk was ever-present in Premier League games until Slot finally rested him for the trip to Brighton & Hove Albion in May, after the title had already been won. It was the first time he had missed a single minute of top-flight football since returning from a two-match suspension in September 2023 following a red card against Newcastle United.

Approaching his 34th birthday, he looked fitter and more domi-nant than ever, but the data only really told half a story. His value to Liverpool went way beyond what he delivered on the field.

'Just let me say hi,' Van Dijk told reporters as he broke off mid-answer during his post-match media duties after a last-gasp

2–1 home victory over West Ham United on 13 April. He had spotted a special guest approaching him.

There was a warm embrace for Liverpool supporter Sean Cox, who suffered brain injuries in an unprovoked assault outside Anfield before the first leg of a Champions League semi-final against Roma in 2018. Cox was accompanied by wife Martina and family. They had been invited by the club to celebrate the Irishman's birthday. The support of Van Dijk and everyone connected with Liverpool, had meant a great deal to Cox's family and friends. 'It's good to see you – it's been a while. I'll come and chat to you guys shortly,' the Dutch defender added.

Van Dijk had provided the perfect gift by heading home an 89th minute winner from Alexis Mac Allister's corner to spark wild scenes inside Anfield. Three minutes earlier, the skipper's head had been in his hands after a mix-up with Andy Robertson led to the left-back scoring an unfortunate own goal.

The Dutchman swiftly changed the narrative. After being mobbed by his team-mates, Van Dijk patted the badge on his shirt in front of the Kop and then planted a kiss on it to rapturous acclaim. 'There was time to make it right, and luckily we did,' he said. 'We train a lot on it and I try to be important.'

It was the perfect way to tee up the big announcement. Four days later it was confirmed that he had penned a two-year extension to keep him at Anfield until the age of 36. With bonuses, he stood to earn around £400,000 per week. Neither Salah or Van Dijk had taken a pay cut.

'It was always Liverpool,' he told LFCTV. 'It was always in my head, it was always the plan and it was always Liverpool. There wasn't any doubt in my head that this is the place to be for me and my family. I'm one of Liverpool. Someone called me the other day an adopted Scouser – I'm really proud to hear these things. It gives me a great feeling.

'I said it from the first day on that it felt right and I think it showed in the years we have spent together up until now. And obviously more years to come. It is the place for me to be, to spend my best years, be successful with the club as we have been over the years and hopefully the future as well. And I love the city, I love the club, I love the fans, I love my team-mates. I love everything that embodies Liverpool. It's a togetherness that I really appreciate. It's an absolute privilege to be here.'

The summer of 2023 was the first time in his professional career that Trent Alexander-Arnold had entered the final two years of his contract. He had previously penned extensions in 2017, 2019 and 2021, with Liverpool regularly rewarding his development and growing importance to the side with improved terms.

Having been appointed vice-captain by Klopp following the departure of James Milner, he had expected Liverpool to open contract talks before the start of the 2023/24 season. It didn't happen.

There was upheaval behind the scenes at Anfield. Julian Ward had stepped down as sporting director, just a year after succeeding Edwards, with Jorg Schmadtke appointed on an interim basis. Contract renewals took a back seat.

Then, in November 2023, the situation was complicated by Klopp informing Gordon that he had run out of energy and would be leaving at the end of the season. Once the news was made public two months later, it was clear that everything would be put on hold until there was clarity about the direction Liverpool were going in. No player was going to commit to fresh terms without knowing who was taking over and where he stood in the new manager's plans.

After Hughes was appointed as sporting director in March 2024, it was telling that his first call in the job involved introducing himself to Tyler Alexander-Arnold, Trent's brother and agent. Talks over a new contract were initiated the following month with the opening offer submitted by the end of April.

Whereas the new Anfield hierarchy were happy to bide their time with Salah and Van Dijk, they knew that, given his age, the clock was ticking with Alexander-Arnold.

The England international understood the circumstances behind why it had taken Liverpool so long to come to the table, but as he approached his final year, he privately started to wonder whether the 2024/25 season could be his last for the club. Interest from Real Madrid was already well known.

'Look, I have been at the club 20 years now. I have signed four or five contract extensions and none of those have been played out in public. This one won't be either,' Alexander-Arnold told reporters following Liverpool's 3–0 home win over Bournemouth in September. Pushed on whether he wanted to stay at Anfield, he added: 'I want to be a Liverpool player this season (as a minimum) is what I will say.'

It was the first and final time Alexander-Arnold stopped in an interview area for print journalists all season. When he conducted interviews with TV rights holders, the topic was strictly off-limits. He kept his counsel as the speculation ramped up.

Privately, he was wrestling with the biggest decision of his life. As well as the emotional bond with his boyhood club, he loved Slot's coaching style and attention to detail. He knew he wouldn't need to leave in order to win trophies.

Slot continued to pick Alexander-Arnold because his attitude and application didn't waver. The head coach knew the lengths to which the academy graduate had gone to make himself available. He had played for Liverpool with the aid of painkilling injections after suffering a side strain on England duty in October. He also returned to action ahead of schedule after damaging his ankle against Paris Saint-Germain in March.

Real Madrid had already been looking for a long-term successor for experienced right-back Dani Carvajal and that pursuit was stepped up after the Spain international ruptured his anterior cruciate ligament against Villarreal in October. Alexander-Arnold was their top target and they didn't want to wait until the summer to secure his services.

Unhappy with reports in the Spanish media that he had already given Real Madrid his word that he would join them, Alexander-Arnold made a yapping gesture with his hand as he celebrated scoring in the 5–0 rout of West Ham United on 29 December.

Twenty-four hours later, Liverpool received an approach from Real Madrid, who were prepared to pay £20 million to sign him in the January transfer window. Edwards, who was contacted by Real Madrid CEO José Angel Sanchez, gave the proposal short shift. Hughes agreed that it was out of the question with Liverpool still competing on four fronts. It was decent money for a player who looked like he could be leaving for nothing six months later, but they put the team's fortunes above finance.

Alexander-Arnold was hurt by accusations that he had actively encouraged Real Madrid to make a move and was adamant he wasn't looking to jump ship mid-season. He had been enjoying a short break in Venice when he was told about the approach being rejected shortly before the news broke in the UK media.

All the noise and criticism undoubtedly affected him against Manchester United in early January when he lost possession 27 times and bore the brunt of the Anfield crowd's frustration before being booked and taken off in the 2–2 draw. His head was scrambled.

Slot defended him publicly and also provided support privately. A week later he gave him the captaincy for the FA Cup tie against Accrington Stanley and the reception he was afforded was much warmer.

Talks over an extension continued until early March as Hughes made a number of improved offers. Liverpool were prepared to make him the highest paid full-back in the Premier League with a hefty increase on his £200,000 per week salary, but received little encouragement.

As a result there was no sense of surprise internally when Alexander-Arnold went to see Slot in his office at Kirkby during the March international break and told him that he had decided to leave when his contract expired at the end of the season. He explained how he felt at this stage of his career he needed to step out of his comfort zone and pursue a new challenge. His agent relayed the same information to Hughes, who had inherited a tricky situation and had done everything he could to find a resolution. There was no animosity.

Ultimately, it didn't matter what Liverpool offered him financially. Alexander-Arnold, who had joined the academy at the age of six, came to the conclusion that he had achieved everything he had set out to do at Anfield. He wanted to experience life in Madrid where he would have to prove himself all over again.

Alexander-Arnold was determined to keep the news under wraps until after the title had been secured to avoid creating any unwanted distractions for the team. When he scored the winner on his comeback from injury away to Leicester City on 20 April, there was an outpouring of emotion as he whipped off his shirt before being mobbed by his team-mates.

'Let the headlines be his great goal and not his contract situation,' Slot told reporters post-match. 'It would be ridiculous if someone argues about his commitment to his club.'

When the shot from Alexander-Arnold hit the net at the King Power Stadium, his close friend Andy Robertson turned to fellow substitute Curtis Jones on the bench and said: 'He called it! That's Trent all over.' Before coming on five minutes earlier, Alexander-

Arnold had boldly told them: 'I'm going to come on here, score and take my top off.' He was true to his word.

A week later Alexander-Arnold was a Premier League champion for the second time – standing in front of the Kop with his arms outstretched as they serenaded him with a rendition of *'the Scouser in our team'* after the 5–1 thrashing of Tottenham.

He could have waited until after the end of the season to publicly clarify his plans but didn't want to be accused of being a coward by slipping out of the back door. He was going to announce his exit on Friday 2 May, two days before Liverpool's trip to Chelsea. However, he was talked out of it by Anfield officials who knew it would dent the party mood in the away end as the title celebrations continued in the capital.

Instead it was agreed that he would wait until the morning after the game at Stamford Bridge. 'After 20 years at Liverpool Football Club, now is the time for me to confirm that I will be leaving at the end of the season,' he posted on social media.

'This is easily the hardest decision I've ever made in my life. I know many of you have wondered why or been frustrated that I haven't spoken about this yet, but it was always my intention to keep my full focus on the team's best interests, which was securing [title] No. 20.

'This club has been my whole life – my whole world – for 20 years. From the academy right through until now, the support and love I have felt from everyone inside and outside of the club will stay with me forever. I will forever be in debt to you all. I've been blessed enough to live out my dreams here and I will never, ever take for granted the special moments I've been fortunate enough to have lived through with you all. My love for this club will never die.'

It divided opinion among the fanbase. Some were philosophical and felt that after clocking up more than 350 appearances and winning the lot with his boyhood club, he had earned the right to open a new chapter and they appreciated the lure of Real Madrid. However, others were angry that a home-grown talent had effectively run down his contract to join a European rival, damaging his legacy in the process.

Alexander-Arnold felt the backlash when Arsenal visited Anfield. Initially, the Kop made their point in a subtle way. As he stood on the touchline waiting to come on midway through the second half, they sang about Liverpool legend Steven Gerrard.

It was a nod to the kind of iconic status Alexander-Arnold had effectively given up by deciding to leave his boyhood club. One of the reasons Gerrard is so adored is that he showed loyalty in the face of regular attempts from European heavyweights to prise him away. The fans also chanted the name of Conor Bradley, who had deputised so well at right-back.

When Alexander-Arnold stepped on to the field, the mood changed. There were boos and the jeers from a significant minority of supporters which grew louder each time he touched the ball. He looked shell-shocked and so did many of his team-mates. Squabbles broke out in the stands as fans argued among themselves over how Alexander-Arnold was being treated. It was toxic and Arsenal fed off the negativity to draw the game and salvage a point.

Anfield season ticket holder and UK member of parliament for Liverpool West Derby Ian Byrne posted on X: 'You never boo a Liverpool player who pulls on that precious red shirt, ever.'

When Slot arrived for his post-match press conference, he knew what was coming and asked the assembled reporters: 'Who is going to start with the first Trent question?' Six of them followed. He treaded carefully, wary of the strength of feeling.

'It's a privilege to live in Europe, where everyone can have their own opinion and express their own opinion,' Slot said. 'All of them were not happy with him leaving the club, a few of them showed it by booing him and a few of them clapped. I owe it to the players in the dressing room to make decisions to try to win the game. If I think there is a better chance of winning it with Trent, I will [play him].'

Robertson added: 'It's crucial in these moments that I don't tell you how to feel and you don't tell me how to feel about it. His legacy at this club is there to see. The trophies he's won, the moments he's had in history, will always be there. I'm extremely proud of him. For Trent, it has not been an easy one, but he's made the decision.'

Salah was considerably less diplomatic when he spoke to Sky Sports the following week as he criticised the 'harsh' supporters who had booed Alexander-Arnold.

'I was surprised because this is not how we act as Liverpool fans, we shouldn't act this way with anyone,' he said. 'We should always appreciate the people that came here even for six months. Imagine someone who gave you his all for 20 years. He has done a lot for the city and done a lot for the club, and is probably [one of] the best players in the club's history. He gave his all and I think he needed a new challenge. He spoke to me about it. I really love him and I think he deserves the best farewell leaving the club. He deserves the fans to treat him the best way possible because he gave it all to the fans.'

Klopp waded in on his return to Merseyside as he prepared to attend the final game of the season against Crystal Palace – his first trip back to Anfield since the end of his managerial reign. He was guest of honour at the LFC Foundation Gala Ball in Liverpool's Anglican Cathedral two days before the trophy lift. During a Q&A he revealed that he had turned his TV off in disgust during the match against Arsenal at the treatment of Alexander-Arnold.

Referring to a montage shown on the big screen of highlights from his tenure, Klopp said: 'Trent was one of the players who made that all happen. It was not me. I didn't score a goal, I didn't cross the ball or do anything on the pitch. This boy was 18 years old and he scored a great free-kick at Hoffenheim and if he doesn't score that we don't go to the Champions League final. Against Barcelona, he did the most cheeky thing in the world [with a quickly taken corner] and set up the goal to make it 4–0. A result in a game that will never happen again.

'I don't tell you, you should not be disappointed or you should not be angry. Just don't forget. I watched the game when he came on and I heard the booing. I am old and I thought it might be my age, so I switched up the volume and the booing again. I needed another 10 seconds. I switched the telly off. Honestly, I could not have been more disappointed in this moment. This is not us. This boy gave everything and I was there every day. If he had not given everything I would tell you now. If someone should feel angry about that it is the owners but they are not.'

Klopp, who took a signed Alexander-Arnold shirt up on stage which was auctioned off for £22,000, made a heartfelt plea to supporters to give the club's vice-captain a warm send-off. 'We are different in a good way. Let's not behave like every other club,' he added. 'I hope that the game on Sunday is the situation where everyone can be around when the trophy is presented. When Virgil gets the trophy it will be one of the greatest days of his life and it should be one of the greatest days in our lives. I am sure you will do it the right way.'

Slot regretted comments he made about Alexander-Arnold in his press conference in the build-up to the Palace game when he mentioned about speaking to the vice-captain about his work ethic in training back in pre-season. It was supposed to be a joke but was taken out of context and provided his critics with more ammunition. The reality was that Slot felt that Alexander-Arnold had behaved impeccably and had given him everything he had demanded en route to clinching the title.

In his programme notes for the Palace game, Slot wrote: 'It is a day for unity and celebration. Nothing can be allowed to get in the way. Whatever might divide us can wait for another day. Whatever could distract us can be put to one side. This is one of the biggest days in the modern history of Liverpool Football Club, so it makes sense that we all contribute to making it as positive as it can be and enjoy it as much as possible.'

The message got through and when Alexander-Arnold replaced Bradley at the start of the second half, he was cheered onto the field. The contrast with a fortnight earlier could hardly have been greater. With his supreme range of passing, he provided a reminder about what Liverpool were waving goodbye to. One chance he created for Darwin Núñez prompted Klopp in the directors' box to declare: 'Wow, what a ball!'

After his parents Dianne and Michael joined him on the pitch during the post-match celebrations, Alexander-Arnold fell into their arms and couldn't hold back the tears. 'I didn't know what to expect stepping out at Anfield after what happened a few weeks ago,' he said. 'I wanted to play for the club one more time and Arne trusted me to play. To get the reception I got means more than anything. I've played hundreds of games for the club but I've never felt so loved and cared for as today. Hand on my heart, I hope one day the fans will be able to recognise the hard work and everything I have done for the team. It's been an honour and privilege to be part of. I'll remember this day. It goes down as the best day of my life.'

Five days later it was announced that Alexander-Arnold would be joining Real Madrid a month early in a transfer worth £10 million to Liverpool. Real CEO José Angel Sanchez had initially got back in touch with Edwards on 5 May, the same day the player announced he would be leaving. Sanchez was keen to thrash out a compensation agreement to sign him on 1 June rather than as a free agent on 1 July so he could play in the group stage of the Club World Cup under new manager Xabi Alonso.

Real Madrid had hoped to only pay around £850,000 but Edwards informed Sanchez that it would take a proper transfer fee for Liverpool to sanction a deal. Edwards knew that the Spanish club would be playing for more than £90 million in prize money from the tournament in America and were desperate to have Alexander-Arnold on board.

A message exchange between Edwards and Sanchez continued and talks gathered pace on the day of the Palace game and during the celebration party in the evening at the city's Municipal Hotel. At one point, Edwards and Hughes went into a side room to discuss the matter further and Sanchez agreed to the terms they had demanded. The finer details were ironed out the following morning with Alexander-Arnold informed just before the trophy parade.

The fee was €10 million (£8.4 million) in a single instalment with no incentive targets to be met. Factoring in Real Madrid taking responsibility for his wages in June and other cost savings, Liverpool valued the overall package at £10 million – around £333,000 for every day Alexander-Arnold had remaining on his deal. He signed a six-year contract in Madrid with a €1 billion release clause. Swapping No. 66 for the No. 12 shirt and rebranding with 'Trent' on the back rather than 'Alexander-Arnold', he was unveiled on 12 June at the Bernabeu, where he stunned the locals by speaking in perfect Spanish for over a minute before ending with the traditional cry of 'Hala Madrid!'

There was less shock at the AXA Training Centre where it was an open secret that he had been learning the language in the preceding few months.

8

PLAYING THE LIVERPOOL WAY

A Liverbird upon my chest,
We are the men of Shankly's best
A team that plays the Liverpool Way
And wins the championship in May.

An old favourite was given a new lease of life.

As Liverpool's pursuit of the Premier League title gathered pace, their supporters adopted the song 'A Liverbird Upon My Chest' as the season's unofficial anthem.

The manner in which it took off both inside and outside grounds around the turn of the year was a source of both surprise and delight for lifelong fan Phil Aspinall, who had written the original version some 40 years earlier.

He had been watching the 1968 Vietnam War film *The Green Berets* starring John Wayne during the mid-1980s when the theme tune, 'The Ballad of the Green Berets', prompted him to grab a pen and a notepad.

'I thought to myself "what a tune that would be for the match" so I got writing,' Aspinall said. 'I did a few verses and the chorus came together. A group of us used to drink in the Albert pub in Anfield on match days and after a couple of goes we had the whole pub singing it with us.

'It made me feel very proud to hear it making a comeback all these years on. I get the biggest buzz in life watching the Reds and it's a song that boosts both the fans and the players. It's great that the younger fans are keeping it alive.'

Over the years more verses had been added, celebrating the achievements of the club's iconic trophy-winning teams and managers, and honouring the 97 supporters who lost their lives at Hillsborough in 1989. It tended to be sung in pubs or on coaches en route to away matches by diehard fans rather than actually at matches.

At the heart of it remained Aspinall's stirring chorus, but for a long time the line about winning the championship in May couldn't be delivered with much conviction.

Liverpool waited three decades to secure their 19th top-flight crown before the painful drought was finally broken during Jurgen Klopp's tenure in 2019/20. And even then the global pandemic meant that fans had to watch from afar when the Premier League title was secured with games being played behind closed doors.

With Arne Slot's side looking unstoppable in 2024/25 and playing a brand of attacking football perfectly in tune with the 'Liverpool Way', it was little wonder that 'A Liverbird Upon My Chest' gained wider popularity and started to be chanted with such gusto again.

The Champions League trip to PSV Eindhoven in late January acted as a real catalyst as footage of the away end delivering a booming rendition was widely shared across social media. It took off and became the soundtrack of the season.

Former Liverpool midfielder Craig Johnston, who played 271 times for the club between 1981 and 1988, was listening with interest from his home in New South Wales, Australia.

During his Anfield career he had been so enamoured with the song that he had mixed it with another terrace favourite 'The Pride of Merseyside' and released a record performed by singer-songwriter Joe Fagin, which reached No. 81 in the UK charts in

1987. Johnston, an entrepreneur who invented the Adidas Predator boots in the 1990s, fared better a year later when he co-wrote 'Anfield Rap' ahead of the 1988 FA Cup final which made it to No. 3.

'It was amazing to hear "Liverbird" again – it brought back a lot of happy memories for me,' Johnston said. 'Coming from Australia, I found the level of football fandom in Liverpool in the Eighties just jaw-dropping, with so many passionate Reds travelling everywhere to follow their team. Sometimes we would have them sleeping on the floor of our hotel rooms on away trips!

'I loved listening to all their songs and I recognised that tune straightaway as my dad used to sing 'The Ballad of the Green Berets' to me when I was young. It was a marching tune with military drumbeats and trumpets.

'The Scousers took it and turned it into something special. The record company back in '87 wanted us to change the tune to avoid paying royalties, but I wasn't doing it for the money, I was doing it as a thank-you to the fans. I'm convinced it would have gone a lot higher in the charts if they had stuck with the original tune. I've still got the original video we filmed in a pub near Lime Street station with my team-mate Sammy Lee and his mates.

'I'm not surprised that a new generation of Liverpool fans have embraced it. It's got everything – the pride of wearing the Liverbird on your chest, the nod to the glorious past with the Bill Shankly reference, the importance of playing a certain way in keeping with the club's attacking ethos, and the bold vow that the title is coming back to Anfield. It's inspiring for those on the pitch.'

With Liverpool already guaranteed a place in the last 16 of the Champions League, Slot left nine of his top stars at home as a youthful squad travelled to Eindhoven for the final game of the league phase.

Despite each victory being worth close to £2 million in prize money, sporting director Richard Hughes was in full agreement with the head coach that it made sense to look at the bigger picture, with a Premier League trip to Bournemouth coming up just three days later. Having largely avoided rotating the squad during the first half of the season as he favoured a settled line-up, Slot knew he had to grasp the opportunities to give some rest to those he repeatedly relied on or the risk of injuries would grow.

For example, Alexis Mac Allister had been granted a week's holiday before Christmas when one-game suspensions from both domestic and European duty meant he wouldn't be eligible to play for a fortnight. There was no training at Kirkby for those left behind on the day of the PSV game and they were told to put their feet up.

Liverpool had earned the right to ring the changes having made it seven wins out of seven in the Champions League earlier in the month against French outfit Lille at Anfield. There was another slice of history as Slot's side set a new club record for most minutes without conceding a goal in Europe.

Remarkably, when Lille's Jonathan David cancelled out Mohamed Salah's 50th European goal for Liverpool shortly after the hour mark, it had been 599 minutes of action since AC Milan's Christian Pulisic fired past Alisson early on matchday one. The previous record of 572 minutes had been set by Rafael Benítez's defending European champions in the 2005/06 season.

'We keep clean sheets not by defending a lot, we keep clean sheets by attacking a lot. The fans prefer it like this as well,' Slot told reporters. 'When you combine the quality of these players with their incredible work rate, it's very difficult to score against this team.'

Having the talismanic presence of captain Virgil van Dijk cajoling those around him certainly helped. He reached a half century of Champions League appearances for Liverpool with 35 wins –

the only player in the club's history who had matched that success rate over 50 games in Europe's elite competition was four-time European Cup winner Phil Neal.

Lille, who were unbeaten in 21 matches in all competitions prior to arriving at Anfield, had Aissa Mandi sent off for two bookings before Harvey Elliott's deflected shot gave the hosts the points. Rather than go for the jugular at 2–1 up, Liverpool had played out time as opposed to taking risks. During their usual post-match debrief over the phone, Slot's father Arend had complained that it wasn't as exciting as previous games.

'I had to try to explain to him you can easily lose these games if you are starting to force all kinds of difficult balls, but he's not always agreeing with me,' chuckled Slot. A picture was painted of a parent who was difficult to please, but the reality was that Arend was deeply proud of his son and the manner in which he had taken managing a club of Liverpool's size and stature in his stride. That was clear on his regular visits to Anfield when he would stand in the background as Slot conducted his media duties.

More records tumbled on an eventful night away to PSV. Academy defender Amara Nallo was sent off for a professional foul just four minutes after coming on for his senior debut as he became the youngest Liverpool player ever to be shown a red card at 18 years and 72 days.

'Amara had never played first-team football before and then to make a debut at Champions League level is probably the hardest way to make it,' Slot said. 'I think he misinterpreted the situation and that's immediately a problem. It's a big moment for him to learn from and it's cruel.'

It was a happier experience for academy midfielder Trey Nyoni, who at 17 years and 213 days became Liverpool's youngest ever player to appear in a major European competition. The long-standing record had been held by Phil Charnock since 1992.

Fellow youngster James McConnell performed to such a high level against PSV that Slot decided he was going to keep him around for the rest of the season rather than sanction a loan move to one of the many Championship clubs vying for his services. The amount of attention Cody Gakpo received during the pre-match walk had been a source of much amusement in the squad on his return to his home city. There was also a hero's reception for Gakpo from the PSV fans inside the stadium.

The 3–2 defeat in the Netherlands was insignificant as Barcelona's failure to beat Atalanta the same night meant that Liverpool still finished top of the 36-team league phase with 21 points from their eight matches. That was some achievement given effectively the same squad had been found wanting in the second tier Europa League competition the previous season.

However, Slot had warned that being seeded wouldn't provide any guarantees about a kinder route in the knockout stages given that under the new format some clubs had been given harder fixtures than others. And he was proved correct as the play-offs between the teams who finished 15th to 18th led to Liverpool being given an unenviable last 16 tie against French champions Paris Saint-Germain, who had demolished Brest 10–0 on aggregate.

Bought to provide cover on the right and ease the burden on Mohamed Salah, Federico Chiesa had largely been a spectator for Liverpool, but there were some signs of promise from him early in the new year.

Chiesa finally opened his account for the club in the FA Cup rout of League Two minnows Accrington Stanley, which saw Rio Ngumoha become the youngest Liverpool player to start a competitive game at 16 years and 135 days. Slot rewarded the England youth international for the manner in which he had lit up training after being promoted from the Under-21s to the senior squad.

Ngumoha was still raw and didn't feature again at first-team level in 2024/25, but Slot loved his attitude and application. The head coach regarded the left winger as a special talent with immense potential who with the right guidance would flourish at the highest level as he developed physically.

Chelsea had been furious to lose him to Liverpool the previous summer. He had been named player of the tournament when Chelsea Under-16s were crowned national champions in October 2023 and having played for their Under-21s at the age of 15, he was viewed as a future first-team prospect. The London club responded to his acrimonious departure by temporarily banning Liverpool's scouts from attending youth games at their Cobham training complex.

However, Liverpool passed the Premier League's five-step review which is standard procedure when a young player wants to move between two category-one academies to ensure that everything is done by the book. There had also been strong interest from Manchester United but they were outflanked by their arch rivals.

Sources close to the youngster dismissed suggestions that the switch to Liverpool was financially motivated. He started off on a scholar's contract of just £1,200 per month with the promise of a first professional contract when he turned 17 in August 2025.

Ngumoha and his family were convinced that the pathway to the first team was clearer on Merseyside having seen the opportunities given to young players such as Jarell Quansah, Conor Bradley, Jayden Danns and McConnell. 'This boy is – and will be – a top, top player,' former Chelsea captain John Terry posted on social media when Nguhoma's exit from the capital was confirmed.

PSV away felt like an important step forward for Chiesa, who had been playing catch-up from the moment he arrived at Liverpool for an initial fee of £10 million the previous August. He had missed most of pre-season with Juventus so wasn't in the right shape to immediately compete for a place in Slot's side.

The Italy international struggled to handle the intensity of the training schedule and picked up a number of muscle injuries. Against PSV he looked fitter and sharper as he completed 90 minutes for the first time since playing for his country at the Euros seven months earlier. He was involved in both of Liverpool's goals.

'Since I joined Liverpool, I've wanted to prove myself and I couldn't for many reasons,' Chiesa said. 'It's hard to play but that's normal. I want to be here. I will be ready for the next opportunity.'

Unfortunately, bullish words were not backed up with actions. Rather than kick on, Chiesa regressed. After his poor display in the FA Cup fourth-round defeat to Plymouth Argyle, he didn't start another game until after the Premier League title had been won. He finished the campaign with just two goals across 466 minutes of action in all competitions.

Yet despite that meagre return, Chiesa still earned cult hero status on the Kop. They admired his enthusiasm and how he was always in the thick of the celebrations. He was similarly popular in the dressing room as he parked his own personal disappointment over such a limited role and supported his team-mates. Ironically, the less he played, the more the song dedicated to him, to the tune of Dean Martin's 'Sway', was chanted on the concourses and in the stands.

Slot had fielded another heavily rotated line-up against Championship opposition Plymouth as he prioritised the upcoming rearranged Merseyside derby at Goodison Park. It was a painful day in more ways than one as Ryan Hardie's penalty dumped Liverpool out and Joe Gomez suffered a serious hamstring injury which meant he didn't play again all season. His early exit led to a debut for youngster Isaac Mabaya.

Preparations had been far from ideal with Curtis Jones ruled out at short notice due to illness after travelling to Devon, while Darwin Núñez had been due to start but was only given a cameo role after returning late from a trip to Spain to attend the birth of his daughter Isabella. Slot still felt he had sufficient firepower with a front three of Chiesa, Diogo Jota and Luis Díaz but the performance was horribly scrappy and disjointed.

'We hardly created anything,' he conceded. 'Sometimes you deserve a bit of luck if you work as hard as Plymouth did.' It would have been easy for Slot to shrug off a shock exit from the FA Cup and paint it as a blessing in disguise given the difficulty of trying to maintain a challenge on all four fronts. It freed up more time to train ahead of matches in more prestigious competitions and with supporters dreaming of bigger prizes, there was little backlash over the defeat.

However, the Dutchman didn't see it that way. He told his squad that losing to Plymouth was unacceptable and insisted that at a club like Liverpool they should expect to compete for every trophy.

By then a trip to Wembley to face Newcastle United in the final of the Carabao Cup had already been secured. A 1–0 deficit was overturned in style with a 4–0 hammering of Tottenham in the second leg of the semi-final at Anfield.

Liverpool channelled a burning sense of injustice from the first leg when their 24-game unbeaten run was ended in controversial fashion. They were furious that referee Stuart Attwell didn't show Lucas Bergvall a second yellow card for clattering Kostas Tsimikas shortly before the Swedish teenager scored a late winner. With Tsimikas off the field following treatment, Liverpool were down to 10 men when the goal went in.

There was more drama on the journey home when thick fog and ice meant the team's delayed flight from London Stansted couldn't land in Liverpool and had to be diverted to Birmingham instead.

The plane eventually touched down in the Midlands around 3 a.m., with the club having to scramble a coach and cars to transport everyone the final 100 miles north.

Staff arriving for work at Liverpool's John Lennon Airport at 5.30 a.m. were surprised to see a shivering Salah in the car park as he struggled to get his vehicle moving in the treacherous conditions. Slot cancelled the planned recovery session at the AXA Training Centre and gave his players the day off to recover.

The second leg at Anfield was plain sailing with Dominik Szoboszlai showcasing what a vital cog he had become in the Liverpool machine.

In the early stages of the campaign, Slot had thrown down the gauntlet to the Hungarian midfielder. 'Something that we have to work on with him is that he's also even more involved in scoring goals and creating chances for us,' he said. 'For an attacking midfielder at Liverpool, his numbers need to go up.'

Szoboszlai's debut season at Anfield following a £60 million move from RB Leipzig in 2023 had been a mixed bag. He got off to a flyer but comparisons with Steven Gerrard, after inheriting the No. 8 shirt worn with such distinction by the club legend, proved wildly premature as he faded badly and ended up losing his place in the team.

Under Slot, he was rejuvenated. After contributing 11 goal involvements (seven goals, four assists) in 2023/24, there were 16 (eight goals, eight assists) of them in 2024/25. In possession, he was Liverpool's fourth attacker with his intelligent movement and eye for a pass. Without the ball, he chased lost causes and never allowed opponents to settle, something he described as 'doing the dirty job for the team'.

Against Tottenham, he had five shots, nine touches in the opposition box, created five chances, won possession nine times and scored. According to Opta, no Liverpool player had recorded those kind of numbers in a match since Philippe Coutinho tormented Slovenian minnows Maribor in the Champions League in 2017.

'Credit to Liverpool,' said Tottenham head coach Ange Postecoglou. 'They were way too good for us. We never got to grips with the game, either with or without the ball.'

In the Premier League, Slot's side had given some hope to the chasing pack by dropping points in their opening two league matches of 2025.

Salah looked to have settled the contest against Ruben Amorim's struggling Manchester United side at Anfield, scoring from the penalty spot after Gakpo had cancelled out Lisandro Martinez's opener. Salah had inflicted more damage on United than any other club during his Liverpool career – this was his 16th goal in 17 appearances against them.

However, Amad Diallo made it 2–2 and the below-par hosts were relieved to see Harry Maguire blaze over a big chance to win the game in stoppage time. The Liverpool players belatedly emerged from the home dressing room to discover Martinez waiting patiently because he wanted the shirt of his Argentine compatriot Mac Allister.

In-form Nottingham Forest were on course for a first league-double over Liverpool since 1962/63 when Chris Wood fired them in front at the City Ground. Approaching the midway point of the second half, Slot's side still hadn't mustered a single attempt on target. They were crying out for some inspiration.

Substitutes Jota and Tsimikas were deep in conversation on the touchline as they waited to be brought on. The duo, who replaced Konaté and Robertson, had been reminiscing about how they had combined for Liverpool's winner at the same venue in the sixth round of the FA Cup in March 2022.

'Let's do it now, recreate your assist, go and take the corner,' Jota told his team-mate. Tsimikas duly delivered and Jota nodded home from four yards out before being mobbed by his team-mates. Talk about an instant impact.

It was the fastest goal scored by a Liverpool substitute on record in the Premier League era – the Portugal international celebrating just 22 seconds after entering the field. 'It was one of those occasions when everything went right,' Jota said. 'I scored with my first touch which I felt gave the team a bit of momentum. But I'm not happy because I think we could have won.'

Jota provided the spark for a frenetic finale and would have been the match-winner but for the heroics of goalkeeper Matz Sels. Slot had carefully managed Jota's game time following his return to action after two months out with a chest injury sustained against Chelsea in October. There had been a minor setback after he scored on his comeback against Fulham before Christmas.

Slot's post-match assessment that it was '98 minutes of total domination' from Liverpool at the City Ground was stretching it, but once again their powers of recovery came to the fore. No top-flight team could better their tally of 23 points earned from losing positions in the Premier League in 2024/25. With Forest sitting so deep, the head coach had thrown caution to the wind by bringing on Jota for Konaté and using Ryan Gravenberch as a makeshift centre-back.

'We brought an attacker in for a defender just to play even more attacking football than we already did because we needed a goal,' Slot explained. 'Scoring from set-pieces was not something I had in my mind.'

Four days later there was another seminal date in the season. Entering stoppage time against Brentford at the Gtech Community Stadium, Liverpool were on the brink of enduring a damaging stalemate. They had been horribly wasteful in the final third.

Thirty-five shots, a record for an away team in the Premier League, had failed to yield a breakthrough.

Darwin Núñez had got a header horribly wrong and ballooned another presentable chance over the bar. Perseverance ultimately paid off. In the 91st minute, Harvey Elliott picked out the run of Trent Alexander-Arnold, whose low cross was turned in by Núñez. The Uruguayan whipped off his shirt and threw it into the air before racing towards the corner flag where he was mobbed by his team-mates. Two minutes later Elliott found Núñez, who took a touch to steady himself and hammered home his second.

'Darwin scored a few important goals, but that first one at Brentford was maybe for him and for us the most important,' said Slot, who had introduced Núñez and Elliott for Díaz and Szoboszlai in the second half.

'It had been so frustrating to watch. We were so close to a goal. We just kept on going and going. We brought on attacker after attacker. We always try to force a win. I had doubts [that the break-through would ever arrive], but the players proved me wrong again.'

As the final whistle sounded, an emotional Núñez clenched his fists and looked up to the heavens. Alisson raced to embrace him and lifted him off his feet. How Núñez had waited for a moment like this. Ridiculed and written off, his confidence had taken a battering. The most expensive signing in the club's history had been relegated to the fringes of Liverpool's title challenge with just two league goals all season before doubling that tally in west London.

Núñez had become used to opposition supporters regularly bait-ing him with the chant of '*You're just a shit Andy Carroll*' – a reference to the striker who scored just 11 goals for Liverpool following a then-British record £35 million transfer from Newcastle United in January 2011. The late drama had silenced the barbs of the Brentford fans.

'You have to stay mentally strong, never give up,' Núñez told Sky Sports. 'There are moments that are very difficult for us players – for me, it's right now, but I never throw the towel in. I always carry on working in training. If I need to stay to practise more, I stay to improve. The work I do on the pitch to help the team, to defend as well, I've always done it well. But I haven't scored goals and people look at that. I'm going through a rough patch but it's really important to keep my head up.'

Van Dijk would regularly put an arm around Núñez's shoulder during difficult times as he provided reassurance that his time would come. 'I told him: "Don't listen to all of you guys [in the media]",' the Liverpool captain told reporters. 'No, I'm joking! Don't take that as a serious comment. I said to him: "Stay calm because you will play again." There will always be an opportunity for him to show himself again. Darwin is in a good place. He is still learning. The South Americans help him with the language. He is part of the group and we need him.'

For FSG CEO of football Michael Edwards and Liverpool sporting director Richard Hughes, Brentford away also provided vindication for their stance in the January transfer window. An intermediary working on behalf of Saudi Pro League club Al-Nassr had reached out to make it clear that they would be willing to pay around £60 million for Núñez.

However, despite Núñez's bit-part role and the generous fee on offer, Edwards and Hughes weren't prepared to weaken Slot's squad with Liverpool still challenging on a number of fronts. They didn't believe that a suitable replacement was available in that window. Al-Nassr ended up signing Colombian striker Jhon Duran from Aston Villa instead.

Edwards and Hughes had also snubbed Real Madrid's attempts to buy Alexander-Arnold, who created the opening goal for Núñez against Brentford. There was a belief internally that if they had been willing to negotiate with the Spanish giants, they could have banked up to £40 million for their vice-captain in January. But the potential value of keeping him until the end of the season was always considered much higher.

If victory felt big when Liverpool's team bus drove away from the Gtech Community Stadium, the value was soon magnified considerably. The squad were sat on a plane awaiting take-off at Luton Airport that evening when the final whistle sounded at the Emirates. Arsenal 2 Aston Villa 2. Mikel Arteta's Arsenal had thrown away a 2–0 lead inside the final half hour. Some Liverpool players and staff had watched the closing stages unfold on their mobile phones as Kai Havertz had a late goal disallowed for handball.

Slot's side had re-established their grip on the title race as they boasted a six-point lead with a game in hand.

The return to action of Ibrahima Konaté in January strengthened Liverpool's backline. The France international presented the club's physios and medical staff with a box of cookies to thank them for helping him get back ahead of schedule after five weeks out with a knee injury.

Initially, the £36 million signing from RB Leipzig played with the aid of painkillers. 'Everyone wants to fight for this club and the fans,' he told reporters. 'At the end, if we reach something nice we will be happy because we have done the sacrifice.'

Konaté's contract situation was becoming a topic of debate as he approached the final 12 months of his existing deal. Hughes had opened talks with his agent over an extension in the autumn, but there was little sign of a compromise being reached. The defender was angered by erroneous media reports – from suggestions that he was on the brink of signing a new contract in November to talk about his high wage demands and that he was planning to leave as a free agent in 2026.

'I just want to say one thing: everything you saw on social media is completely fake,' he said. 'I didn't even ask for something from the club. They made me an offer, and I replied to them with something, that is it. The rest, that I want to wait until the end [of my contract], all of it is completely fake. In November [it was claimed] I was very close to signing the deal. It was not true and that is why I was a little bit mad. I knew at one moment people would think I didn't want to sign the contract, but I was never close to signing it. We'll see what will happen.'

Konaté was back to his best and playing pain-free by the time Liverpool followed up an emphatic 4–1 win over lowly Ipswich Town at Anfield with a 2–0 triumph at in-form Bournemouth.

A smile creeping across his face, Slot delivered a balanced assessment of a hard-fought victory at the Vitality Stadium. He praised Andoni Iraola's side for giving the Premier League leaders one of their sternest tests of the campaign and acknowledging that good fortune had played a part in the outcome. 'Having Mohamed Salah definitely helps in a game like this,' he said.

Salah kept his nerve to score from the spot following a long wait for the VAR check, which confirmed that Gakpo was both onside and had his heels clipped by Lewis Cook when he burst through. Liverpool lived dangerously in the second half before Salah eased anxiety levels with a sublime curling finish into the far corner of the net.

It meant the Egyptian attacker had broken the 20-goal barrier in the top-flight for the fifth time in eight seasons at Liverpool (his lowest league tally had been 18 in 2023/24).

Having been given two days off, the squad travelled from the south coast up to London for a team-bonding night out organised by Van Dijk. They dined on black cod, sushi platters and Wagyu beef in Japanese-Peruvian restaurant Pirana in the heart of affluent

Mayfair. It was a rare chance to relax and socialise together given the crowded nature of the schedule.

'Smashed it,' declared Jurgen Klopp as he walked out of his final pre-match press conference at the AXA Training Centre in May 2024.

There was a last-day-of-school feeling as the outgoing Liverpool manager got plenty off his chest. Klopp argued that the excessive demands placed on players was the reason why English clubs had fallen short in Europe that season. 'The Premier League is the best league in the world. It is not over-rated, the players are over-worked,' he said.

Klopp described Liverpool being asked to play four away games in the space of 10 days as 'a crime … absolutely insane … I was waiting for Amnesty International to go to them!'

Rounding on UK broadcaster TNT Sports, who had given Liverpool the dreaded 12.30 p.m. kick-off slot on a Saturday six times in 2023/24, the German coach vowed never to watch the channel again and asked its executives to remove him from their list of subscribers.

Klopp was demob happy but it was in keeping with his out-spoken approach on a range of issues throughout his reign. In stark contrast, Arne Slot sought to avoid making headlines as he didn't see the point in publicly bemoaning the cards Liverpool had been dealt.

The Premier League's decision to bring forward the trip to Aston Villa due to the fixture clash with the Carabao Cup final at Wembley was far from ideal. It meant that Liverpool faced five league matches in the space of a potentially season-defining 15 days in February. They would then play just one league game in the whole of March.

Slot took it on the chin. It was in keeping with his laidback, composed demeanour on the touchline, but when the first game of that gruelling run ended in controversial fashion, the red mist descended.

James Tarkowski's volley eight minutes into stoppage time salvaged a point for Everton as the final Merseyside derby to take place at Goodison Park ended 2–2.

Slot was convinced that Konaté had been impeded by Beto in the build-up, but to his dismay the goal stood after a lengthy VAR check for both offside and a possible foul. The gleeful chant of 'We won the league at Goodison Park' from the away end proved premature.

Abdoulaye Doucoure's goading of the Liverpool supporters in the Bullens Road Stand after the final whistle sparked more chaotic scenes. Curtis Jones raced to confront him and both sets of players waded in as police and stewards tried to restore some order amid the din.

Having dismissed Doucoure and Jones for second yellow cards, referee Michael Oliver then also sent off both Slot and his assistant Sipke Hulshoff for angrily confronting him on the field to continue their protests over the equaliser.

'It's not easy to accept,' said Van Dijk, who had acted as a peacemaker. 'We all know this is their cup final. You saw how they celebrated the goal. Doucoure wanted to provoke our fans. Curtis didn't think that was the right thing to do. There was a little tussle. I don't think the referee had the game under control. I said that to him. It's a fact.'

Slot didn't conduct any media duties post-match but Van Dijk, Robertson and Mac Allister all fronted up. Calm and measured, staff regarded it as a real show of leadership as they took the sting out of a difficult situation.

As well as the challenge from Beto on Konaté, Slot was furious over the amount of stoppage time added, and Oliver's decision not to penalise a blatant trip on Salah by Charly Alcaraz shortly before

Tarkowski scored. Given Everton's physical approach, the Dutchman was baffled that the stats showed that 20 of the 29 fouls given in the game had been committed by his team.

'There were a lot of things that were hard to take in that added time,' Slot told *The Athletic* when we sat down at Kirkby in May. 'I am usually quite calm. But the whole situation meant it was not a place to be calm in. Their fans were very loud with it being the last derby at their stadium.

'Many things happened that were not okay. But we're all human beings, we all make mistakes. We're talking about the foul on Mo, we're talking about the foul on Ibou [Konaté], we're talking about the fourth official who tells me there are only 60 seconds to play after there was an injury for them where he then gave the ball to them when we had the ball. That meant they could put another long ball in. They scored after 80 seconds. I could feel that the referee was waiting for the moment when we would kick the ball away. But after 60 seconds he should have blown the whistle.

'That was a bit too much, even for me! It felt at that moment in time like we had dropped two very important points. Looking back at it now, we have to thank Michael Oliver because that late goal meant we could win the title in our stadium [against Tottenham].'

Misconduct charges from the Football Association inevitably followed, with Slot fined £70,000 and given a two-match touchline suspension. Hulshoff got the same two-match ban with a £7,000 fine. Liverpool were fined £50,000 and Everton £65,000 for failing to ensure their players behaved in a proper manner after the final whistle.

Having apologised and admitted that 'emotions got the better of me ... I should have set a better example', Slot accepted his punishment but disputed Oliver's version of events to the independent regulatory commission.

Oliver claimed that while aggressively shaking his hand on the field, Slot had told him: 'If we don't win the league, I'll fucking blame you.' The Liverpool head coach was adamant that he had in fact said: 'If we don't win the league, I will have you to thank for that.'

Slot felt that the psychological impact of being denied victory at Goodison Park lingered. When Wolverhampton Wanderers came to Anfield four days later, Liverpool were cruising at 2–0 up before losing their way alarmingly.

After Matheus Cunha halved the deficit midway through the second half, there was a collective bout of the jitters both on the field and in the stands. But for Alisson's outstanding save from Marshall Munetsi, Vitor Pereira's side would have left with a share of the spoils.

It was the first time since Opta records began in 2003/04 that Liverpool had played an entire half of league football at Anfield without registering a single attempt on goal. Wolves had 10 shots to zero after the break as the hosts made a catalogue of errors.

'Conceding in the last minute against Everton was in our heads a bit,' said Slot. 'When the boys came in, I felt that they were a bit down. They weren't so happy. I said to them this win was maybe even a bigger accomplishment than outplaying Tottenham here 4–0. In a season, if you want to achieve something, good football is the basis of success. But if you don't have the mentality to win difficult games, you will never achieve something.'

During the closing stages, Andy Robertson had gestured to the Kop to calm down after they had voiced their irritation at him for playing a backpass to Alisson. The atmosphere was anxiety-laden as Liverpool grimly held on to move seven points clear of Arsenal.

The sense of longing for title glory at Anfield was palpable. Supporters had been hurt by previous agonising near misses, as well as not being able to celebrate properly in 2020 due to the pandemic. Slot made the point that five years earlier Klopp's side had been so far ahead that dealing with pressure never really came into it.

Both in the dressing room and in his message to fans, Van Dijk urged everyone involved to relax and embrace the opportunity.

'We are all human beings and I totally understand anxiety or nervousness can kick in but we have to just keep going,' the Liverpool captain told reporters. 'We need the fans in the best shape of their lives and they need us to be in the best shape of our lives as well. Hopefully by the end of the season we can all enjoy it even more.

'We just have to buckle up, enjoy the ride. There will be a lot of twists and turns. If you're not ready for it – and we have been there already – it will be a difficult couple of months for you, but I feel like we as a team are ready for it and we will give it everything we've got.'

However, the next test in that pivotal five-game run brought more recriminations at Villa Park. Having equalised through Alexander-Arnold's deflected strike, Liverpool were on top at 2–2 when substitute Conor Bradley sent Dominik Szoboszlai scampering through on goal. As goalkeeper Emiliano Martinez came out to meet him, the Hungary midfielder unselfishly squared to Núñez, who somehow conspired to fire over the bar from six yards out with the net gaping.

A disbelieving Slot had his hands on his head on the touchline before asking the fourth official: 'Not offside?' No, there was nothing to spare Núñez's blushes. Data firm Opta gave the chance an xG (expected goals) value of 0.75.

Núñez cut a lonely figure at the end as he walked off the pitch with his head bowed. He hadn't scored in eight appearances since that match-winning late double at Brentford. Rather than leaping to his defence in the face of stinging criticism, Slot gave a withering assessment of Núñez's performance.

'I can accept every miss,' Slot told reporters the following day. 'What was a bit harder for me to accept was his behaviour after that chance – and by behaviour I mean I think it got too much in his head – where he wasn't the usual Darwin that works his ass off and makes sure he helps the team.

'It is not about the chance for me, it's more about the 20 minutes afterwards I want to talk to him about. The most important message is you can miss a chance but you can't miss out on work-rate. It's part of your life as a No. 9 that you sometimes miss when people expect you to score. It is not part of your job as a No. 9 to then slow down in work-rate.'

It was the only time Slot publicly criticised a player all season – a sign of his growing frustration with the misfiring South American. The stats backed Slot up. Núñez only had 10 touches during his 24 minutes on the field against Villa, completed just two passes and won just one of the five duels he contested. Slot had also been riled by a perceived lack of effort after bringing Núñez on in the previous game at home to Wolves. His days at the club were numbered.

The Anfield hierarchy felt that the 2–2 draw with Villa had effectively guaranteed Champions League qualification with a third of the campaign remaining.

The importance of retaining their place among Europe's elite was huge given that Liverpool's self-sustaining business model relied on maximising revenues with all income then reinvested.

It was only February but Slot had already achieved the main target set by the owners the previous summer. The Dutchman wasn't in the mood to celebrate. There was silverware to be won and next up was a showdown with Manchester City at the Etihad – a venue where Liverpool hadn't won in the league for nearly a decade.

9

ENGINE ROOM

'We have really good midfielders who came to the club around the same time as me. We are complementing each other really well and we are so happy to play with each other.'

Alexis Mac Allister

The industrial city of Szekesfehervar is just over an hour's drive south-west of the Hungarian capital Budapest.

Situated down a quiet residential street on the outskirts, there's a talent factory. Zsolt Szoboszlai is waiting at the entrance with a firm handshake before offering a guided tour.

With two indoor seven-a-side pitches and a small gym, facilities inside the Fonix Gold academy are modest. But the cabinets packed full of trophies and the walls adorned with framed photographs of celebrated triumphs provide proof of an impressive track record in developing footballers.

Their most famous graduate is Zsolt's son, Dominik. This is where the Liverpool midfielder spent much of his childhood. Fonix Gold was co-founded by Zsolt in 2007 when Dominik was seven years old. From an initial intake of 20, by 2024 it had expanded to 250 youngsters, aged five to 19, some travelling from up to 100 miles away to attend training sessions.

Dominik had initially started off in the youth ranks at local top-flight club Fehervar FC (then known as Videoton due to a sponsorship deal), but Zsolt took the bold decision to take him out and launch his own academy. He had played professionally in Hungary and in neighbouring Austria before turning his attention to coaching after suffering a serious Achilles injury.

'I felt that youth football needed some different ideas,' Zsolt told *The Athletic*. 'We placed a big emphasis on technical ability. The more technically skilled a player is, the more able they are to solve problems during a match.

'As soon as Dominik started walking, he had a ball at his feet. From the age of three, I was giving him some small practice drills to do. With my background, it was natural that I wanted to pass on some of my football knowledge. The main thing was to learn everything about the game. The aim wasn't to become a professional footballer, it was to be as good as you can.'

Those drills at home included arranging a collection of water bottles across the living room floor for Dominik to slalom his way through. If one was knocked over, he would have to start all over again. If Zsolt was feeling generous he would fill them with water to make it easier.

There was a competitive edge to everything they did – from who could get dressed first in the morning to racing each other to the front door when the doorbell rang.

In small-sided training games at the academy, Zsolt gave youngsters on the same team matching coloured headbands rather than bibs to wear as he believed it encouraged them to look up in order to pick the right pass to a team-mate. They also had a golf ball in each hand to prevent them from pulling an opponent's shirt, designed to teach players to use their body to get in front of an opponent.

Fonix Gold's blossoming reputation led to invitations to prestigious European youth tournaments involving clubs such as Austria's Red Bull Salzburg and Germany's Bayern Munich. Zsolt points to a framed collage of photos from when they upset the odds to lift the 2011 Cordial Cup. Dominik, then 10, stands proudly in the front row with his winner's medal draped around his neck.

'Dominik was the driving force of the team,' Zsolt says. 'He was always playing with older kids. He was born in 2000 but always played with those kids born in '98 and '99. He played all over the pitch but was always a midfielder.'

Offers from clubs across Europe soon followed. He spent time at Atalanta in Italy and ADO Den Haag in the Netherlands before accepting the opportunity to join Salzburg when he turned 16. His outstanding form for their reserve team FC Liefering led to a Salzburg first-team debut when he was 17.

When Dominik wanted a quote from former Liverpool captain Steven Gerrard as a tattoo, Zsolt told him he could get it done on one condition – he had to finish top of all the fitness testing in pre-season. Dominik duly delivered and got 'God gives you talent but if you don't work and sacrifice a lot it will mean nothing' inked in Hungarian on his left arm.

'Even today, those records at Salzburg are still held by Dominik from when he was 17,' Zsolt states proudly. 'When he wanted to buy his own car, I said, "Yes, if Salzburg qualify for the Champions League and you have something to do with them getting there." They played Maccabi Tel Aviv [in the final qualifying round in September 2020] and he scored in both legs so he was able to get the car.'

Zsolt believes his son's development benefited from having relatively small feet [UK size seven], but he dismissed reports he had put him in boots that were too small in an attempt to try to stop his feet from growing.

'Oh yeah, we cut back his toes!' he says laughing. 'No, there is only one rule we have with the kids when it comes to boots: you don't buy a bigger boot than you need. If the boot is too large your foot will slip and slide, and your ankles will come up at the side.

Having small feet helped Dominik as you can control [the ball] better and it's easier to learn the finer touches.'

Having been part of four league title wins in Austria, more success followed after Szoboszlai moved to Bundesliga outfit RB Leipzig in 2021 with back-to-back German Cup triumphs. At the age of 22 he was appointed captain of Hungary following a players' vote, and in July 2023 became the most expensive Hungarian footballer in history when Liverpool triggered his £60 million release clause. It was a big commitment financially with most of the fee having to be paid up-front.

Good fortune played a part. Liverpool had initially pursued Mason Mount, who only had one year remaining on his contract at Chelsea. But Mount preferred a move to Manchester United and Liverpool also felt he was overpriced at £55 million. After turning their attention to Szoboszlai instead, they had no regrets.

'Leadership has always been part of his personality,' his father adds. 'Some consider it strange, as I was quite strict with him, but he's also a real personality and that helped make him the man he is. The ability to deal with pressure is one of the reasons why he became captain. This is how he grew up – always under some kind of pressure, but in a positive sense. He's built up in stages, from Salzburg to Leipzig to Liverpool. He was always motivated. The harder you work, the more chance you have of achieving something.'

When the final whistle sounded at the Etihad Stadium on 23 February 2025, an exhausted Szoboszlai dropped to the turf and lay motionless on his chest. He had run himself into the ground.

It was the abiding image from Liverpool's first away league win over Manchester City since November 2015. With Arsenal having lost to West Ham United 24 hours earlier, Arne Slot's side had moved a commanding 11 points clear at the Premier League summit.

The travelling Kop were sufficiently emboldened to deliver the first booming rendition of '*We're gonna win the league*'. There was also a gleeful chant of '*Hand it over Manchester*' following the 2–0 victory.

By the time Szoboszlai climbed back to his feet, he was greeted by the outstretched hand of City manager Pep Guardiola, who wanted to show his appreciation for what he had witnessed.

'Dom is so important,' fellow Liverpool midfielder Alexis Mac Allister told reporters post-match. 'You could see physically that he is really good. He can score, he can assist and he is doing really well. We have really good midfielders who came to the club around the same time as me. We are complementing each other really well and we are so happy to play with each other.'

Slot had kept a settled midfield all season. With Ryan Gravenberch operating in the holding role, the two other spots had been shared between Mac Allister, Szoboszlai and Curtis Jones. No other Liverpool midfielder started a top-flight match until after the title had been won.

At the Etihad, Slot sprung a tactical surprise by starting without a recognised striker and playing Szoboszlai and Jones as two No. 10s, with Mac Allister and Gravenberch offering protection behind them. With Cody Gakpo and Diogo Jota not fully fit, Slot decided that an extra midfielder would benefit Liverpool more out of possession than putting his faith in Darwin Núñez to lead the line. It worked perfectly.

The opening goal was particularly satisfying for Slot as it came from a set-piece routine which first-team individual development coach Aaron Briggs had worked on with the players during training at Kirkby 24 hours earlier. Mac Allister's corner was delivered low to the near post where Szoboszlai swept it into the path of Mohamed Salah, whose first-time strike from close to the penalty spot was deflected past City keeper Ederson.

Salah returned the compliment before the break as he raced onto Alexander-Arnold's lofted pass and picked out Szoboszlai, who drilled the ball into the bottom corner. Having established a position of control, Liverpool sat back in the second half and defended in numbers to protect their lead. The fact that Alisson only had one serious save to make was testament to the visitors' organisation, concentration and endurance. By the end they had enjoyed just 34 per cent possession – their lowest amount in a league win since Opta's records began in 2003.

Slot had warned his players they would need to 'suffer' to beat City and Szoboszlai epitomised that selfless team ethic as he repeatedly tracked back to break up attacks. Whereas in his first season at Anfield his influence had waned after such a bright start, this time he was getting stronger.

'Dom has grown into such a key player for us,' left-back Andy Robertson told reporters. 'His quality is one thing, but his energy is second to none. He's played in different positions and he takes it on. He knows what he needs to do for the team. Defensively, we did so well as a team. The wingers put in such a shift, helping me and Trent out at times when we needed them. Curtis and Dom at the top end of the pitch pressed so well. We limited a good team to very few chances.'

Szoboszlai's playful exchange with Salah in front of the TV cameras post-match at the Etihad illustrated their close bond. 'Finally, Mo could find me! It doesn't happen all the time,' the Hungarian smiled when asked about his sixth goal of the season. 'He's still a kid,' was Salah's swift riposte.

Their friendship had developed with the pair regularly meeting up in their spare time for food and to play backgammon, their favourite board game. Aspiring to the kind of lofty status in world football Salah occupies, Szoboszlai knew he could learn a lot from the Egyptian's mentality and attention to detail.

After the victory over Man City, Slot's phone buzzed with a congratulatory message from Jurgen Klopp. The duo regularly exchanged messages over the course of the season. Slot made it clear to Klopp that he had an open invitation to attend matches, but the German coach didn't want to create any distractions and decided not to return to Merseyside until after the title race had been settled. It wouldn't be long before he could start making travel plans.

'Everybody felt in that game at Man City that if we could bring that win over the line then we would be getting very, very close,' Slot told me in May.

'The boys fought so hard to get that result. Mo was almost playing as a full-back in the second half! That tells you how hard we had to work and it also tell you how good City still are. If you can play against us and still have so much ball possession then you are a very good team. How tired Dominik was at the end – that tells you everything. Partly from running but also mentally because if you are under so much pressure with attack after attack, it drains you mentally as well.'

As the Liverpool players returned to the away dressing room at the Etihad, Ballon d'Or winner Rodri was waiting by the door to congratulate each of them. It was a classy touch from the Spanish midfielder, who was recovering from an anterior cruciate ligament injury. Those present regarded it as an acknowledgement from City that they were handing the league title over after four years of domestic dominance.

Friendly conversations followed between international teammates such as Salah and Omar Marmoush, and Van Dijk and Nathan Ake. Salah also had a lengthy chat with Guardiola. It was all very cordial – the spikiness of the rivalry from previous years just wasn't there with Liverpool so far in front.

* * *

When Liverpool discovered that Alexis Mac Allister had a release clause of £35 million in his contract at Brighton, they could hardly believe their good fortune.

As the club embarked on rebuilding their midfield after a disappointing 2022/23 season, the Argentina international was their top target.

He was a World Cup winner and at the age of 24 had already proved that he could handle the demands of the Premier League. He had been named Brighton's player of the year after helping them achieve European qualification for the first time in their history. He was also durable, having only missed four league matches due to illness and injury in three and a half years on the south coast.

Senior recruitment figures at Liverpool were convinced that he was worth at least double and possibly even treble what they paid to secure his services. The scouting reports which had been compiled over the course of 18 months praised his consistency, versatility, athleticism, composure under pressure and game intelligence. The data provided by Liverpool's director of research Will Spearman marked him out as 'the complete midfielder' with no obvious weakness.

Mac Allister was also wanted by Manchester United but the chance to play for Klopp heavily influenced his decision. Liverpool feared that Real Madrid would try to hijack the deal so moved quickly to get it done in early June 2023 as he penned a five-year contract.

'It's a dream come true,' said Mac Allister, who requested the No. 10 shirt which had been vacant since Sadio Mané's move to Bayern Munich a year earlier. 'It's amazing to be here and I can't wait to get started. Since I won the World Cup I said that I want to win more trophies and I think that this club will help me to do that.'

Born in the city of Santa Rosa in Argentina's La Pampa province, Mac Allister had a ball at his feet from the moment he could walk. His father Carlos was a tough-tackling left-back who played for Argentinos Juniors, Boca Juniors and Argentina. His uncle Patricio was a striker who also represented Argentinos Juniors.

Alexis, like his two older brothers Francis and Kevin, dreamed of following in their footsteps. Their dad used to tell them stories around the dinner table about playing alongside his friend Diego Maradona.

By the age of five, Alexis was training twice a week on the small pitches at Club Social Parque, the academy in a working-class district of Buenos Aires. As a Boca fan, he grew up idolising Juan Román Riquelme. 'The boys lived in that club,' Carlos told *The Athletic*. 'Because first one would train, then the other, then the other, and you take them all and they all stay there. I think the three of them were born to be footballers because they grew up with everything that had happened to my brother and me as foot-ballers.'

After a short spell at Club JJ Batista, Alexis and his brothers joined the youth ranks at second-tier outfit Argentinos Juniors. Based in a middle-class neighbourhood of Buenos Aires, the club had produced Maradona, Riquelme and Fernando Redondo.

In October 2016, aged 17, Alexis was handed his senior debut against Central Cordoba and went on to help them win promotion back to the top flight. The following season, all three brothers were involved in the same league game against San Lorenzo – a source of great pride for the family. 'It was emotional and we look back on that day with a lot of fondness,' Alexis said. 'We are so grateful because the club made us grow so much as people and players. It has a special place in our hearts.'

Among the collection of tattoos on his left arm are the names of his parents and brothers. There are also significant dates, such as when he made his debut for Argentinos Juniors and when they won promotion. The roulette wheel around his elbow features the shirt numbers worn by him and his brothers. There's also the face of Jesus Christ and an image of himself as a child wearing a No. 10 shirt and walking up some steps with a ball in his hand.

Alexis' performances for Argentinos attracted the attention of Brighton's South American scouts. The Premier League club's data-led approach had flagged him as a gifted youngster to monitor closely.

In January 2019, Brighton bought him for £8 million before sanctioning loan spells at Argentinos and then Boca as he waited to get a work permit to play in England. He belatedly arrived in January 2020, but within two months the global pandemic hit and the season was halted. 'I lost momentum and stagnated as a player,' he admitted.

After a difficult start, he adjusted to the pace and physicality of the Premier League. He flourished under the guidance of Brighton managers Graham Potter and then Roberto De Zerbi. Having forced his way into Argentina's 2022 World Cup squad, he proved to be one of the stars of the tournament in Qatar as he linked up expertly with Lionel Messi. When Gonzalo Montiel scored the winning penalty against France in the final, Mac Allister burst into tears before blowing kisses to his family in the stands.

Argentina were world champions for the first time since 1986 and the gravity of what he had achieved hit home during the trophy parade around Buenos Aires. 'I was overwhelmed with emotion,' Mac Allister said. 'It was mad – five million people on the streets celebrating with us.'

Recruitment staff at Liverpool talk about players who 'take the stairs rather than the elevator' to the top. Mohamed Salah and Virgil van Dijk fit into that category, having overcome adversity and setbacks earlier in their careers.

The Anfield hierarchy saw the same steely resilience in Mac Allister. He had been overlooked by his country until the Under-20s age group and hadn't even completed 90 minutes for Lionel Scaloni's senior team prior to the World Cup in Qatar.

Affectionately nicknamed 'Macca' by his team-mates, Liverpool supporters quickly took him to their hearts. 'Super-smart tactically, super influential, he's fulfilled all our expectations. How can you not love a boy like him? He is incredible,' raved Klopp.

Having been signed predominantly to play as a No. 8, he found himself initially playing a lot of games deeper in the holding midfield role. After selling Fabinho, who had been a vital cog in Klopp's title-winning team of 2019/20, Liverpool missed out to Chelsea on the signings of Moises Caicedo and Romeo Lavia, while Wataru Endo needed time to adapt to what Klopp demanded from him after arriving from Stuttgart. When Klopp started to put his faith in Endo in the second half of 2023/24, Mac Allister was given more freedom to get forward.

'The way Macca protects the ball, I've never seen before,' Curtis Jones said. 'He does this thing where he receives the ball, sticks his bum out and you can't take the ball from him.'

Under Slot, Mac Allister went to the next level. He relished the more patient approach and the usual 4-2-3-1 formation suited him perfectly, with Gravenberch alongside and either Szoboszlai or Jones operating ahead of him.

'When I think about Macca, I cannot come up with a poor performance from him all season,' Slot said. 'He is so involved in every game we play. He is so important for us defensively as well. There's a reason why he is a World Cup winner because he shows up when really you need him in terms of his mentality.'

*   *   *

Mike Kolf takes a seat in his office at the Damsko Football Academy, a 15-minute taxi ride from Amsterdam's Central Station. One of Ryan Gravenberch's Ajax shirts is in a frame on the wall outside the door.

Kolf divides his time between here and nearby amateur club AVV Zeeburgia, where he has been head of youth since 1998. Zeeburgia have 850 youngsters on their books aged between four and 23. Remarkably, since the late 1990s, around 650 of their players have gone on to join professional clubs. Gravenberch, who grew up in the nearby leafy neighbourhood of Watergraafsmeer, is one of their great success stories.

'I've known Ryan since the day he was born,' says Kolf, who played amateur football in the Dutch capital with Gravenberch's dad, Ryan senior. The pair remain close friends.

'Ryan was five when he started off with us, but he always seemed older. He got bigger, stronger and better. He stayed here until he joined Ajax at the age of eight. Growing up around here in Amsterdam East was good for Ryan. It's an area with many open spaces to play so boys don't sit at home on their PlayStations.

'These days there are so many distractions for kids. Some say, "Yeah, I want to become a footballer", but then go off doing other things. Ryan was always in love with football. If after a game you said to him, "Do you want to go and play for that team?" he would always play again. When he was seven, he was playing with the nine-year-olds. I think he slept with a football. He was always smart, always laidback like his dad.'

At Ajax, he progressed so quickly that at times he came across as complacent. One of his youth coaches, Dennis de Haan, tells a story about giving a team talk, where after explaining how they would set up tactically, he asked if anyone had any questions. 'What time does the canteen open because I want to eat a grilled cheese sandwich?' asked Gravenberch.

He became the youngest Ajax player in history to grace the Eredivisie when he made his debut against PSV Eindhoven in September 2018 at 16 years and 130 days – beating a record previously held by the great Clarence Seedorf.

His upward trajectory stalled after signing for Bayern Munich as he started just three Bundesliga matches during the turbulent 2022/23 season under Julian Nagelsmann and his successor Thomas Tuchel. Gravenberch's stay in Bavaria proved to be brief as Liverpool bought him for £34 million.

It went right down to transfer deadline day, 1 September 2023. Bayern had initially been adamant he wasn't for sale but ultimately decided to cash in rather than keep an unhappy player. Liverpool were delighted, having missed out to the Bundesliga giants when he left Ajax a year earlier.

Slot's decision to play him at the base of Liverpool's midfield transformed Gravenberch from a decent squad player into a leading light. He went from clocking up 1,837 minutes for the club in all competitions under Klopp in 2023/24 to 4,207 minutes in 2024/25. Missing out on Real Sociedad's midfielder Martin Zubimendi had proved to be a blessing in disguise for Liverpool.

'It didn't surprise me because when Frenkie de Jong left Ajax [in 2019], Ryan played as the No. 6,' Kolf told *The Athletic*.

'Slot knew he could do it. Ryan makes it look so easy at times. It's his reading of the game that's so impressive and the way he creates space. Just watch how he lets the ball roll across his body, how he gets out of tight areas because he knows where the space is. He inspires the kids here so much. I always talk about Ryan to them.

'Our boy made it to Ajax, Bayern Munich and now Liverpool. Everyone is so proud of the level he has reached and he's still so young. He could play for Holland for the next 10 years and become one of the greatest players this country has ever produced.'

Gravenberch made more high turnovers (44) and won possession back from opponents (193) more times than any other Liverpool player in the Premier League in 2024/25. His tally of 60 interceptions was only beaten in the top-flight by West Ham's Aaron Wan-Bissaka (66) and Fulham's Antonee Robinson (62).

The Netherlands international handled his vastly increased workload under Slot by taking advice from captain Virgil van Dijk about getting more sleep as well as using the ice baths and the sauna to aid recovery between games. He felt that opponents increasingly targeted him as the season went on in a bid to reduce his impact, but he knew this created more space for his teammates.

The midfield rebuild was such a key element of Klopp's legacy. Initially, Liverpool had pursued Borussia Dortmund's Jude Bellingham but they dropped out of the race when the scale of what they needed to do in the market became clear. Bellingham subsequently joined Real Madrid in a £115 million deal.

Gravenberch, Mac Allister, Szoboszlai and Wataru Endo were signed in the summer of 2023 for a combined total of £145 million, with £52 million recouped from the sales of Jordan Henderson and Fabinho, while James Milner, Naby Keita and Alex Oxlade-Chamberlain left as free agents.

'It's not only the midfielders we brought in but also the development of someone like Curtis,' says Klopp's former assistant manager Pep Lijnders.

'It was the natural evolution of the squad. Some key players left who were so important and won many prizes for us. How to replace Fabinho? How to replace Hendo? How to replace Millie?

'What a signing Macca has been. He's the motor in the middle. Dom is so athletic and so consistent. Very few No. 6s in world football are able to bring the ball out from the back like Ryan. We were always careful with the signings we made.

'We knew Ryan had massive talent and big potential, but the way he played that No. 6 position was an eye-opener for everyone. It gave the team offensively a new weapon, a new strength. I'm so happy for Ryan because he's such a great boy. I still remember when we played Ajax and we saw him for the first time – how he rolled with the ball, his first touch was like glue. You know a yo-yo? It was like he had the ball on a short piece of string. That's how he treated it.'

Three days after beating Manchester City at the Etihad, Liverpool swept Newcastle United aside 2–0 at Anfield. Once again their midfield unit shone brightly. After Szoboszlai scored the opener, Mac Allister settled the contest in style. Winning the ball back inside his own half, the Argentine burst forward, exchanged passes with Salah, and arrowed a shot beyond Nick Pope into the top corner.

With second-placed Arsenal held to a goalless draw at Nottingham Forest the same night, Liverpool's advantage at the top of the Premier League was extended to 13 points. In the space of 15 days in February, a crunch five-game spell saw the leaders collect a healthy return of 11 points out of a possible 15. The irritation and unease generated by the draws at Everton and Aston Villa had abated. No harm had been done.

Slot's focus immediately shifted to the Champions League and the first leg of their last-16 tie away to Paris Saint-Germain. After a slow start to the league phase with defeats to Arsenal, Atlético Madrid and Bayern Munich, Luis Enrique's side had clicked into gear. They had fought back from 2–0 down at home to Manchester City to win 4–2 before demolishing Stuttgart 4–1.

After the extravagance of assembling a star-studded frontline of Lionel Messi, Neymar and Kylian Mbappé had failed to secure the European glory their Qatari owners craved, PSG had moved in a different direction with a younger, hungrier, more cohesive unit under Enrique.

During the January transfer window they had bolstered their ranks with the signing of winger Khvicha Kvaratskhelia from Italian club Napoli for £59 million. Liverpool had long since retained an interest in the gifted Georgia international, but the timing wasn't right for them to rival PSG for his signature as they already had Luis Díaz and Cody Gakpo to pick from on the left flank.

Slot regarded PSG as the toughest possible test, with the underlying data he was presented with reinforcing that belief. Their 15th-placed finish in the league phase belied their true status. For defender Ibrahima Konaté, it was a homecoming and when Liverpool arrived in the French capital, he arranged for some cakes to be delivered to the team hotel from his favourite Parisian patisserie.

Under the lights at Parc des Princes, Liverpool were outplayed as the scintillating attacking trio of Kvaratskhelia, Ousmane Dembélé and Bradley Barcola caused them a stack of problems. The hosts' relentless pressing rattled Slot's side and repeatedly forced them to go long and give the ball away cheaply.

PSG had 70 per cent possession, 27 shots and created an xG (expected goals) of 1.8, but they couldn't find a way past an inspired Alisson, whose total of nine saves was the most on record by a Liverpool goalkeeper in a Champions League game. 'The performance of my life,' was how the Brazilian described it.

Liverpool pulled off the ultimate smash-and-grab raid in the French capital when they scored with their solitary attempt on target through substitute Harvey Elliott, three minutes from time.

Just 47 seconds separated Elliott replacing Mohamed Salah and him coolly slotting past Gianluigi Donnarumma with his first touch after Núñez teed him up. There was a joyous knee slide before he was mobbed by his team-mates. PSG's 22-game unbeaten run was over.

As Elliott joined his fellow substitutes for the post-match warm-down, he was serenaded by the jubilant 2,000 travelling fans who had been kept behind by the French police and stewards in an otherwise deserted stadium. Having been consigned to the periphery for so much of Slot's first season, he suddenly found himself in the spotlight and deservedly so.

Playing for Liverpool meant everything to the England Under-21s international. He had arrived from Fulham at the age of 16 in the summer of 2019, with a tribunal setting a compensation fee of up to £4.3 million after the two clubs couldn't agree on a figure.

His dad Scott, a lifelong Liverpool supporter, had taken him to Anfield for the first time when he was just three years old to watch a Champions League qualifier against Maccabi Haifa in 2006. He grew up idolising Liverpool legend Steven Gerrard.

At the age of 15 years and 174 days, Elliott became Fulham's youngest-ever first team player and the youngest in the history of the League Cup when he came on against Millwall. Earlier in the day he had sat an exam at Coombe Boys' School, and on his return to the classroom the following morning he was given a standing ovation by his fellow pupils. 'Fearless' was the assessment of Fulham academy director Huw Jennings, who spoke about his 'Messi-like style'.

Real Madrid, PSG, Manchester City, Chelsea and Arsenal all wanted to sign him in 2019, but once Liverpool made their move while he was on a family holiday in Portugal following his GCSE exams, his mind was made up. Madrid's charm offensive had included giving him a tour of the Bernabeu and offering to arrange a meeting with their long-serving captain Sergio Ramos.

'No, it's okay thanks,' Elliott replied. 'I don't like him after what he did to Mo Salah.' It was a reference to Ramos dumping Salah on his shoulder and forcing him out of the 2018 Champions League final in Kyiv which Elliott had attended as a Liverpool fan.

The youngster quickly endeared himself to Klopp: 'An exceptional talent and a nice kid as well. It's easy to be convinced about Harvey when you see him in training. He could have gone pretty much anywhere but he wanted to be part of Liverpool.'

Despite spending the 2020/21 season on loan at Blackburn Rovers in the second tier of English football, and being sidelined for five months of the following season with a fractured and dislocated ankle, by the time Slot took over Elliott already had 119 senior Liverpool appearances under his belt. He was still just 21.

He started 27 matches in all competitions in Klopp's final season but under Slot that number dwindled to just six in 2024/25. A broken bone in his foot kept him out for two and a half months before Christmas, and on his return to fitness he couldn't force his way into the team.

'This is my club and I'll fight for my place,' Elliott told reporters as he dismissed speculation about his future after coming off the bench to play a part in both of Núñez's goals in January's dramatic win at Brentford.

The reality was that Slot simply preferred the greater physicality offered by Szoboszlai and Jones in an advanced midfield position. Elliott could also operate wide on the right but given Salah's durability and output, game time was always going to be sparse for him there.

In the bowels of Parc des Princes, Elliott talked about channelling his 'anger' at such a limited role. 'It's not about everyone being able to see I'm frustrated, it's about being there for the team,' he said. 'You just need little moments where confidence becomes bigger and better and hopefully more opportunities come. The manager has his decisions and his tactics and you have to respect that.'

There was also an acknowledgement that PSG would have been out of sight but for the heroics of Alisson. 'He's the best in the world,' added Elliott. 'Without him, I don't think we would be anywhere near where we are this season.'

Elliott's attitude remained impeccable but eager to play more regularly, he left to join Aston Villa at the end of the summer transfer window. Liverpool agreed to a season-long loan with an obligation for the Midlands outfit to buy him for £35 million in 2026.

Prior to the second leg against PSG, Liverpool had what should have been a straightforward league assignment at home to rock-bottom Southampton. However, a dismal first-half display ended with the visitors taking a shock lead as Will Smallbone took advantage of a defensive mix-up. No matter what the scenario, the players had become used to Slot delivering calm, articulate half-time team talks, complemented by video analysis to illustrate where they needed to improve.

This time it was different. Slot, who had been watching from the directors' box alongside assistant Sipke Hulshoff as they completed two-match touchline bans, made his way down the stairs and erupted after the dressing room door slammed shut behind him. He unleashed a furious tirade about his side's lack of energy and intensity both with and without the ball.

'He had every right to be angry,' said Van Dijk. There was a triple substitution with Mac Allister, Elliott and Robertson introduced for Szoboszlai, Jones and Tsimikas.

The response in the second half was emphatic. Liverpool turned an embarrassing 1–0 deficit into a comfortable 3–1 win thanks to Núñez's equaliser and two penalties from Salah. Staff felt that Slot's bollocking had been so effective because it was so out of character.

* * *

Having been so fortunate to emerge triumphant in Paris, luck deserted Liverpool in the return game at Anfield.

There was an unwanted piece of history as they were eliminated from Europe for the first time after winning the first leg away from home. It was also the first time the six-times winners had lost a penalty shootout in the competition, having won the finals of 1984 and 2005, as well as the 2007 semi-final against Chelsea.

It was a tale of what might have been against PSG, who went on to knock out Aston Villa and Arsenal before thrashing Inter Milan 5–0 in the final in Munich.

If only Salah had been more clinical early on before Dembélé scored against the run of play to wipe out Liverpool's narrow lead. If only Alexander-Arnold hadn't limped off with an ankle injury. If only substitute Quansah's header hadn't bounced back off the inside of the post, late in normal time. The offside flag had been wrongly raised and the goal would have stood. Ultimately, it came down to spot-kicks with Núñez and Jones both thwarted by PSG keeper Donnarumma. As PSG celebrated winning the shootout 4–1, Salah couldn't hold back the tears.

'The best game of football I was ever involved in. Incredible intensity,' was Slot's verdict. 'If you have to go out, then go out in the way we did against one of the best teams in Europe, making such a fight out of it. Every fan around the world was hoping this game would just keep on going.'

Slot refused to be downbeat. Tactically, he regarded it as up there with Liverpool's best displays of the season, given the contrast to the one-sided nature of the first leg. He tried to lift chins off the floor by reminding the players that Liverpool hadn't even been involved in the Champions League the previous season, and that two years earlier they had been humbled 6–2 on aggregate by Real Madrid in the last 16. 'We have to accept it and come back stronger next season,' he told them.

Three days later, I was sat with Curtis Jones at the AXA Training Centre. Some would have cancelled media commitments after the heartache of missing a penalty in a pivotal Champions League clash, but how he handled that setback spoke volumes about the mentality which had enabled him to succeed at his boyhood club. He had no regrets about volunteering to step up.

'I went home and slept fine,' he insisted. 'I see it as part of my journey. I'm a confident lad and I've got trust in myself. My attitude is that I want the team to rely on me. That comes with risk and the possibility of failure.

'I don't just want to be seen as a guy who coasts around in games or is happy just to be there and part of the team. I want to be seen as a lad who is a big part of things. I have to step up with that weight on my shoulders. You see all the greats around the world in sport. There are times when they succeed, times when they fail. But they are great because they do it again and again. You have got to be fine with missing. I'm fine if I go up there and I miss, but I'm not fine if I'm driving home knowing I was too scared to take a penalty.'

Fatherhood helped provide a sense of perspective. His long-term partner, Saffie, had given birth to their daughter Giselle the previous October. 'I could score a hat-trick or have a bad game, but as soon as I see her, I forget all those other things around me. It's all about spending time bonding with her,' he explained.

Jones, who grew up close to Liverpool city centre and joined the academy when he was nine, had come a long way since making his debut against Wolves in the FA Cup at the age of 17 in January 2019. Back then, he was a skinny and skilful teenage winger. Under the guidance of Klopp and then Slot, he had developed into a tactically disciplined and versatile central midfielder.

Over the course of 2024/25 he played 46 times (27 starts) in all competitions and became Liverpool's first academy graduate since Alexander-Arnold to clock up 150 appearances for the club. His pass completion rate of 93.1 per cent was the highest among all Premier League midfielders. His club form deservedly led to England recognition and by the summer he had already collected six caps.

'Where I'm from, we didn't have much, so you were always like the underdog,' he told *The Athletic*. 'We used to play out on the street or climb over the fence into my school to play on the field. You had to make the most of what you had. Being a Scouser at the academy coming through, the lads who got brought in from other clubs were always seen as the first ones who needed a chance because the club had paid money for them. Again, you're the underdog.

'I never cared about the names around me. My attitude was always: "I'll show you." It's served me well with all the stuff that's happened over the years. The injuries, being left out of squads, people saying he needs to go out on loan or leave the club. I stayed here and stuck to my plan: "I'm going to make it here." I've come out the other side.'

The energy-sapping Champions League defeat to PSG undoubtedly contributed to Liverpool losing the Carabao Cup final to Newcastle United. It was a deflating week with the first back-to-back setbacks of the Slot era as talk of a possible treble or double was silenced.

The Dutchman had given his players the Thursday off in an attempt to inject some freshness. Caoimhin Kelleher, Andy Robertson, Diogo Jota and Conor Bradley were among those who joined club staff for a trip to Cheltenham Racecourse. Van Dijk stayed closer to home as he watched his daughter Jadi perform in the school play *Fantastic Mr Fox* before helping with her science homework.

However, Liverpool were off the pace and a distant second best in the Wembley final on 16 March. They got bullied by Newcastle's direct approach – winning just 43 per cent of duels overall and only 32 per cent of aerial duels. Eddie Howe's game plan had been to bypass Liverpool's high press with a succession of long balls and Newcastle deservedly lifted their first domestic trophy for 70 years. Dan Burn's header was followed by Alexander Isak making it 2–0 before substitute Federico Chiesa pulled one back deep into stoppage time.

With the March international break, it was 17 days before Liverpool played again. Slot headed to Ibiza to relax. He had found the long stretch from November through to the Carabao Cup final particularly gruelling, especially with his family still living in Holland. It was the first time he had experienced such an intensive period, having been used to a winter break during his time managing in his homeland.

Van Dijk vowed to ensure that nobody felt sorry for themselves with a Premier League title still to be won. They sat 12 points clear of Arsenal with nine games remaining.

'We have to turn this around,' the captain told reporters at Wembley. 'It's how football works: in five days you lose twice and the world is sinking. Two weeks before everything was sunshine and rainbows everywhere. No-one expected us to be challenging for the Premier League. It's the most difficult prize to get. There's a lot at stake. We have to work our ass off for it.'

Slot decided to give the players some extra time off following the completion of their national team commitments. The squad didn't reconvene at Kirkby until the Saturday before the midweek Merseyside derby at Anfield. He waited until the Monday before addressing the full squad about what had gone wrong at Wembley. During a frank team meeting he told them: 'Don't ever accept being outworked by an opponent.' He described the manner of the final defeat to Newcastle as 'almost unacceptable'.

However, having used video analysis to highlight flaws in their performance, he finished with a selection of more positive clips from other matches to emphasise what he knew they were capable of.

Over time, Slot regretted not rotating his squad to a greater extent. Although the continuity provided by a settled line-up had heavily contributed to their consistency, relying so much on a small pool of talent had left some feeling fatigued.

Slot had only made three changes for the visit of Southampton between the two legs against PSG, when Enrique had rested eight of his players. Nine of Liverpool's 10 outfield players at Wembley also started both games against the French champions. It had taken its toll and the Dutchman concluded that he would need a change of approach in his second season if Liverpool were going to last the pace both domestically and in Europe.

The 246th Merseyside derby belonged to Diogo Jota. He picked the perfect night to end a 10-game goal drought. It was classic Jota as he darted away from Idrissa Gueye and James Tarkowski before hammering a shot low past goalkeeper Jordan Pickford. There was joy and relief in abundance as he jabbed a finger towards the badge on his shirt before Jones jumped on his back.

Mac Allister had been fortunate to escape serious injury after a reckless challenge from Tarkowski, who somehow escaped with a yellow card from referee Sam Barrott. 'Was I surprised? No,' Slot said bluntly.

Liverpool's 26-game unbeaten Premier League run was ended at Fulham but when Van Dijk's late header secured victory at home to West Ham they were on the brink of glory. Slot had reached 50 games in charge of Liverpool with 36 wins, more than any other manager in the club's history. The previous best was Joe Fagan and Kenny Dalglish on 29.

Plans were put in place for a possible celebration at Leicester City with LFCTV sending former players Phil Thompson and

David Thompson as part of an expanded crew. But Arsenal's win at Ipswich ensured that the champagne remained on ice after Alexander-Arnold's goal relegated the Foxes.

It was a similar story the following Wednesday evening when players and staff gathered at the AXA Training Centre to watch Arsenal play Crystal Palace on a big screen which had been set up in the sports hall. They wanted to be together in case a Palace victory handed them the title.

'Mo Salah was watching almost scared that Liverpool were going to win the league that night,' recalls one staff member present.

'Particularly those senior players who had been part of the last title-winning team in 2020, you could sense that they were desperate to win it themselves out on the field rather than getting a favour from Palace.'

Nobody was disappointed that the contest at the Emirates ended 2–2 as it meant Liverpool needed just a point to clinch the title on home turf when they faced Tottenham four days later. Tickets were changing hands for thousands of pounds on the black market with the stage set for a momentous occasion.

10

NOW YOU'RE GONNA BELIEVE US

'I feel proud and blessed. We got the job done and we truly deserve to be champions of England. The most beautiful club in the world and we deserve all of this.'

Virgil van Dijk

As Liverpool's team bus crawled along Anfield Road through a dense cloud of red smoke, thousands of supporters lined the route, lighting flares and roaring their encouragement in the spring sunshine. That was the moment when the magnitude of what his team were on the brink of achieving hit home for Arne Slot.

'Every time I think about it, it makes me feel a bit emotional,' he said.

'All our fans were passionately singing: "*Now you're gonna believe us, we're gonna win the league*". You could feel what it meant to them.

'We still needed a point to clinch it. That came with responsibility and a bit of anxiety. But when we arrived at the stadium, with the fans with us like that, everyone inside the bus felt that it would be impossible for us to lose this game of football.'

It was 27 April 2025 and the street sellers outside Anfield were doing a roaring trade selling 'Champions of England' merchandise. There was a new addition to the array of banners on the resplendent Kop which read: 'It was always Liverpool.' It was a nod to captain Virgil van Dijk's comments after he signed a new two-year contract. The Dutch defender had urged supporters to arrive dressed in red and they didn't disappoint him.

With his hands in his pockets as he stood in his technical area, Slot couldn't have looked more relaxed early on, but Tottenham briefly gave him cause for concern. James Maddison's corner was inviting and former Liverpool striker Dominic Solanke punished some slack marking as he sent a header past Alisson.

The response both in the stands and on the pitch was emphatic as the volume and tempo were cranked up. Within four minutes, Liverpool were level. The offside flag initially curtailed Luis Díaz's celebrations, but when a VAR check confirmed that the Colombian was actually onside, Anfield erupted.

Díaz was serenaded by the home fans and soon it was Alexis Mac Allister's turn to get the same treatment after he unleashed a 20-yard thunderbolt beyond Guglielmo Vicario.

The breathing space Liverpool craved arrived before the break courtesy of Cody Gakpo, who worked his way into space and produced a clinical finish into the bottom corner. Gakpo took off his shirt to show off a vest which was emblazoned with the message: 'I belong to Jesus.'

It was 11 years to the day since Steven Gerrard's cruel slip against Chelsea, which was punished by Demba Ba and effectively wrecked Liverpool's Premier League title dream under Brendan Rodgers at Anfield. This time they would not be denied.

In the second half, Mohamed Salah slammed home the fourth to move clear of former Manchester City striker Sergio Aguero into fifth place in the Premier League's all-time list of scorers on 185. The Egyptian celebrated by taking a selfie with the elated Kop behind him. Initially, it looked like he had borrowed the mobile phone from a supporter at the front, but it had actually been given to him by the club's photographer as part of their commercial partnership with Google Pixel.

'Since the beginning of the season, I've always taken a selfie [after each game] with the players who scored so for this one I said: "Okay, I have to think of something special because this picture is going to be there forever",' Salah explained to Opus Sport. 'So I worked my mind a little bit around that idea and it was fine.'

After Destiny Udogie turned the ball into his own net to make it 5–1, red balloons were unleashed from the stands and the chant of 'champions' spread around Anfield like wildfire. Shortly before the final whistle, Slot turned and blew a kiss to his wife and children in the Main Stand. Liverpool's title party – ending Manchester City's record-breaking run of four consecutive Premier League titles – was underway.

'I feel proud and blessed,' Van Dijk said. 'We got the job done and we truly deserve to be champions of England. The most beautiful club in the world and we deserve all of this. Let's let it sink in.'

Salah, like Van Dijk, had been part of Jurgen Klopp's Liverpool team which had ended the club's 30-year wait for the league title in 2019/20. But this time it was different as they shared the moment with a joyous capacity crowd.

'This is way better, 100 per cent,' Salah told Sky Sports. 'Without Sadio [Mané], Jurgen, Bobby [Firmino], with everybody … it feels more special with the fans.'

Salah recalled a conversation he had with Slot at the start of the season: 'I told him "as long as you rest me defensively, I will provide offensively". He listened a lot and you can see the numbers.'

With the official presentation still a month away, Ryan Gravenberch danced on the pitch with a cardboard cut-out of the Premier League trophy.

There was the wholesome sight of Andy Robertson and Alisson inviting over the ball boys from the club's academy, who had been grouped together just off the pitch, to join their heroes in a huddle.

Robertson had recognised 16-year-old Scottish left-back Cameron Williams, who he had previously trained alongside on international duty.

'Waking up that morning, it felt like we had a cup final,' Robertson said. 'It was the longest morning ever. The scenes coming into Anfield on the bus were the best we've ever seen. Nothing was going to stop us. After going 1–0 down, we bounced back so well. It was party time. The fans let out so much emotion. Being able to secure the title in front of our fans was the cherry on the top.

'We showed a level of consistency all season that no other team was able to match. Credit to the manager for how he implemented his tactics. Sometimes you'd be sat in meetings before games thinking: "There's no way we're getting beat today".'

Former Liverpool striker John Aldridge, an Anfield regular since the 1960s, described the atmosphere against Tottenham as among the greatest he had ever experienced.

'I was there for St Etienne [1977], Chelsea [2005] and Barcelona [2019], the iconic European nights under the lights, but that day against Spurs belongs right up there,' he said. 'From start to finish, the whole ground, not just the Kop, was absolutely bouncing. I'd never heard the entire place like that. Winning the title meant that much more because the fans hadn't been allowed in the ground in 2020. Thirty-five years is a long time to wait to celebrate something like that together. Some had never seen it happen. It meant everything.'

Similar sentiments were repeatedly relayed to Slot over the days that followed. 'That's what probably makes me the most proud,' he said. 'To hear people who have worked at the club or been a fan of this club for so many years, and with all the success this club has had, to still be able to do something that is more special to them than anything else, is probably the highest you can achieve. To do something at a club which will always be remembered, for people to say "this was probably one of the most special days I've ever been at Anfield", yeah that brings emotions even for a calm and collected guy like me.'

Scientists at the University of Liverpool revealed that fans at Anfield that day caused a series of tremors. The most significant after Mac Allister's goal registered 1.74 on the Richter scale. 'Their enthusiasm was literally powerful enough to move the earth,' said Professor Ben Edwards.

Midfielder Curtis Jones gave young supporter Harry Whitehurst a memory to cherish forever as he lifted him from the Kop and took him onto the field to join in the celebrations. Earlier in the season, the LFCTV cameras had captured some touching footage of Jones making a surprise visit to meet Whitehurst, who suffers from the rare genetic condition Williams syndrome, while he was volunteering at Homebaked community cafe close to the stadium.

A clip went viral of Darwin Núñez trying to drench Salah with what appeared to be a bottle of champagne. However, alcohol-free Nozeco was used out of respect for Liverpool's Muslim players. On his return to the home dressing room, Núñez sat puffing on a large cigar.

When the lap of honour was complete, Fenway Sports Group's CEO of football Michael Edwards and Liverpool sporting director Richard Hughes were waiting to embrace Slot and his coaching staff. Principal owner John W. Henry and FSG president Mike Gordon also offered their congratulations.

'For them to trust me to be in this position, maybe now everybody says: "That makes complete sense." But the moment they signed me, maybe not everyone was as convinced as they are now,' Slot said. 'So that tells you also what a special club this is that they don't always go for maybe the most simple or obvious choice. They make the choice that they think is best for the club.'

In his post-match press conference, Slot explained why he had felt compelled to lead a chant of Klopp's name after taking the microphone in the centre circle.

'I did it because of what he did before I even arrived here,' referencing how his predecessor had done the same for him 343 days earlier when he symbolically passed on the baton. 'I think that is something not one manager ever did before. That definitely helped me. But apart from that, he helped me even more by the team he left behind and the culture he left behind. The quality the players have was obvious for everyone, but the culture of hard work has been incredible and that is one of the reasons why we could achieve what we have achieved this season. It was a nice moment to thank him as well.'

Two hours after the game, Ibrahima Konaté re-emerged from the mouth of the tunnel and walked to the back of the first tier of the deserted Main Stand before taking a seat. He spent a few minutes in quiet contemplation. The French defender had finally landed one of football's biggest prizes. Two years earlier he had experienced defeat to Real Madrid in the Champions League final and lost the World Cup final to Argentina.

'I don't have words to describe what I felt,' Konaté said. 'I said to my brother: "I want to see how it is to sit in the stand if I watch a game." I tried to act like a fan. I just wanted to enjoy the moment on my own. We won it with 60,000 fans and us on the pitch. I just wanted to feel something different and I am very happy now. I was close to crying. It's crazy, unbelievable, and we have to really enjoy it now. I'm the first French player from Liverpool to lift it.'

Paying tribute to his manager, Konaté added: 'I saw him on the pitch and he didn't really want to take the praise. He walked behind us and it's crazy to be humble like that. Okay, we are on the pitch and we run and do everything, but he has done a lot as well for us. Thanks to him.'

Slot, who gave everyone two days off, vowed that he would enjoy 'a glass of beer or two or three' and was true to his word. The party for players, staff, family and friends took place in the Carlsberg Dugout, a plush sports bar in Anfield's Main Stand and went on until 3 a.m. Having become the first Dutch manager to win England's top-flight, Slot soaked up the occasion with his family.

The dance floor was packed for most of the night with a DJ taking requests. 'Sultans of Swing', which had been first on the dressing room Spotify list after each cherished victory, again went down a storm.

It was all very informal with no speeches. John W. Henry and his wife Linda Pizzuti made an appearance but said their goodbyes before midnight. Liverpool actor James Nelson-Joyce was also there, along with former British super-middleweight boxing champion Paul Smith, and his younger brother Liam Smith, the former world light-middleweight champion.

Some of the players, including Van Dijk in his club tracksuit, took the opportunity to go back out on to the pitch to have photographs taken in front of a deserted Kop with their loved ones.

More than three hours after the final whistle, the scenes outside the ground were remarkable. Thousands of fans who hadn't attended the game had converged on Anfield as fireworks and red flares lit up the sky.

Walton Breck Road, behind the Kop, should have long since reopened to traffic but was impassable due to the sheer number of supporters celebrating. Many clambered up railings, lamp posts or onto nearby roofs as the songs kept coming. At one stage, Andy Robertson left the club party to take a look for himself as he soaked it all in.

'Super grateful for the past,' Klopp posted on Instagram with an image of Liverpool's players and staff standing together in front of the Kop during a rendition of 'You'll Never Walk Alone' after the demolition of Tottenham. 'Super, super happy about the present, extremely positive about the future! Congratulations – YNWA. Thank you Luv.'

As a major clean-up operation got underway early on the Monday morning, Liverpool wasted no time in getting both the Champions Wall outside Anfield and the Walk of Champions inside the ground updated to reflect the fact that they had won a 20th top-flight title.

Supporters from the Irish Kop, an online forum set up by Dublin-based fan Paul Larkin in 2003, started planning a make-over themselves. They are responsible for one of Anfield's most iconic banners. Six metres wide and three metres high, it featured the faces of six cherished managers from Liverpool's illustrious history – Bill Shankly, Bob Paisley, Joe Fagan, Kenny Dalglish, Rafael Benítez and Klopp.

It was based on a painting by artist David Neve, who had been inspired by the Five Heads of Communism symbol depicting Karl Marx, Friedrich Engels, Vladimir Lenin, Joseph Stalin and Mao Zedong. The criteria was that you had to have managed Liverpool to either Premier League or Champions League glory. Klopp had been added to the initial banner after winning the latter in 2019. Now they needed to commission a new version to include Slot ready for the start of the following season and they quickly raised the €1,000 required via a crowdfunding page.

With 82 points and still four games remaining, Slot could have broken Sir Kenny Dalglish's record for the most points won by a manager in his first season at the club, set with 88 in 1985/86.

However, the Dutchman looked at the bigger picture. With the title secured and key players jaded, he prioritised giving them a rest. Slot fielded a much-changed line up at Stamford Bridge where Chelsea, who were chasing Champions League qualification, provided the customary guard of honour for the champions. Gravenberch was left out of a Premier League game for the first time all season and, unsurprisingly, intensity levels dropped with little at stake.

A 3–1 defeat in the capital didn't come close to bursting the bubble of delight in the away end. Red balloons spelt out 'champions 20' and they never stopped singing. Chelsea midfielder Romeo Lavia, who had turned down a move to Liverpool in 2023, was met with a chant of: '*You could have won the league.*' The young Belgian saw the funny side.

When Arsenal arrived at Anfield a week later, their manager Mikel Arteta was greeted by a banner in the Kop depicting him in a red dress holding a posy of flowers with the words: 'Always the bridesmaid, never the bride.'

It was a reference to the fact that the Londoners, who hadn't won a major trophy since the 2020 FA Cup, were destined to finish second in the Premier League for the third successive season. In the build-up to the game, Arteta, who had bemoaned the impact of injuries and suspensions on his side, said that winning silverware was about 'being in the right moment in the right place'. He also claimed after their Champions League semi-final exit at the hands of Paris Saint-Germain that Arsenal had been the best team in Europe over the course of the campaign.

'Liverpool have won the title with less points than we have in the last two seasons,' Arteta said. 'With the points of the past two seasons we have two Premier Leagues.'

Given that Liverpool could still have beaten Arsenal's final points totals of 89 in 2023/24 and 84 in 2022/23, the Spaniard's comments didn't stand up to scrutiny. Slot smarted at the suggestion that Liverpool had somehow been fortunate. He pointed to their lack of spending in the transfer market and how they had blown their rivals away with a 26-game unbeaten league run.

'When it comes to tournaments like the Champions League, FA Cup, World Cup, Euros, then it's about being in the right place at the right time,' Slot said. 'But not in a Premier League season. I don't buy into that way of thinking. Nine times out of 10, the best team wins the league. The one time we won the league at Feyenoord, 14 players left before the beginning of the season. That is something different to not changing anyone.'

'I did it now in two different leagues in two different ways. All the excuses that have always been made if a team doesn't win the league, all these excuses you could give to Liverpool or Feyenoord, with us maybe not spending or with 14 players gone. It's nice that if you have all these excuses that you don't have to use them.'

As Liverpool raced into a 2–0 lead against Arsenal, Anfield glee-fully chanted '*Best team in Europe, you're having a laugh*' in the direction of Arteta. The party atmosphere turned sour in the second half: substitute Trent Alexander-Arnold was booed following his announcement he would be leaving his boyhood club in the summer. All the negativity helped the visitors secure a point – despite the dismissal of Mikel Merino for two yellow cards.

There was a disconnect between how Alexander-Arnold's deci-sion to leave was viewed by a section of the fanbase compared to his team-mates. That was epitomised by the sight of midfielder Dominik Szoboszlai dismissively lifting his hands towards the Kop as some continued the jeering after the final whistle, while the vice-captain applauded all four stands.

The players put a collective arm around Alexander-Arnold. Dealing with the fallout was helped by the fact that the squad headed straight to Dubai for a four-night title celebration. They stayed at the five-star Atlantis The Royal on Palm Jumeirah. The trip was partly subsidised by the fines collected over the course of the season for poor timekeeping and wearing the wrong attire, with Liverpool also making a sizeable contribution.

While Van Dijk and co were drinking cocktails and unwinding on a luxurious yacht on the Persian Gulf, Slot and his coaching staff were partying on the Spanish island of Ibiza.

They headed for the O Beach resort in San Antonio, which is co-owned by Wayne Lineker, the brother of former England striker Gary. Slot was given the VIP treatment as he stood in the DJ booth being serenaded with 'We Are The Champions' by Queen. The footage soon went viral online.

'It's not so easy to party when people constantly recognise you and film you,' he said. 'That's one of the things that's changed in my life.'

'Imagine telling someone nine months earlier as we entered a new era without such an iconic manager that a fortnight before the end of the season Arne would be on holiday with the league title already wrapped up,' chuckled one senior club official.

'Arne's attitude was that everyone had given absolutely everything and deserved some down time. But it would be wrong to view that final month as just one big party. It was calculated. Arne was like: "I need you to do it all again next season." So the plan was to get some rest in when the games were less important and then reap the benefits of that further down the line.'

Players and staff reconvened on Merseyside on the Friday with a light training session followed by Alexander-Arnold's leaving party inside the grounds of the AXA Training Centre. The carnival-style 'Summer of 66' event featured a barbecue, outdoor bar, ice cream van, performers on stilts, flamethrowers, crazy golf and a designated kids' zone. The England international was joined by parents Diane and Michael, brothers Tyler and Marcell, and other family members and friends.

Given how emotions were running high ahead of his departure, the plan had been to keep it private, but when photos were published on social media over the weekend, there was an inevitable backlash, with the club criticised for hosting it. However, the reality was that Alexander-Arnold had thrown the party with the club's blessing as a thank-you to his team-mates and staff. He picked up the cost himself. Brazilian forward Roberto Firmino had done the same prior to leaving Anfield as a free agent two years earlier.

By the time Liverpool travelled to Brighton & Hove Albion on the Monday, their plan for replacing Alexander-Arnold was already in place. They agreed to trigger the £29.5 million release clause in the contract of Bayer Leverkusen's Netherlands international Jeremie Frimpong and they also got academy graduate Conor Bradley tied down to a new four-year contract as they recognised his exciting development with improved terms.

Slot decided to leave Alexander-Arnold on the bench for the 3–2 defeat at Brighton. For the first time since 2004, Liverpool lost a league game in which they had led twice. It was no coincidence that with Van Dijk rested, having played every minute of the club's previous 69 league matches, Alisson found himself having to pull off more saves (nine) than he had ever previously made in a Premier League game. Liverpool did nonetheless become only the third side in Premier League history to score in all their away games in a season, after both Arsenal and Manchester United did so in 2001/02.

On the Thursday before the final game against Crystal Palace at Anfield, Mohamed Salah boarded a private jet and flew to London to receive the Football Writers' Association Footballer of the Year award. He was joined on stage for the presentation by Ian Rush, the highest goal scorer in Liverpool's history.

Van Dijk had finished second in the vote followed by Newcastle United's Alexander Isak and Arsenal's Declan Rice.

'It means a lot winning this award, it's incredible,' Salah said after taking to the stage in the city's plush Landmark Hotel. He collected the award for a third time, equalling the record set by former Arsenal striker Thierry Henry.

'I always feel special winning this award, something from the writers is so special. I will try to win it again next season. Winning the Premier League and having that impact on the team, I never felt that much happiness in the club as in that moment when we won the title against Spurs.'

The following night it was Klopp receiving a standing ovation as the guest of honour at the LFC Foundation Gala Ball in Liverpool's Anglican Cathedral. At the turn of the year he had started work in an advisory role as head of global soccer for Red Bull's network of clubs. He looked refreshed: life away from the stresses of management clearly suited him.

Comedian John Bishop, one of the hosts, asked him if returning to the city just after Slot had guided Liverpool to the Premier League title was like 'splitting up with your missus and then the next time you see her, she's lost weight, been to Turkey, got new teeth and looks fantastic!'

A smiling Klopp responded: 'No, it would be like if I split up with my missus, she gets a new guy and I like the guy and I cheer them on and think: "Wow, that fits much better than I thought!" I am over the moon about what Arne and the team did. It's exactly what I dreamt of. It came true and we are champions of England again.'

Away from the cameras, Klopp paid a visit to the AXA Training Centre on the Saturday. It was emotional as he hadn't been back since clearing his desk the previous May. Chauffeur-driven, he timed his arrival for around 12.30 p.m. just as the players were going out to train as he didn't want to disrupt the schedule.

After the session, he met Slot face to face for the first time and congratulated him on the job he had done. Mutual respect abounded as they chatted about how the season had panned out.

Klopp had kept in contact with a lot of the players via WhatsApp messages over the course of the campaign and there were warm embraces as they were reunited.

Earlier in the week a photograph had been taken of the squad with all the club staff based at the training ground, including those involved in catering, security, administration, medical, media and recruitment. Van Dijk insisted on it being included alongside his column in the matchday programme for the match against Palace.

'While it's the players who get the recognition when a club is successful, anyone who has worked in football knows that nothing would be possible without the work of the people behind the scenes,' he said. 'You have played your part and you are appreciated each and every day.'

Sir Kenny Dalglish made a presentation on the pitch pre-match to George Sephton, affectionately known as 'The Voice of Anfield', who was stepping down after 54 years of service as the stadium announcer. 'It's been the honour of a lifetime but the time is right to pass the microphone on,' Sephton said.

As Van Dijk led Liverpool out to rapturous applause, mosaics across three stands read: 'LFC – Campione – 20'. The skipper ensured that the hosts returned the compliment and gave Palace their own guard of honour in recognition of their FA Cup final triumph over Manchester City a week earlier.

Klopp was joined in the directors' box by fellow former managers Dalglish and Rafael Benítez, ex-club captains Steven Gerrard and Jordan Henderson, and the Fenway Sports Group trio of Henry, Gordon and Tom Werner. A banner spanning almost the width of the Kop read: 'A team that plays the Liverpool Way and wins the championship in May.' The chant of 'champions' was deafening.

It had been 35 years and 24 days since Liverpool last lifted the league trophy in front of their supporters. Before that there was an inconsequential game to play.

When Ismaila Sarr's goal was followed by the dismissal of Gravenberch for a professional foul on Daichi Kamada after the break, Slot's side looked set to sign off with a defeat. However, Salah's strike from Cody Gakpo's nod down with six minutes to go earned them a draw.

It meant that having already shattered the record for most goal involvements (47) in a 38-game Premier League season, Salah also equalled the record set jointly by Alan Shearer and Andrew Cole over a 42-match season. With 29 goals, he collected his fourth Premier League Golden Boot and with 18 assists, there was a second Premier League Playmaker award for him.

'Ridiculous numbers,' Van Dijk said. 'He's a fantastic player. I am really happy that me and Mo signed for another two years. Mo had an amazing season. He gets the applause he deserves. If he wins the Ballon d'Or then I think no-one could argue.'

Having only taken two out of the last 12 points on offer, the 10-point gap to second-placed Arsenal in the final standings didn't really do justice to the scale of Liverpool's dominance.

Van Dijk had been heavily involved in planning the presentation. He wanted Mark and Jo McVeigh from the Owen McVeigh Foundation to bring out the trophy dressed in its red ribbons and place it on the plinth. When Liverpool CEO Billy Hogan made the call to inform them, Mark had been reduced to tears.

'It's just a bit of a shock, isn't it?' Mark told the *Liverpool Echo*. 'I've followed Liverpool all my life and it isn't lost on me the enormity of this. I am just humbled beyond belief. Virgil has always been wonderful to us.'

It was recognition for how they had enriched the lives of so many children with terminal illnesses and provided support to families across Merseyside through the work of the foundation which they set up following the tragic death of their 11-year-old son Owen to leukaemia in December 2015. Van Dijk and his wife Rike were both long-standing supporters of the charity but never sought publicity for the events they helped to organise and subsidise.

Van Dijk also requested that former Liverpool skipper Alan Hansen was invited to hand out the medals and give him the trophy. Not only had Hansen been captain when Liverpool last won the league in front of their fans in 1990, but the Scotsman is also widely regarded as one of the greatest centre-backs to ever play for the club. Hansen, who clocked up 620 appearances across 13 years of service, winning eight league titles and three European Cups, had been recuperating after a serious health scare.

'It was a huge honour for Al, especially after such a tough year, and a touch of class from Virgil,' Dalglish said. 'We all know the soft spot Al still has for this club.'

As the precious prize was handed from one legendary figure to another, it was the perfect finale.

'I was very determined to make sure that Alan was going to be the one who handed the trophy to me,' Van Dijk said.

'I suggested it and I am happy it worked out. I'm glad he's looking well. After the trophy lift, we took some pictures together, I wanted him to be there. Apparently he had already gone upstairs so they got him back. I was glad I got him on the pitch. He deserved that moment in front of the Kop.'

The Dutchman became just the 11th player to captain Liverpool to a top-flight title as he followed in the footsteps of Henderson, Hansen, Graeme Souness, Phil Thompson, Emlyn Hughes, Tommy Smith, Ron Yeats, Willie Fagan, Donald MacKinlay and Alex Raisbeck.

'To join that list of captains, it's something really special,' he added. 'I never ever dreamed about it, only because it was too far for me to think this could happen. That's the beauty of it. It shows that anything is possible if you keep believing, keep working hard. I'm glad I've managed to write history with my team.'

Van Dijk was delighted with the send-off Alexander-Arnold received as he made his final appearance for the club before completing a move to Real Madrid.

'We all wanted Trent to stay,' he said. 'You saw again the quality he brings to the team. There is no debate. We're all gutted he's leaving. But he made that decision with his family that unfortunately his time at Liverpool has ended and we all have to deal with it. I'm glad he got the farewell he deserved.'

As the celebrations continued on the field, Alisson climbed on to the crossbar at the Kop end to orchestrate a rendition of 'campione, campione, olé olé olé.'

Klopp's former assistant Pep Lijnders was watching it all unfold on TV at home in Holland with his sons Benjamin and Romijn. 'It's a big thing to be able to look in the eyes of the fans when you win something and share it with them,' he said.

'That was something we missed out on in 2020 because the world was in such a difficult place. Liverpool couldn't have wished for a better transition than this. Arne was the right man, at the right place, at the right time. Very smart, very calm, a lot of good decisions. He kept the big ideas but put his own stamp on the team like with the changes to the team's pressing and a bit more man marking in the middle. We left behind a squad full of power but all the credit belongs to Arne and his staff.'

A few weeks later, Lijnders, who had been out of work since being sacked by Red Bull Salzburg in December, was back in football as Pep Guardiola's new assistant coach at Manchester City. He had been interviewed for the manager's job at Norwich City prior to receiving the surprise job offer. Guardiola had called Klopp to ask for his blessing before approaching the Dutchman.

After the trophy lift at Anfield, players and staff headed into the city centre for the party at the Municipal Hotel. As the drinks flowed, Curtis Jones performed a rendition of 'Band4Band' by the rapper Central Cee. Musical expertise arrived the following day in the form of award-winning Scottish DJ and record producer Calvin Harris, who Van Dijk had roped into performing on the team bus for the victory parade.

Torrential rain did little to dampen spirits as more than a million supporters lined the 10-mile route which started in the south of the city. Some hung off lamp posts and traffic lights, others climbed up scaffolding or on top of cars to gain the best possible vantage point.

'Just look at it. I told you this is the best city in the world,' Jones told LFCTV. 'It's my second Premier League title but this one feels more special as I've played a bigger role this time. This city is red.'

Cody Gakpo waved a wrestling style LFC belt above his head, while Van Dijk stood in dark sunglasses with the trophy aloft. Slot waved a 'champions' flag and signed Liverpool shirts and footballs which had been thrown from the crowd before tossing them back. 'This is unbelievable – you cannot imagine what you see here,' Slot said. 'Of course I have won a few things before but you cannot compare this to anything. So many people. It's beyond my dreams.'

Alisson, who had been part of the previous parades in 2019 and 2022, said: 'We worked so hard for this and it's a lot of celebrating to be honest. I am too old to do that now! It's been four weeks of celebration. I am really happy. I just want to enjoy it as much as we can.' As he spoke, Van Dijk planted a kiss on his cheek.

The crescendo came as the open-top bus made its way through a red fog along the city's iconic waterfront as fireworks were set off from the Liver Building. Sir Kenny Dalglish watched the spectacular scenes unfold alongside Klopp.

'Yeah, not a bad first trip back for Jurgen,' smiled Dalglish. 'He enjoyed himself. He might have left the club, but the club will never leave him. What I liked was that he never did anything to take the glory away from Arne. There's huge respect between them.

'Jurgen deserves a lot of credit for how he handled everything with the handover – going back to when he sang Arne's name on the pitch. Arne has been magnificent for this club. He's never tried to be someone he isn't. I liked how he didn't rush into bringing in new players. He gave everyone a chance. Getting off to a great start was key for him as momentum just grew from there.'

Shortly after the parade, the mood in the city suddenly changed as jubilation was replaced by fear and panic. More than 130 people were injured when a Ford Galaxy car was driven into a crowd on Water Street as supporters started to head home. Miraculously, there were no fatalities.

Slot had been due to travel to London the following day to receive both the Premier League Manager of the Season and the Sir Alex Ferguson Trophy for Manager of the Year from the League Managers Association (LMA), but didn't attend the awards dinner out of solidarity with those impacted by the incident. In his acceptance speech, delivered in his absence, he paid tribute to the efforts of the emergency services and the bystanders who had helped in the aftermath. 'Football is and always should be a game built on rivalry, but it is also a great source of comradeship, especially at times like this,' he wrote.

Klopp, who was inducted into the LMA Hall of Fame 1,000 Club, said: 'It just showed the two faces of life. The most beautiful face for a long, long time. The parade was incredible. Then from one second to another everything changed. We learned again that there are more serious things in the world than football.'

The LFC Foundation and the club's former players association Forever Reds donated £50,000 to the Liverpool Spirit Appeal, which was set up to provide financial support to those who had experienced physical or psychological injuries. The total amount raised soon climbed beyond £150,000 with Jamie Carragher's 23 Foundation contributing £10,000.

Thankfully, over the weeks that followed, all those hurt were discharged from hospital.

Liverpool chairman Tom Werner pulls up a seat in his office at Boston's Fenway Park. A replica of the European Cup is on the shelf beside him and he conducts his own trophy lift.

It's late June but the buzz of being at Anfield for the final day of the season against Crystal Palace a month earlier clearly remains for the affable billionaire American television producer and business-man.

'The overriding emotion for me was a great sense of pride,' he says. 'You know even more than me how hard it is to win a Premier League title. Even though we won it five years ago, it didn't compare to this because of what happened with Covid and the fact that the fans couldn't participate in it.

'The relationship between Liverpool supporters and the club is unique. It's unlike any other relationship in professional sports. The connection is so special. When Virgil hoisted the trophy, all the singing, all the dancing, you realise what an important moment that was in their lives – an achievement they will never forget. When everyone went down to the Kop end and sang "You'll Never Walk Alone", you'd need to have had ice in your veins not to have goosebumps.'

The 75-year-old, the second largest individual shareholder in Fenway Sports Group, braved the elements as he joined the players and staff on the open-top bus for the four-hour trophy parade. 'I had the honour of seeing a million fans, seeing their joy. It's quite difficult to fully articulate what it was like. When you see a boy and his grandfather both pointing in delight towards Arne Slot, who is holding the Premier League trophy, you see how a moment like that is a dream come true for young and old alike. No other club could have produced scenes like that.

'I have a lovely relationship with a number of the players and it was nice to meet the wives and the girlfriends. I've got so much admiration for how humble and kind they are. It's a really special group of athletes who play for Liverpool.'

I take him back to November 2023 when Klopp first informed the owners that he would be stepping down at the end of that season. There must have been a feeling of trepidation about the future.

'First of all, Jurgen is an extraordinary coach and an extraordinary man. It's an honour to call him a friend. When he told us he was going to leave, my first feeling was "you've been a transformational manager for Liverpool, thank-you for everything you've done, we'll respect your decision and move on". The job is relentless. He did it for nearly nine years. There are so many different constituencies that you have to deal with from the players to the medical department, the physios, the recruitment guys, the academy, the media, the football authorities, and most importantly the supporters.

'When I think back to that period, John W. Henry, Mike Gordon, Billy Hogan and I also saw it as an opportunity to find somebody … not to replace Jurgen, but someone who could come in and write the next chapter.'

How important in launching the new era was the return of former sporting director Michael Edwards as FSG's first CEO of football? 'You've met Michael, you know he's extremely bright, extremely successful. His record is peerless. He was critical in rebuilding the structure, which included not just appointing Richard Hughes as sporting director, but also the staff under him like the scouts.

'They say success has a thousand fathers and failure is an orphan. Well I'd say Michael is probably the preeminent father of success.

Without his leadership, which was so important in identifying Hughes and identifying so many of the players who have been so critical to the success we've enjoyed, we wouldn't be where we are now.

'Did he need much persuading? Yes and no. He's a very talented man and I'm sure he had a lot of competing offers. But Liverpool is Liverpool. Key for Michael was our commitment to purchasing a second club. That's very much still the plan but it has to be the right opportunity. We've looked at a number of clubs and it just hasn't been the right fit yet. I do believe eventually that will happen.'

FSG had trusted Edwards' judgement when it came to Hughes and they were quickly impressed by how the Scotsman went about his business, especially when it came to dealing with the contract sagas involving Salah, Van Dijk and Alexander-Arnold.

'I'm pleased to say that Richard is a friend of mine. And what I like about him as a friend translates into why he's a great leader. He's got a very kind and thoughtful outlook on life. He's not overwhelmed by the job. His experience at Bournemouth was really helpful and the ability he had shown there to identify talent.

'My impatience is balanced by his patience. I'd call him frequently and say "Richard, how are things going with Mo Salah and his contract?" And he would say: "Tom, it will all be good in the end." I think all the agents who deal with him would say that he conducts business in a very respectful way. He has a plan and he executes it.

'We were delighted that the new contracts for Mo and Virgil were sorted. But you know what? If Richard had called and said, "The chasm is too big", I would have respected that too. John, Mike and I try to find people who are excellent at their jobs and let them do their jobs. We don't meddle, we just provide support and advice from our point of view. There's a lot of trust. I can't say enough wonderful things about Richard.'

From the owners' perspective, there was no resentment over Alexander-Arnold's decision to turn down a new deal and sign for Real Madrid. Werner and Hogan had a cappuccino with the vice-captain at the coffee bar inside the players' entrance at the AXA Training Centre the day before his farewell game against Palace.

'The message I wanted to give him was how grateful we were for everything that he had contributed to the club,' Werner reveals.

'Trent showed me a picture on his phone of him at Liverpool when he was seven years old. He bleeds Liverpool red. I have so many memories of his remarkable contributions like the corner he took quickly for the assist against Barcelona [in 2019]. He saw going to Real Madrid as an opportunity. Of course we were disappointed, but he did what was right for him and I understand that. He will always be part of our family and I don't think it's trite to say I love him.'

In the spring of 2024, FSG had put their faith in Edwards and Hughes to find the perfect successor to Klopp and they certainly delivered with the appointment of Slot.

'With Michael and Richard on board, we had enormous confidence that they would find the right person. Arne was always their first choice and he's shown why that was the case. It's a surprise to everyone that his first year went quite so wonderfully, but it's been a source of delight. One of Arne's great attributes is his authenticity. He's not trying to be Jurgen Klopp, he's not trying to be Pep Guardiola. He's his own man and he's quite brilliant in all the things that he does.

'I think he saw this as a great opportunity for him. He came into a club which was very strong. He inherited a squad which was enormously talented. He felt he could work with them and help improve some of their performances. He's a wonderful strategist.

He took something that was already in very good shape and moulded it to his liking. His humility is balanced with a real inner belief that he knows what he's doing. I had an opportunity to watch training before the final game of the season and it was very impressive. The fact that Arne as head coach was able to focus solely on coaching worked well. The dynamic is good between him, Richard and Michael.'

So what did the owners seriously think was realistic before the start of the season? 'I thought we would be in the top four but I also felt that Manchester City would win the league again. Our victory over City at Anfield in early December was a real game-changer for the way I looked at the season. That's when I started to believe "we could actually win this."'

Exceeding expectations had been helped by a much-improved record under Slot when it came to avoiding injuries. The total number of days lost in 2024/25 was just 764 compared to 1,383 in Klopp's final season.

'I'm glad you mentioned that,' Werner says. 'Keeping players healthy was a big reason for our success and that's testament to the work of Arne and his staff, and everyone on the medical and sports science side. Arne was very focused on reducing both the number of days a player would be absent and also the number of players who sustain injuries.

'In all the years I've been involved in professional sports, I know that you cannot win unless you're able to field a healthy team for the majority of the season. When players go down injured, it changes everything – the chemistry. The person who comes in might not be perfect for that particular role. Injuries also dent the mood in the camp.

'When we did lose a key player to injury in Alisson, Caoimhin Kelleher came into the team for 10 games and was outstanding. I didn't feel that enough credit was given to Kelleher's contribution.'

There had been plenty of criticism over Liverpool's lack of spending on transfers before Slot's first season in charge, but winning the title had vindicated the decision to ignore the outside noise and stick to the plan of keeping a settled squad. 'We have a fair and a very high payroll. Over the years the priority has been to ensure that we get our best players tied down to new contracts. That's been supplemented by making transfers at the right time where necessary. We were confident that our strategy last summer was the right one.

'The fans would like you to sign the most expensive players every transfer window. We are responsible for saying: "Okay, we just want to make sure that we're improving the team." There's no point signing someone for £40 million or £50 million unless they are going to have a significant role. Last summer we felt the squad was already strong.'

The iconic title celebrations and the parade around the city had been followed by the sight of Paul McCartney joining Bruce Springsteen on stage during a series of sell-out concerts at Anfield. They did a duet of the Beatles song 'Can't Buy Me Love'.

Those weeks with the eyes of the world on Merseyside provided a snapshot of the heights Liverpool had reached both on and off the field with the help of shrewd leadership and a passionate, energised fanbase. Over the course of FSG's reign, two sides of the stadium had been redeveloped at a cost of £200 million – increasing capacity from 44,000 to 61,000.

'We are enormously proud of the improvements we've made at Anfield,' Werner admits. 'After we acquired the club back in 2010, we were looking at plans that the previous owners had for building a new stadium but we felt that there was such a great history at Anfield. The choice really wasn't stay at Anfield or build a new stadium. The question in front of us was: "How do we renovate Anfield? How do we make it bigger, better and louder? How do we give the fans the amenities that they would get at other first-class stadiums in England?"

'I use the metaphor of the virtuous circle. The success we have on the pitch, the more we generate through matchday, commercial and media streams, it all goes back into the club and allows us to do all the great things we do. We are relentless. We can always grow. Our focus is always on winning more trophies.'

Bold words were backed up with deeds as Liverpool embarked on the biggest spending spree in their history in the summer of 2025. Twice, they shattered their transfer record. They beat off competition from Bayern Munich and Manchester City to complete a £116 million deal for Bayer Leverkusen's attacking midfielder Florian Wirtz.

Then at the end of the window they made striker Alexander Isak the most expensive signing in the history of British football when Newcastle United finally sanctioned a £125 million move to Anfield after an acrimonious saga.

Slot talked about wanting to add 'new weapons' to his squad to make Liverpool a more potent attacking force with Hugo Ekitike another exciting arrival in a £79 million move from Eintracht Frankfurt. Including performance related add-ons, Liverpool's total outlay on signings was around £449 million with up to £262 million recouped from sales.

It was an unprecedented summer which underlined both their pulling power and their financial muscle after winning the Premier League title.

'When you have the opportunity to sign players of that calibre then you have to go for it,' Werner adds. 'Take someone like Florian, he's a remarkable talent. We could be looking at a future Ballon d'Or winner. Out of all the things that have been said about Florian, if even half of them come true then he'll be a huge contributor for us.

'This summer was a different scenario to last summer. We felt there were players available who could strengthen us and I'm sure those fans who always want us to spend money in the transfer market are happy with some of the decisions we took.

'It's hard climbing Mount Everest once. It's hard climbing it the second time. In fact it might even get harder each time because the intensity you have when you achieve something together for the first time is so strong. From my vantage point, I'm glad we've changed the make-up of the squad. Often in the history of professional sports, if you bring back the same players, whether it's football, the NFL or the NBA, it's very hard to repeat what you did.

'The signings should improve what's already a wonderful situation but I think also the chemistry will improve as well by bringing in fresh faces who are hungry. I hope we're not at the pinnacle. I hope that when we're sat here chatting in five years we have more incredible memories to look back on.'

11

HIS NAME IS DIOGO

*'We will always carry him with us in our hearts,
in our thoughts, wherever we go.'*

Arne Slot

Diogo Jota's journey to the top shaped him both as a footballer and as a man.

The Portuguese forward didn't come through the ranks at an elite academy in his homeland. He wasn't one of those tipped for stardom at a young age.

Scouts and coaches questioned whether he was tall enough or strong enough to make it at the highest level. Establishing himself as a professional involved total dedication as he sought to prove his doubters wrong.

It was a topic of conversation when I interviewed him for the first time for *The Athletic* in December 2020 – just three months after he had completed a £45 million move from Wolverhampton Wanderers to Liverpool.

'I was still paying to play football when I was 16 years old,' he revealed.

'These days kids who are 14 or 15 have already been offered professional contracts, but that wasn't the case with me. Until I was 16, I was just playing for fun really. I was lucky enough to have a team where we were all like a family. We played all together for like nine years.'

That team was Gondomar Sport Club in the small city where he grew up. Porto's impressive home, Estadio do Dragao, was just a 15-minute drive away but none of Portugal's top clubs were convinced about his potential. Christened Diogo José Teixeira da Silva, he had decided to go by the name Diogo J to distinguish himself from other youngsters called Diogo Silva. With 'Jota' being the Portuguese pronunciation of the letter J, it stuck.

When he finally moved on from Gondomar in 2013, it was to small top-flight club Pacos de Ferreira. He made his senior debut for them at the age of 17 and went on to score 18 goals in 47 appearances.

'Although I did some training with the bigger clubs, I never stayed there,' he explained. 'There were small setbacks as you always want to go higher. But in the end, it all worked out well. I think my journey shows that the secret is that you should never give up.

'Every experience you have, every setback, it always makes you stronger and that was the case with me. You always have to keep striving for what you want to achieve.'

Jota laughed as he recalled how, at the age of six, he had been crying and begging his father Joaquim to cancel the swimming lessons he had signed him up for because they clashed with football training. He had 'one passion' and was determined to ensure that nothing got in the way.

He had been inspired by watching Portugal's run to the final of the 2004 European Championships, where a side including Cristiano Ronaldo, Luis Figo and Deco were ultimately beaten by Greece on home soil.

'Cristiano was my hero,' he said. 'He was only 19 but was already playing at the Euros with so much quality. We always looked upon him as our main reference.' He talked about how surreal it was to share a dressing room with Ronaldo at international level for the first time and how he had initially been too shy to strike up a conversation.

Jota was still a teenager when Atlético Madrid signed him from Pacos in 2016 but he never played a competitive game for the Spanish club. After a pre-season under manager Diego Simeone, he was loaned out to Porto for the 2016/17 season where he scored nine times in 38 matches.

In summer 2017 he headed to England to join Wolves on loan. The move was made permanent for £12.8 million the following year, after his 17 league goals helped Nuno Espirito Santo's side win promotion to the Premier League.

'I don't regret going to Atlético,' Jota said. 'They were playing in the Champions League final the season before. The opportunity to go there and have all the pre-season with them meant a lot to me and I learned a lot. In the end, leaving was the best option for me at that time in terms of my career. Every experience you have allows you to develop as a player and person.

'Even if it's not what you expect at the beginning, everything that happens in your life you can learn from and you can take advantage of it in terms of the experience.'

After three seasons at Wolves yielded 44 goals in 131 games, he was ready to take the next step. On the day he signed for Liverpool in September 2020, his message to supporters was: 'My job is to score goals and provide assists. That's what they can expect from me. Now I'm one of them. I will give my best.'

Jota certainly delivered on that promise. He scored just nine minutes into his Premier League debut for Liverpool, against Arsenal, and went on to become the first player in the club's history to hit the back of the net in his first four home top-flight matches. Affectionately nicknamed 'Jots' by his team-mates, he quickly fitted into the dressing room dynamic. He grew close to the South American contingent but was universally popular.

'A pressing monster,' was how former assistant manager Pep Lijnders described him. 'When Jota is in this angry mood, he wants to run against the world and can do incredible things.' That combative edge and willingness to chase lost causes was one of the reasons why Liverpool supporters took him to their hearts. Another was his thirst for scoring goals.

Referencing his humility and strong work ethic, Jurgen Klopp said he was 'easy to like ... an incredible package of personality and technique'.

Liverpool's first-choice front-three of Mohamed Salah, Roberto Firmino and Sadio Mané had been set in stone, but Jota's impact shook up the established order. He cherished the matchball signed by his team-mates following his hat-trick against Atalanta in the Champions League. Trent Alexander-Arnold wrote on it: 'Congrats, the first of many.'

Watford's Ismaila Sarr and Gent's Jonathan David had also featured on Liverpool's three-man shortlist for attacking reinforcements back then but they never had any cause to regret opting to sign Jota instead.

In that December 2020 interview we chatted about his passion for Esports and in particular the *FIFA* and *Football Manager* franchises. He loved playing as a lower league club and challenging himself to guide the underdog to Champions League level against the odds – it struck a chord with him. He was in the process of launching his own professional gaming team. Prior to joining Liverpool, he had been crowned champion of the ePremier League Invitational FIFA 20 tournament after beating Alexander-Arnold in the final and joked that his new team-mate was out for revenge.

He admitted towards the end of that initial interview that he 'felt something was missing' with games being played in empty stadiums in 2020/21 due to the global pandemic. 'Feeling the

Anfield effect is the thing I am looking forward to the most,' he said. 'Football without fans is nothing.'

How he fed off that energy from the stands when supporters returned in 2021/22. He scored 21 goals in all competitions and made huge contributions to Liverpool lifting both the League Cup and FA Cup. There was a clinical double away to Arsenal in the semi-final of the League Cup and the winner at Nottingham Forest in the last eight of the FA Cup.

There was a period when he was ranked as the top *FIFA* player in the world, but he had to send his apologies and forfeit his place in one online tournament because it clashed with Liverpool's Premier League game against Southampton. After scoring the first of his two goals that day, Jota sat on the Anfield turf cross-legged and mimicked that he was on his PlayStation. The celebration became synonymous with him.

Hamstring and calf injuries hampered his progress the following season and forced him to sit out the World Cup in Qatar. However, his knack of scoring vital goals remained. Liverpool had conspired to throw away a 3–0 lead at home to Tottenham when, deep into stoppage time, he coolly and clinically dispatched a low left-footer beyond Fraser Forster to spark wild celebrations in the stands.

Jota was a master at catching goalkeepers off-guard with a sweetly struck first-time shot. His aerial threat was also remarkable for a man who stood at just 5 ft 10 ins.

When Sky Sports pundit Jamie Carragher described him as the club's best finisher of the Premier League era it wasn't hyperbole. The prolific Salah was rewriting the record books, but if a game was on the line and you got one final chance, you wanted it to fall to Jota.

In July 2024, I was among a small group of reporters who sat down with him at Philadelphia's Four Seasons Hotel during Liverpool's pre-season tour of the United States.

A short walk away from the Rocky Steps, he talked about overcoming adversity. He had contributed 15 goals in Klopp's last season in charge, but had also endured plenty of misfortune. A hamstring strain, knee ligament damage and a hip problem had limited him to 32 appearances. He missed the League Cup final triumph over Chelsea at Wembley and was sidelined during the run-in when the team's title challenge wilted.

'When you know you are injured and you are going to be out for a while, it's like a knockout,' he said. 'But you need to get up again. I had three injuries in three good moments. Each time my momentum was stopped. Mentally, it was tough.

'We're playing in the best competitions in the world, so it's not so easy to get into form and make the difference. But I did that last season every single time I was on the pitch. If I can stay fit, my numbers will be good and I can help the team. I know what I'm capable of.'

Jota was refreshed after a family holiday in Italy and eager to make his mark as a new era dawned under Arne Slot. He was awaiting the birth of his third child with long-term partner Rute Cardoso. They were happy and settled in the Blundellsands area of Crosby, a coastal town north of Liverpool, with sons Dinis and Duarte, and their three Beagle dogs Mel, Nikki and Luna.

He scored the first goal of Slot's reign in the opening weekend victory at newly promoted Ipswich Town and then got the winner away to Crystal Palace. However, he was forced off in pain against Chelsea at Anfield in October 2024 after Tosin Adarabioyo inadvertently landed on his ribs, and he didn't play for two months.

On his comeback off the bench against Fulham before Christmas, he needed just seven minutes to make his mark as he salvaged a precious point for 10-man Liverpool.

Jota only scored nine times in 2024/25, but so many of them resonated. There was the equaliser with his first touch against

Nottingham Forest at the City Ground in late January. Having only been on the pitch for 22 seconds, it was the fastest goal scored by a Liverpool substitute in the Premier League era.

When Everton arrived at Anfield in early April, Slot's side were in need of a lift after being dumped out of the Champions League by Paris Saint-Germain and beaten by Newcastle United in the League Cup final. After being frustrated by their neighbours for nearly an hour, it was Jota who brought the contest to life. He dispossessed James Garner just outside the penalty area and then collected a flick from Luis Díaz. Alert to the space that could be exploited, he left two defenders trailing before producing a cool finish in front of the Kop. 'I always believe in myself,' he told reporters post-match. 'That's the feeling I look for when I play football. That's why you put all your life, all your efforts into moments like that. Moments where you can decide a game. It's what makes you keep going.'

Captain Virgil van Dijk saluted Liverpool's match-winner: 'We all know how good Diogo can be and he showed it with his goal. It was big for us. A few injuries haven't helped but he always works so hard in order to be important for this team and his quality on the ball is so high.'

His close bond with the supporters was illustrated by the scenes which followed the 5–1 thrashing of Tottenham which wrapped up the title. He stood in front of the Kop as the song dedicated to him reverberated around the stadium:

> *Oh, he wears the No. 20,*
> *He will take us to victory,*
> *And when he's running down the left wing,*
> *He'll cut inside and score for LFC,*
> *He's a lad from Portugal,*
> *Better than Figo don't you know,*
> *Ohhh, his name is Diogo.*

Jota belted out the lyrics with them while twirling a red and white scarf above his head. 'It's an unbelievable song that makes me really proud,' he said. The following day he was spotted cycling through the town of Crosby wearing his special 'Champions 24/25' home shirt.

When Liverpool received the Premier League trophy a month later, he had the Portuguese flag wrapped around his waist. During the celebrations he was joined on the pitch by Rute, Dinis, Duarte and their baby daughter Mafalda, as well as his parents Joaquim and Isabel, as they posed for pictures with the silverware.

'When I was a kid, I wanted to play in the Premier League but I didn't even imagine to win it, I just wanted to be there,' he told LFCTV.

'I fulfilled my dream when I played for Wolverhampton. But when you achieve a dream, you unlock another phase, another level, another step. When I came to Liverpool I knew that was possible.

'To arrive at this season with a title that I was chasing for a lot of years in the best league in the world, finally we did it. It's a moment that I will cherish forever. I will always remember this city, this club, my three kids were born here. It changed my life completely.'

Jota requested a photograph from the club which he wanted to get framed to hang on the wall in his house. It said much about his character that it wasn't one of him celebrating, but instead an image of all the players and staff standing together in front of the Kop.

More glory followed as he won his 48th and 49th international caps in helping Portugal clinch the UEFA Nations League with wins over Germany and Spain. When his football commitments for the season were finally completed on 8 June, he headed to his hometown to prepare for an even more important assignment.

On 22 June he married his childhood sweetheart Rute at Igreja da Lapa in central Porto. As they kissed at the entrance to the

Catholic church, confetti rained down on them. The ceremony was followed by a reception with family and friends 40 minutes east of the city at Obras do Fidalgo, a stunning eighteenth-century unfinished baroque facade.

Renowned Michelin starred chef Rui Paula, a friend of the couple, did the catering, a band played and guests danced late into the night in a large glass dome. Liverpool team-mates Andy Robertson and Caoimhin Kelleher were among those present.

Rute posted a selection of photographs to her Instagram page with the caption: 'My dream came true.' Jota swiftly replied: 'But I am the lucky one.'

The initial reaction was one of denial. I thought it must be some kind of dreadful misunderstanding. The idea of it being true was too awful to comprehend.

Around 9 a.m. in the UK on 3 July, reports in Spain emerged stating that Jota and his younger brother Andre Silva, 25, had died in a car accident on the A52 motorway near Palacios de Sanabria, in the north-western province of Zamora.

The horrific reality was soon confirmed by a short statement from the Portuguese Football Federation followed by one from Liverpool. A dream summer had been so cruelly, so brutally, so abruptly cut short.

The previous evening Jota had enjoyed dinner with his family at a coastal resort near Porto before embarking on the journey back to Merseyside ahead of the start of pre-season training. Having recently undergone minor surgery, doctors had advised him against flying.

As a result, he had decided to drive six hours to Santander and then catch a ferry to Plymouth, which is around 300 miles south of Liverpool. Andre Silva, who was a professional footballer with Penafiel in Portugal's second division, had volunteered to accompany him. They planned to stop halfway to rest before completing the drive to Santander.

Spanish police said their rented Lamborghini Huracan crashed after a rear tyre blowout while overtaking another vehicle at around 12.30 a.m. local time. Less than 24 hours earlier, Jota had shared a video montage of his wedding on social media which he described as 'a day I will never forget'.

'It doesn't make sense. Just now we were together in the national team, you had just got married,' said Portugal captain Cristiano Ronaldo.

Sir Kenny Dalglish, the former Liverpool player and manager, said: 'Football is not important at this sad time. You feel so helpless, knowing there's so little we can do to ease the pain for his wife of just two weeks, his three beautiful children, and their heartbroken family.'

Jurgen Klopp wrote: 'This is a moment where I struggle. There must be a bigger purpose but I can't see it. Diogo was not only a fantastic player but also a great friend, a loving and caring husband and father. We will miss you so much.'

As Anfield's flags were lowered to half-mast and a book of condolence was opened, supporters descended on the stadium en masse to pay their respects. Some sat on benches consoling each other as they wept.

The grass area behind the Main Stand was soon transformed into a shrine with thousands of floral tributes. Shirts, scarves, hats, flags and handwritten notes were also laid down. One read simply 'Thanks for the memories Diogo', another described him as 'the eternal champion'.

Banners declaring 'Diogo lives forever' and 'RIP Diogo YNWA' were tied to the railings. To witness a scene of such sadness, it was hard to believe that just five weeks earlier this same spot had been a place of such unbridled happiness.

There were no rivalries at a time like this. Manchester United and Everton shirts also sat among the memorabilia. Their managers Rubin Amorim and David Moyes paid visits in the days that followed.

Jota's return of 65 goals in 182 appearances for Liverpool across five seasons didn't come close to explaining why he was so widely adored by their supporters. It was more about the manner in which he went about his business – how tenacious he was on the field and how grounded he was off it. No ego. A proper team player.

He was also well known for his generosity when it came to good causes and would regularly send videos of support if he heard about a supporter going through difficulties or about to embark on a challenge for charity. He knew that small gestures had a big impact.

It was the first time in the club's modern history that a current first-team player had passed away. The acute sense of shock and pain meant that it was early evening on the Thursday before senior club figures felt able to issue tributes.

'What can anyone say at a time like this when the shock and the pain is so incredibly raw? I wish I had the words but I know I do not,' Arne Slot said.

'All I have are feelings that I know so many people will share about a person and a player we loved dearly and a family we care so much about. My first thoughts are not those of a football manager. They are of a father, a son, a brother and an uncle and they belong to the family of Diogo and Andre Silva who have experienced such an unimaginable loss.

'My message to them is very clear – you will never walk alone. The players, the staff, the supporters of Liverpool Football Club are all with you and from what I have seen today, the same can be said of the wider family of football.'

The last time they had spoken on the phone, Slot had congratulated Jota on winning the Nations League and wished him good luck for his wedding. The Dutchman described him as 'a person who never sought popularity but found it anyway, not a friend to two people, a friend to everyone'.

In a joint statement, Liverpool's owners said they were 'numb with grief' and that Jota had 'a zest for life that was utterly contagious'. Fenway Sports Group CEO of football Michael Edwards and sporting director Richard Hughes described themselves as feeling 'utterly bereft' and 'consumed by shock and sorrow', adding: 'We have lost someone truly irreplaceable.'

Behind the scenes, Hughes and Slot spearheaded the club's response to the tragedy with the stance that the wishes of Jota's family had to be at the forefront of everything they did. Supporting them was their overriding priority.

Early on the Thursday, with the assistance of other senior staff, Hughes and Slot contacted as many members of Liverpool's first-team squad as possible in an attempt to ensure that they found out directly from the club rather than via the media. Some were still on holiday, with Cody Gakpo in the south of France and Harvey Elliott in Ibiza when the devastating news reached them.

The first group of returnees, including new goalkeeper Giorgi Mamardashvili, had been due to report back to the AXA Training Centre for pre-season testing but that was immediately cancelled.

Hughes was the key link with Jota's family. Having established that in keeping with Portuguese traditions the wake and funeral would be held promptly, a flight was immediately chartered for the Friday for Liverpool players and staff. The club's director of first-team operations and travel Phil Holliday coordinated everything.

The wake took place on the Friday afternoon at Saó Cosme Chapel in Gondomar with Portugal's president Marcelo Rebelo de Sousa and prime minister Luis Montenegro among those in attendance.

The locals turned out in force to pay their respects and were keen to relay tales about acts of kindness from Jota. Gondomar's academy had been named after their most famous graduate. His image was at the entrance with one of his quotes: 'It's not about where we come from, but where we're going to.' He would return whenever his schedule allowed to help inspire the next generation, handing out signed Liverpool shirts and tickets to matches. He had never forgotten his roots.

It was a similar story at Pacos de Ferreira, who had been able to build a new stand with the money they received from selling Jota to Atlético Madrid in 2016. His connection with the club remained strong and he had provided advice for youth players during a tournament the previous summer.

The joint funeral on the Saturday was at the seventeenth-century Igreja Matriz de Gondomar church. Captain Virgil van Dijk and Andy Robertson led the way for the Liverpool contingent with floral tributes in memory of the two brothers in the shape of their football shirts, No. 20 for Diogo and No. 30 for Andre.

Current players and staff were joined by ex-assistant manager Pep Lijnders and ex-first-team development coach Vitor Matos, and former players including Jordan Henderson, James Milner, Fabinho and Thiago.

Before flying to Portugal, Henderson had returned to Anfield to lay flowers and spend some time reading all the messages. The note he left read: 'Rest in peace my friend, along with your brother Andre. We will all miss you. Love Hendo and family.' Henderson, who was captain when Jota joined Liverpool in 2020, remembered all the good times they had enjoyed together, the laughs they shared in their joint mission to wind up Milner: 'Thank you for everything you brought into this world.'

Milner had initially intended to drive to Liverpool after finishing training at Brighton on England's south coast and board the club's charter flight. However, after getting stuck in traffic, he had to fly out from Luton instead. He told *The Athletic*: 'I was privileged to be able to pay my respects with the other lads and to spend a small amount of time with his wife and his family, which was important. It's horrible to see a family go through that, but it's the least we can do, to show them we're there for them. As you go through life, you get these reminders that every day is precious.'

Ahead of the 24th season of Milner's Premier League career, the 39-year-old midfielder changed his shirt number to 20 in honour of Jota. 'Loved him as a player, loved him even more as a team-mate and a friend,' he added. 'We were only together at Liverpool for three seasons and you might not have thought we had much in common – different nationalities, very different ages – but we hit it off immediately. Maybe it was because we were both so stubborn. Honestly, people say I'm stubborn, but Jots could give me a run for my money.

'He was an unbelievable guy, one of my favourite team-mates I've had in all my time playing. He was always up for a laugh, always winding people up. He was one of those you could put in any corner of the dressing room, next to any other player, and he would click with them straight away.'

Portuguese duo Ruben Neves and Joao Cancelo, who had been visibly distraught during a minute's silence at their Club World Cup clash for Al-Hilal against Fluminense the night before, were also at the funeral, despite playing in the United States just over 12 hours earlier.

Former Wolves clubmates Joao Moutinho and Rui Patricio were there, along with Manchester City's Bernardo Silva and Ruben Dias, who played alongside Jota for Portugal, and his national team boss Roberto Martinez. 'It's a really sad day but we are together. Their spirit will be with us forever. Today we are one football family,' Martinez said.

Delivering the eulogy, parish priest José Manuel Macedo said: 'Our faith in God is going to give a new life to these two deceased young men. We must have faith and hope and we have to believe in resurrection, in a new life. Those who believe, they will live eternally.

'I could say a lot about Diogo and Andre, their father prayed in the church and both Diogo and Andre made it [as professional footballers] because of their effort, their dedication, their sacrifices. They were very respectful to others, both local fathers and quiet and dedicated to their families.

'Extraordinary people, they were. That is why so many people are here. Two responsible, serious men of faith, known all over the world because of sport. Football brings people together and builds bridges between different people when it is done with honesty, values, discipline, team work, no ego, respect, peace and understanding.' The hour-long mass ended with the hymn 'Ave Maria'.

Robertson had jokingly nicknamed his close friend 'MacJota' because he regarded him as the 'most British foreign player I've ever met'. Jota loved watching darts, snooker and horse racing in his spare time. They had been among a group of players and staff who went to Cheltenham Racecourse in March and enjoyed a day to cherish.

In a poignant tribute, Robertson said: 'I want to talk about my mate. My buddy. The bloke I loved and will miss like crazy. I could talk about him as a player for hours, but none of that feels like it matters right now. It's the man. The person. He was such a good guy. The best. So genuine. Just normal and real. Full of love for the people he cared about. Full of fun.

'The last time I saw him was the happiest day of his life – his wedding day. I want to remember his never-ceasing smile from that magical day. How much he was bursting with love for his wife and family. I can't believe we're saying goodbye. It's too soon, and it hurts so much. But thank you for being in my life, mate – and for making it better. Love you, Diogo.'

Van Dijk added: 'Man, I can't believe it, I don't wanna believe it. Absolutely devastated and in total disbelief. What a human being, what a player, but most importantly what an unbelievable family man.

'You meant so much to all of us and you always will. For your family to lose two sons, a husband and a father is just unimaginable. So cruel and unfair. My heart is breaking for all of your beautiful family, for Rute and for your kids. I promise you that in these difficult times and beyond we will always be there for your family. A champion forever, number 20 forever. We will miss you beyond words and never forget you. Your legacy will live on.'

Kelleher, who by then had completed a move to Brentford, recalled how they would always do the quiz in the programme together pre-match at Anfield. 'A fun, genuine, normal, down to earth and loving family man,' he said. 'It's gonna hurt for a long time and I'm gonna miss you so much but I feel so lucky to have got to know you and have such a good friend.'

Everyone had their own special memories. For Conor Bradley, it was the evening he accepted an invitation to play him at *FIFA* for the first time during an away trip and found himself 5–0 down at half-time. Typically, Jota had gone out of his way to help him settle in when the young Northern Irish full-back was promoted from the academy to the senior set-up.

The words of Mohamed Salah underlined what a challenge it would be for Liverpool to plot a way through one of the most heart-wrenching chapters in their history.

'Until yesterday, I never thought there would be something that would frighten me of going back to Liverpool after the break,' he said. 'Team-mates come and go but not like this. It's going to be extremely difficult to accept that Diogo won't be there when we go back.'

Following their return from Portugal, Hughes and Slot held a meeting on the Sunday to try to map out what the week would look like. There was input from director of medicine and performance Jonathan Power and performance psychologist Lee Richardson as Liverpool sought to ensure the right support network was available.

Tuesday 8 July was the day when most of the squad reported back. They knew it would be emotion-fuelled – walking past Jota's locker for the first time, the void in the dressing room.

It was decided that some pre-season testing would take place but the traditional six-minute race test, where players try to cover as much ground as possible within the allotted timeframe, was shelved. Having a competitive edge on that Tuesday just didn't feel right. There was no meeting, with the players given space to mourn.

Rather than head home to Cheshire that afternoon, Slot drove to Anfield with his wife, Mirjam, to lay flowers at the memorial shrine that was continuing to expand at the stadium. Soon it spread the entire length of the Main Stand and beyond. 'Diogo, we had the same dream and we fulfilled it together,' said the heartfelt message from the Slot family, including children, Isa and Joep. 'Andre and yourself will forever be in our hearts.'

After giving the squad the Wednesday off, it was the Thursday when Slot decided they would effectively try to restart training. 'If you can't, if it's too much, there's no pressure on anyone,' Slot told his players during a team meeting on the Thursday. 'My door is always open. You've got the doc and the psychologist too. Come and talk to us.'

The message was 'do it like Diogo' – be authentic. Grief hits people in different ways and no-one would be judged. There would be empathy and compassion in abundance.

The squad made it clear that they were keen to visit Anfield to see the outpouring of sentiment for themselves and that was arranged for the Friday. They were joined by Rute, Jota's parents Joaquim and Isabel, and other family members. The players each carried two roses, one red and one white, to lay among the tributes.

Rute also paid a visit to the 'Forever 20' wall on the corner of nearby Sybil Road and added a message to the hundreds that had been left by supporters on the side of a house. A short walk away, a mural of Jota had already been completed outside the Halfway House pub.

Fittingly, at 8.20 that evening it was announced that Liverpool had permanently retired the No. 20 shirt across all levels of the club. It was the first time such an honour had been bestowed on anyone in the club's history.

Edwards said: 'As a club, we were all acutely aware of the sentiment of our supporters – and we felt exactly the same way. It was vitally important to us to involve Diogo's wife, Rute, and his family in the decision and to ensure they were the first to know of our intention. This is a unique tribute to a uniquely wonderful person.

'By retiring this squad number, we are making it eternal – and therefore never to be forgotten. Diogo joined us in 2020, he won us number 20, and he wore – with honour, distinction and affection – the number 20. As far as Liverpool Football Club is concerned, he will be forever our number 20.'

Slot added: 'We will always carry him with us in our hearts, in our thoughts, wherever we go. To retire his shirt is the one thing we could, should and have done.'

As well as offering counselling to current players, Liverpool reached out to those who had recently left the club like Trent Alexander-Arnold, Kelleher and Jarell Quansah.

At the start of the week it had been unclear in what form the opening friendly at Preston North End on 13 July would go ahead. Was it too soon? Would they need to send an Under-21s team to fulfil the fixture?

Senior players had discussed among themselves whether they would be in the right frame of mind to play. But the longer the week progressed, the more of them felt that they needed to get back out there and wanted to be involved.

Speaking candidly to LFCTV pre-match, Slot reiterated publicly some of the messages he had relayed to the squad privately. 'Nothing seems to be important if we think of what has happened, but we are a football club and we need to train and we need to play again, if we want it or not,' he said.

'It's very difficult to find the right words because we constantly debate what is appropriate. Can we train again? Can we laugh again? Can we be angry if there's a wrong decision? I've said to them that maybe the best thing for us to do is handle this situation like Jota. And what I meant with that is that Jota was always himself. It didn't matter if he was talking to me, to his team-mates, to the staff, he was always himself. So let us try to be ourselves as well. If we want to laugh, we laugh. If we want to cry, we're going to cry. If they want to train, they can train; if they don't want to train, they can not train. But be yourself, don't think you have to be different than your emotions tell you.

'What I take comfort in is that in the last month of his life, Diogo was a champion in everything. A champion for his family, which is the most important thing, because he got married. A champion for his country because he won the Nations League, with a country that he cared about so much. And of course, a champion for us by winning the Premier League.'

If Slot showcased his coaching acumen in securing title glory in his maiden season at Liverpool, the compassion and leadership he demonstrated during a period of such heartache was arguably even more impressive.

The touching scenes at Preston – 40 miles north of Anfield – will live long in the memory. The road back to anything resembling normality would be long and winding, but the first tentative steps were taken at Deepdale.

The Championship club proved to be the classiest of hosts with their captain Ben Whiteman laying a wreath in front of the away supporters before kick-off while singer Claudia Rose Maguire performed 'You'll Never Walk Alone'.

Conor Bradley pointed to the heavens after opening the scoring, Darwin Núñez did both the baby shark and PlayStation celebrations so closely associated with Jota, and then Cody Gakpo held up '20' with his fingers after netting Liverpool's third.

For seven minutes after the final whistle, players and staff stood on the edge of the penalty area applauding the 5,600 Liverpool supporters amassed in the Bill Shankly Kop as the Jota song remained on loop. One banner being held up read 'Diogo Jota 1996 to 2025. Forever Red'. The tears flowed both in the stand and on the pitch. There was comfort to be taken from such a touching show of unity and togetherness. It was part of the healing process.

'If you play for this club, it's unbelievable when you win things, but in moments of tragedy, I think it's also unbelievable what these fans are doing,' Slot said.

'The fans cannot have better players to play for them, but us as players and staff can't have better fans to support us. To represent this club in this city now even means more to me and to my wife than it did before.'

Long-serving club chaplain Bill Bygroves sat and prayed with those players who turned to him. He spoke powerfully during LFCTV's tribute show to Jota as the channel resumed broadcasting after being taken off air for four days as a mark of respect. Bygroves described tears as like 'safety valves of the heart when too much pressure is on them' and said it was 'bad theology to bottle everything up'.

Performance psychologist Lee Richardson was another important figure. He had earned the squad's trust since joining Liverpool during Klopp's reign in 2019.

The former Blackburn Rovers and Aberdeen midfielder had initially gone into management at the end of his playing days before opting for a change of career. His door at the AXA Training Centre was usually open for those wanting to chat about dealing with pressure, loss of form, the impact of injuries or personal issues. Now it was players and staff grieving a gifted colleague and much-loved friend.

The previous October, Jota had volunteered to mark World Mental Health Day by sitting down with Richardson to be filmed discussing some of the challenges elite players face.

'Sometimes speaking to someone, saying the problem out loud helps,' Jota said. 'One thing that's important and it happens to me, I have it here [points to his head], but when you say it out loud, it already gives you a different feeling. That's one of the good reasons why you should speak to someone. It helps you clear your thoughts. Recognising a problem is the first step to solving it.'

What really hit home watching that back was hearing Jota talk about how stepping onto the field acted as a welcome distraction. 'I feel like when I enter the pitch, everything clears,' he said.

For his team-mates, it became a place of refuge. More powerful tributes followed as the club's pre-season schedule took them to Hong Kong, Japan and then back to Merseyside before facing Crystal Palace in the Community Shield at Wembley.

Liverpool unveiled plans for a memorial sculpture at Anfield. The players came together and decided to wear a 'Forever 20' emblem on their shirts for the duration of the 2025/26 season and the LFC Foundation vowed to launch a grassroots football programme in Jota's name.

'It is the least we can do,' Gakpo said. 'Obviously, he was an outstanding player, but he as a person was even more wonderful. He was good with everyone. Everyone loved him, and that is also what you saw with how everyone reacted.

'So yeah, it's more that we want to remember who he was to us. Not as a player, because the player we can see on the highlights on YouTube, but more as the person he was. He will be missed this season, but he will also be missed by everyone in this team and in this club, and by his family, for the rest of our lives. We will not forget him.'

The Netherlands international was the first player to open up about the impact of the tragedy when he sat down with reporters in Tokyo's Conrad Hotel at the end of the tour of Asia.

'Yeah, it's been very difficult,' he added. 'A lot of us were still on vacation when the situation happened. We came together as a team and as a club as soon as possible. We tried to be there as much as we could at that moment for the family and together as a team to help wherever we could. The family of Diogo hopefully felt the love we have for them, and for Diogo and his brother. We really try to be a family.'

The sense of loss was also profoundly felt at Wolves as they inducted Jota into their Hall of Fame and announced plans for a permanent tribute.

His wife Rute and his parents Joaquim and Isabel Silva were at Molineux on the opening weekend of the new season as a stunning tifo image – a banner held up by fans – of Jota stretched the height of the South Bank before kick-off. It read: 'We'll remember you when you walk in fields of gold.' It was a reference to Sting's 'Fields of Gold', the forward's favourite song.

The previous night had seen Jota's family return to Anfield for Liverpool's game against Bournemouth. Special mosaics across two stands displayed 'DJ 20' and 'AS 30' during the minute's silence. A banner declared: 'Rute, Dinis, Duarte, Mafalda – Anfield will always be your home.' Rarely has 'You'll Never Walk Alone' been delivered with so much feeling.

After the final whistle, a tearful Salah, who had wrapped up a 4–2 win by scoring deep into stoppage time, stood on his own in front of the Kop applauding as the Jota song echoed around Anfield. It was incredibly moving – a reminder of what everyone associated with the club was still going through.

Liverpool's defence of the Premier League title was up and running, but their thoughts were with their eternal No. 20.

ARNE SLOT'S FIRST SEASON AT LIVERPOOL

 Virgil van Dijk became the first player from the Netherlands to captain a side to the English top-flight title. He played every minute of every league game in 2024/25 before being rested for the trip to Brighton after the title had already been won.

 Arne Slot became the first Dutch coach to win the Premier League title.

 For the first time in the club's history, Liverpool scored in every single away league game in 2024/25. They became just the third side in Premier League history to do so after both Arsenal and Manchester United in 2001/02.

 Mohamed Salah became the first player in Premier League history to hit double figures for both goals and assists before Christmas in a season.

 Mohamed Salah moved above Billy Liddell and Gordon Hodgson into third place in Liverpool's all-time scorers' list on 245 goals.

 Arne Slot became just the fourth manager in Liverpool's history to win the league in his first season in charge after Matt McQueen (1922/23), Joe Fagan (1983/84) and Kenny Dalglish (1985/86).

 Mohamed Salah's number of away league goals, which equalled the club record for a season set by Jimmy Smith in 1929/30. It also equalled the Premier League record for most away goals in a single campaign in the competition – level with Kevin Phillips (1999/00) and Harry Kane (2022/23).

ARNE SLOT'S FIRST SEASON AT LIVERPOOL

11 The number of matches Mohamed Salah both scored and assisted in during 2024/25 – a new Premier League record.

29 Mohamed Salah's league goals in the 2024/25 season. He won both the Premier League Golden Boot for those goals, and the Playmaker award after contributing 18 league assists.

36 The number of Arne Slot's total wins in his opening 50 matches at Liverpool. That was higher than any other manager in the club's history. Joe Fagan and Kenny Dalglish had set the previous best of 29 victories.

42 The number of points Liverpool finished this Premier League ahead of Manchester United – the biggest ever gap in points between the two rivals at the end of a top-flight campaign.

47 The record-breaking number of goal-involvements for Mohamed Salah over a 38-game Premier League season. The record was previously held jointly by Arsenal's Thierry Henry (2002/03) and Manchester City's Erling Haaland (2022/23) with 44. Salah also equalled the record of 47 set by Newcastle United's Andrew Cole (1993/94) and Blackburn Rovers' Alan Shearer (1994/95) over a 42-game season.

234 The number of days Liverpool were top of the Premier League table across the course of the 2024/25 season. They hit the summit when they leapfrogged Manchester City on 2 November and never looked back.

ACKNOWLEDGEMENTS

It was 27 October 1990. Row 14, seat 3 in the old Main Stand.

Liverpool 2 Chelsea 0. Ian Rush and Steve Nicol scored inside the opening 20 minutes for the reigning champions of England.

You don't forget your first trip to Anfield – walking up the steps and seeing that pristine playing surface, the noise and splendour of the Kop.

I was 12 years old and my dad got the tickets as an early birthday present. I've still got the scrapbook in which I scrawled a short match report and stuck in my ticket stub when we got home.

Writing about the club I grew up supporting was all I ever wanted to do and I feel very fortunate that I've been able to call it 'work'.

I owe so much to so many people. To Neville Smith for giving me my first job in journalism as a trainee reporter at the *Bath Chronicle* in 2000 and John Thompson for taking me on at the *Liverpool Echo* five years later.

I always wanted to return to the city after loving life as a student there in the 1990s and it's been home for more than 20 years. The fact that some of my boyhood heroes I now regard as friends feels as surreal as having my first book published.

Joining *The Athletic* in 2019 as their first Liverpool FC correspondent required a leap of faith as they expanded into the United Kingdom, but proved to be one of the best decisions of my life. I'm grateful to them for all the help and support since, and in particular to editor-in-chief Laura Williamson for allowing me to embark on this project.

A huge thank-you to Liverpool chairman Tom Werner for being so generous with his time. The transformation of the club under the ownership of Fenway Sports Group has been remarkable. Having the opportunity to sit down with Arne Slot at the AXA Training Centre shortly after the Premier League title was wrapped up to look back on his first year at the helm was another great honour.

Thanks to talismanic captain Virgil van Dijk, who fronts up to the media after every game, for the contributions he made over the course of the season. He's a class act – both on and off the pitch.

I massively appreciate the insight and anecdotes provided by all the club staff who helped me along the way. Thank-you for trusting me with this story.

I'm also grateful to Jonathan de Peyer and everyone at the publisher HarperNorth for giving me the opportunity to write this book. When Jonathan first contacted me to suggest the idea in January, I wrestled with whether it was feasible within the timescale while juggling the day job, two kids, a dog and a cat. Self-doubt set in but the belief you showed ultimately convinced me to take it on and I'm so glad I did.

On a personal level, to Holly and Max for being so understanding about all the anti-social working hours. Being your dad is the best job in the world and I couldn't be prouder of you.

To Claire, I couldn't have done this without your love and encouragement.

ACKNOWLEDGEMENTS

Finally, a big thank-you to all the readers and listeners who have supported me along the way. From Melbourne to Michigan, Bangkok to Baltimore, I've met so many amazing people while covering the fortunes of Liverpool. The passion for the club across the globe never ceases to amaze me.

For more unmissable reads,
sign up to the HarperNorth newsletter at
www.harpernorth.co.uk

or find us on socials at
@HarperNorthUK

Harper
North